Himouto (干物妹)

A lazy little sister who never lifts a finger around the house.
"At home, Umaru is a himouto."
Origin: a portmanteau of imouto (little sister) and himono (a woman who is elegant and polished in public, but secretly a slob at home).

From Shueisha's *Imouto Dictionary*.

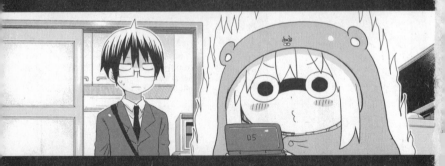

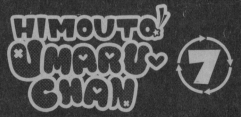

7

Characters Inside

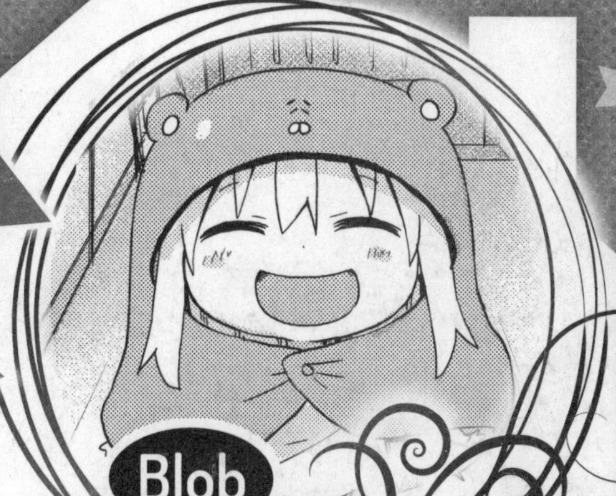

Blob

Inside Umaru

Master

Siblings

Taihei's little sister. Once she steps across the threshold of her home, she turns into an irresponsible slob whose motto is, "Eat, sleep (Zzz...), play!"♪

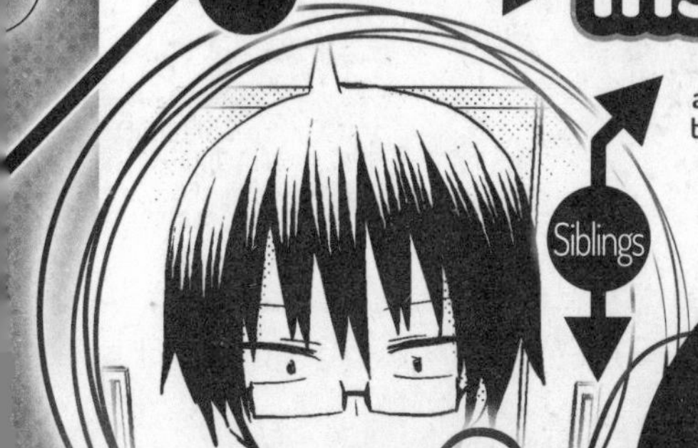

Taihei

Umaru's big brother. He has an office job, but he also works a second job doing chores and generally being a "house-husband."

Story

Inside, Taihei's little sister Umaru is a lazy little sloth all year round, spending her days indulging in snacks and video games, with a cola always in one hand. ♪ But once she steps outside, she turns into a super-perfect, super-popular achiever?! Or at least, that's the way it usually goes. This summer, Umaru suddenly announces that she's ready to graduate from the Lazy Life! Is this the end of the himouto?!

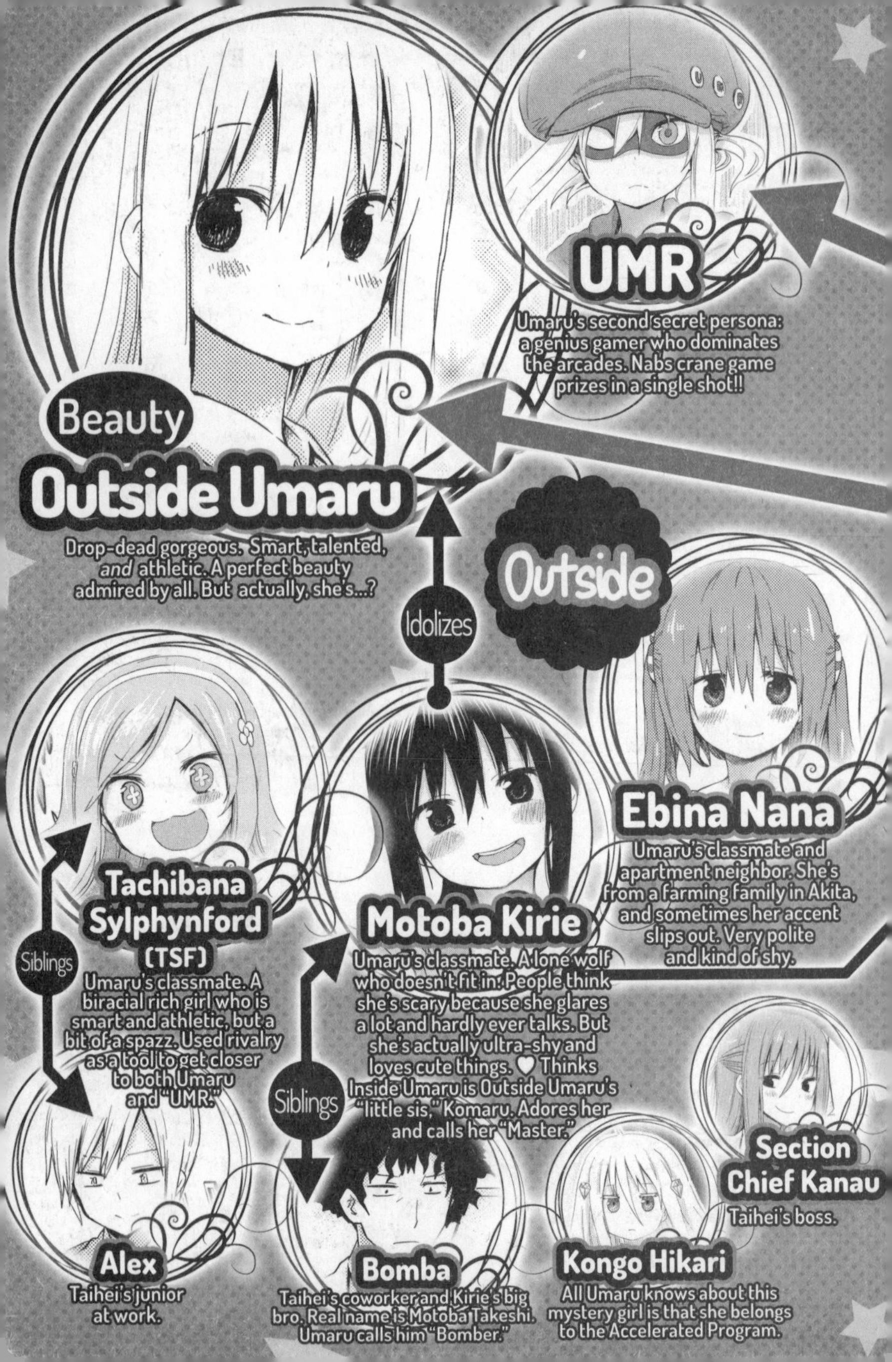
UMR
Umaru's second secret persona: a genius gamer who dominates the arcades. Nabs crane game prizes in a single shot!!
Beauty
Outside Umaru
Drop-dead gorgeous. Smart, talented, *and* athletic. A perfect beauty admired by all. But actually, she's...?
Outside
Idolizes
Ebina Nana
Umaru's classmate and apartment neighbor. She's from a farming family in Akita, and sometimes her accent slips out. Very polite and kind of shy.
Motoba Kirie
Umaru's classmate. A lone wolf who doesn't fit in. People think she's scary because she glares a lot and hardly ever talks. But she's actually ultra-shy and loves cute things. ♥ Thinks Inside Umaru is Outside Umaru's "little sis," Komaru. Adores her and calls her "Master."
Tachibana Sylphynford (TSF)
Umaru's classmate. A biracial rich girl who is smart and athletic, but a bit of a spazz. Used rivalry as a tool to get closer to both Umaru and "UMR."
Siblings
Siblings
Section Chief Kanau
Taihei's boss.
Alex
Taihei's junior at work.
Bomba
Taihei's coworker and Kirie's big bro. Real name is Motoba Takeshi. Umaru calls him "Bomber."
Kongo Hikari
All Umaru knows about this mystery girl is that she belongs to the Accelerated Program.

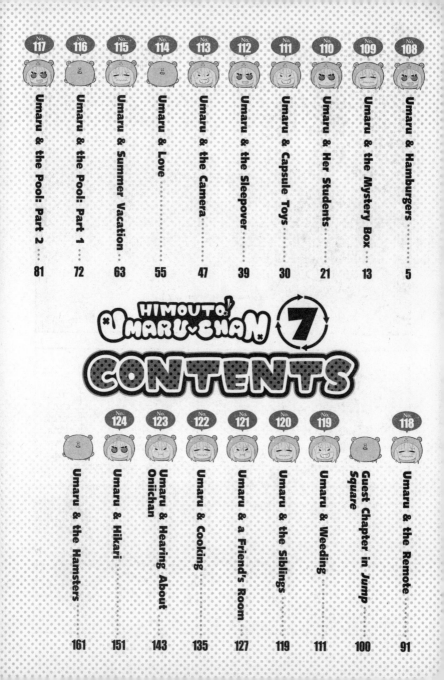

HIMOUTO! UMARU-CHAN 7 CONTENTS

No. 108 Umaru & Hamburgers

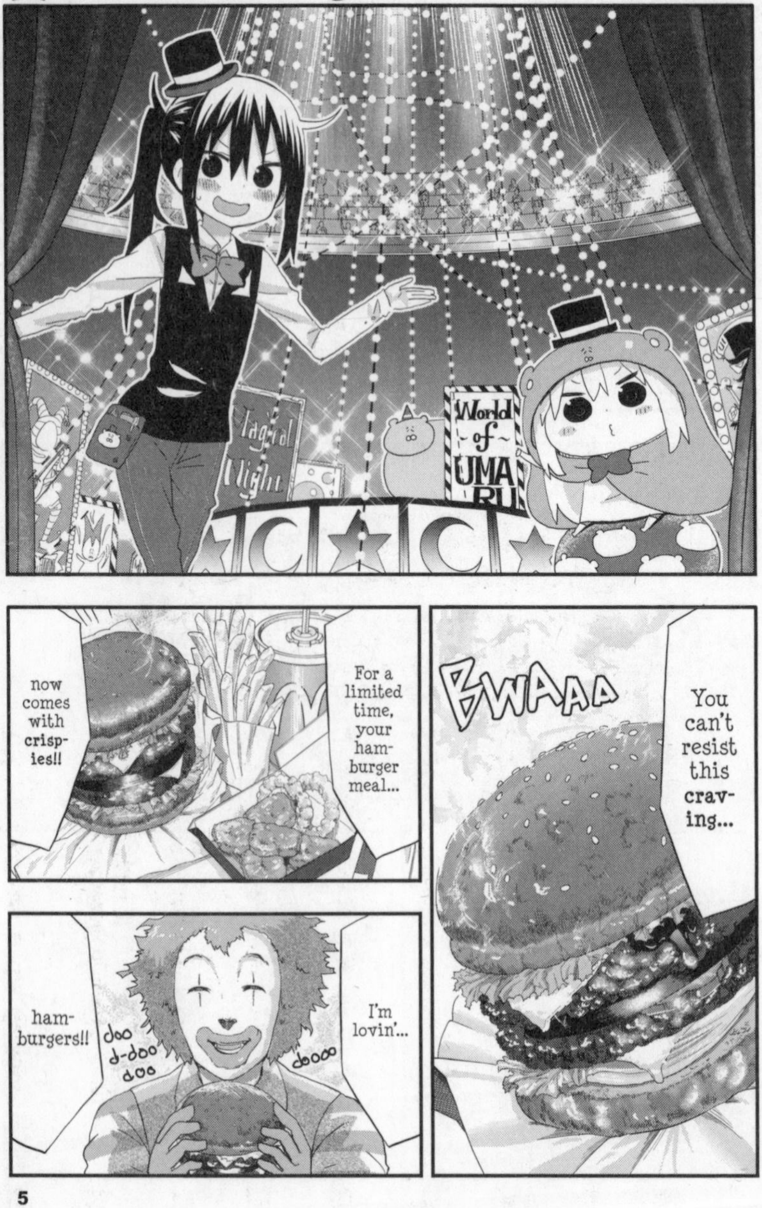
World of UMARU
BWAAA
You can't resist this craving...
For a limited time, your hamburger meal...
now comes with crispies!!
I'm lovin'...
doooo
doo d-doo doo
hamburgers!!

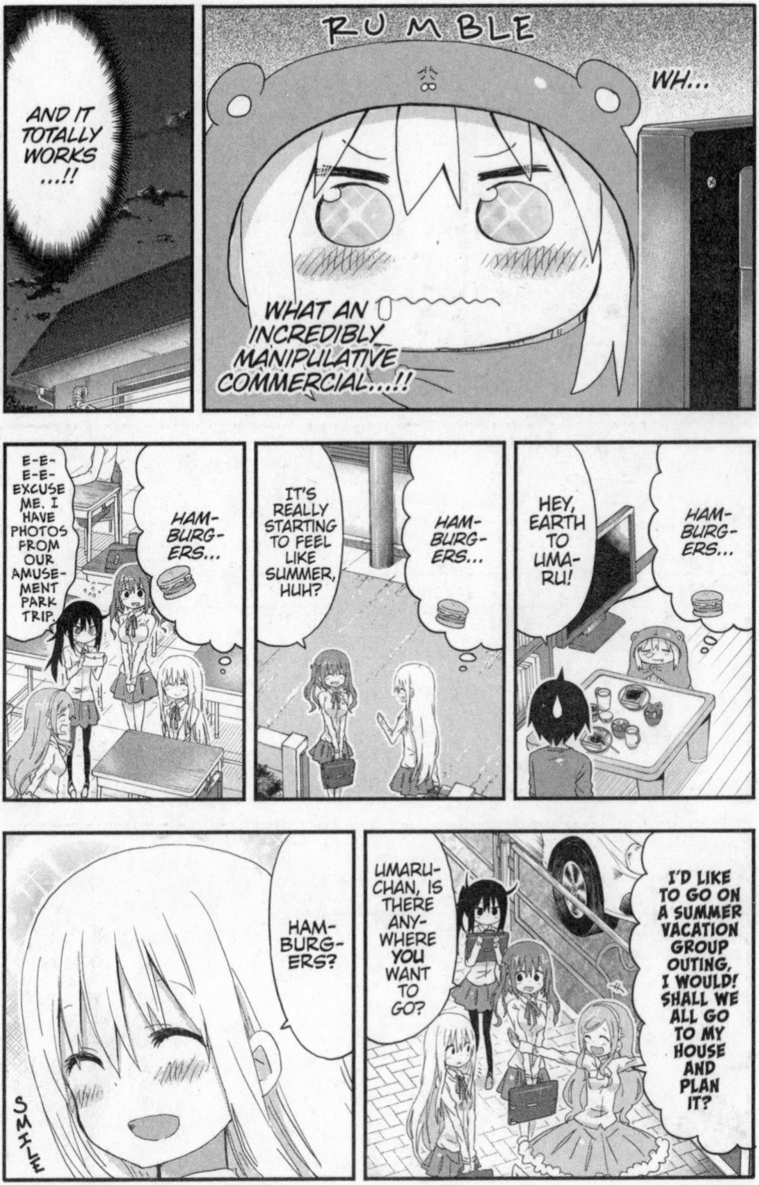
RUMBLE
WH...
WHAT AN INCREDIBLY MANIPULATIVE COMMERCIAL...!!
AND IT TOTALLY WORKS ...!!
HAM-BURG-ERS...
HEY, EARTH TO UMA-RU!
HAM-BURG-ERS...
IT'S REALLY STARTING TO FEEL LIKE SUMMER, HUH?
HAM-BURG-ERS...
E-E-E-E-EXCUSE ME. I HAVE PHOTOS FROM OUR AMUSEMENT PARK TRIP.
I'D LIKE TO GO ON A SUMMER VACATION GROUP OUTING, I WOULD! SHALL WE ALL GO TO MY HOUSE AND PLAN IT?
UMARU-CHAN, IS THERE ANY-WHERE YOU WANT TO GO?
HAM-BURG-ERS?
SMILE

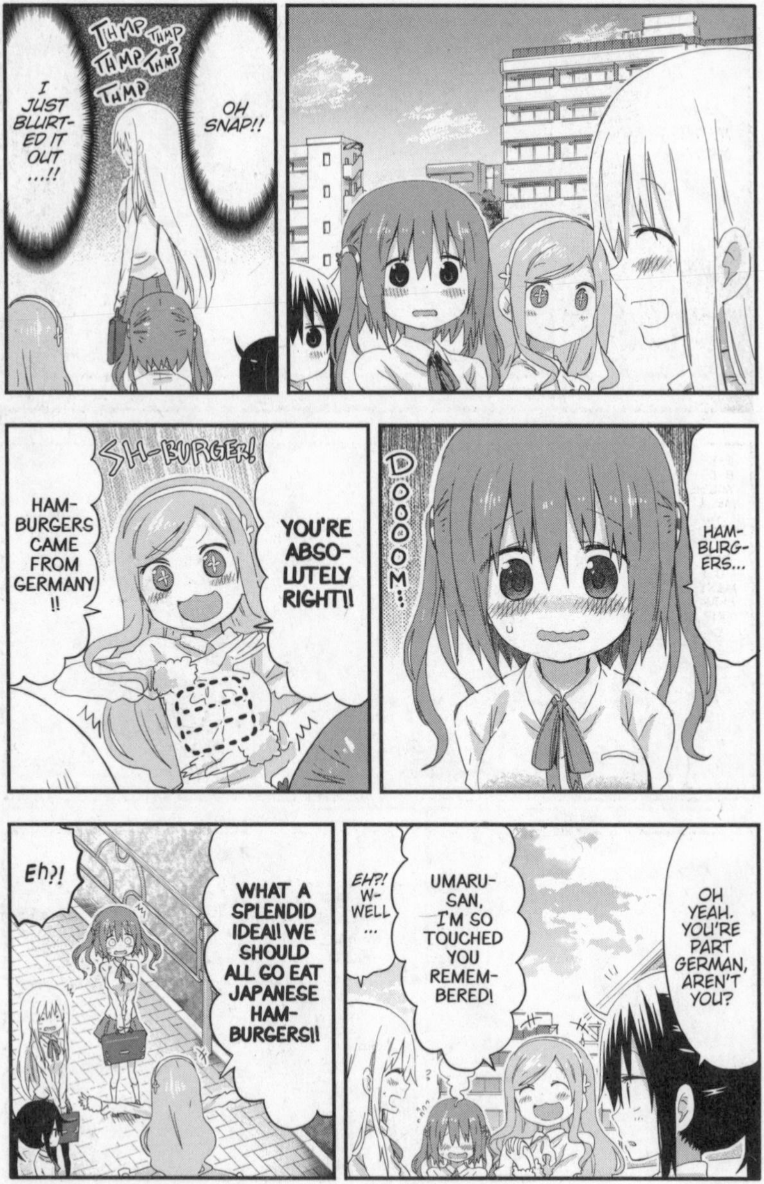
OH SNAP!!
THMP THMP THMP THMP THMP
I JUST BLURTED IT OUT ...!!
HAMBURGERS...
DOOOOOM...
YOU'RE ABSOLUTELY RIGHT!!
SH-BURGER!
HAMBURGERS CAME FROM GERMANY !!
OH YEAH. YOU'RE PART GERMAN, AREN'T YOU?
UMARU-SAN, I'M SO TOUCHED YOU REMEMBERED!
EH?! W-WELL ...
WHAT A SPLENDID IDEA!! WE SHOULD ALL GO EAT JAPANESE HAMBURGERS!!
Eh?!

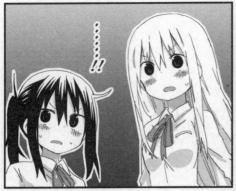

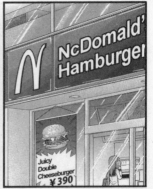

NcDomald's
Hamburger
Juicy Double Cheeseburger ¥390
......!!
IT'S ...
IT'S MY FIRST TIME HERE...
M...
ME TOO...
OH? IS IT TRULY?
RRRUMBLE
THIS IS FORBIDDEN GROUND FOR KIDS WITHOUT FRIENDS...
GAB GAB
...
THMP THMP THMP THMP
D...
DO YOU ORDER OVER THERE...?
INDEED, YOU DO! YOU SHOULD ASK FOR IT AS A MEAL!
Super Meal
01 Juicy Double Cheeseburger
02
03
04
CrinKLe...

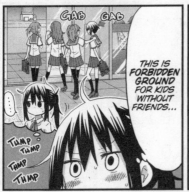

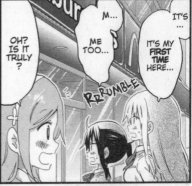

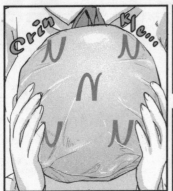

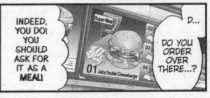

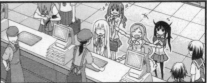

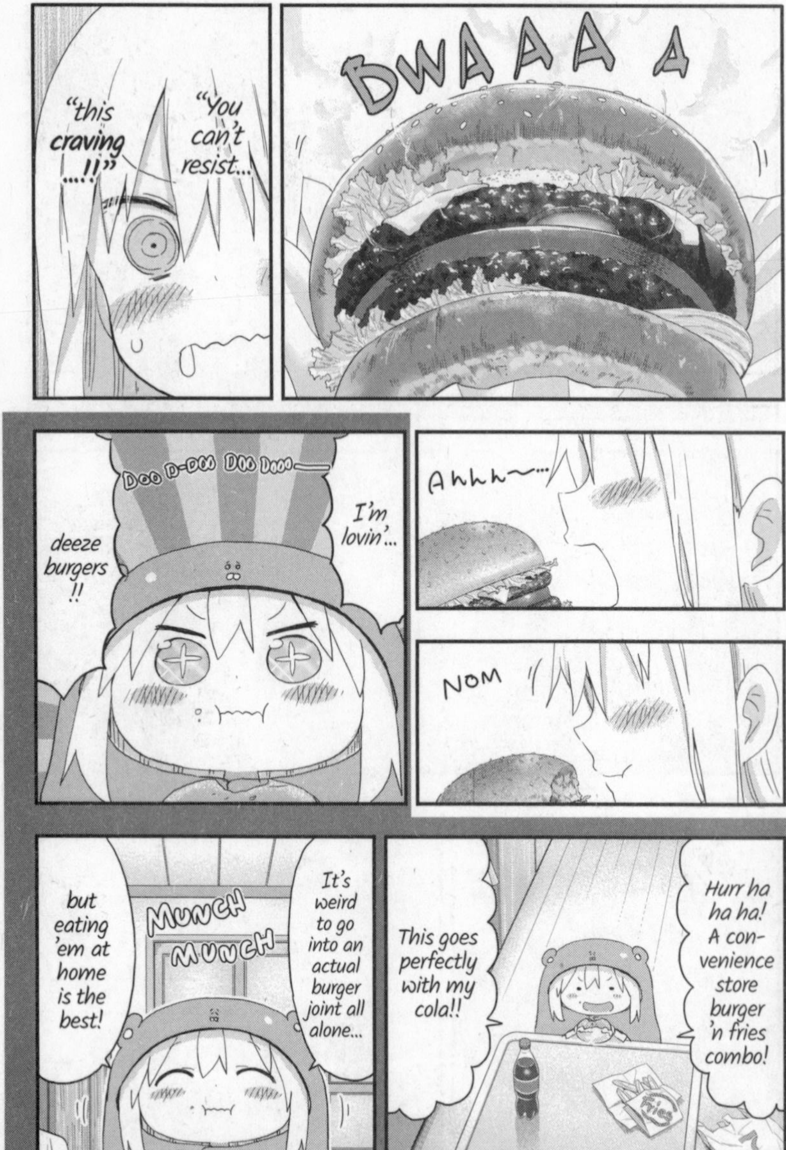
BWAAAA
"You can't resist...
"this craving ....!!"
Ahhh~....
NOM
Doo D-doo Doo Dooo—
I'm lovin'...
deeze burgers !!
Hurr ha ha ha! A convenience store burger 'n fries combo!
This goes perfectly with my cola!!
fries
It's weird to go into an actual burger joint all alone...
MUNCH
MUNCH
but eating 'em at home is the best!

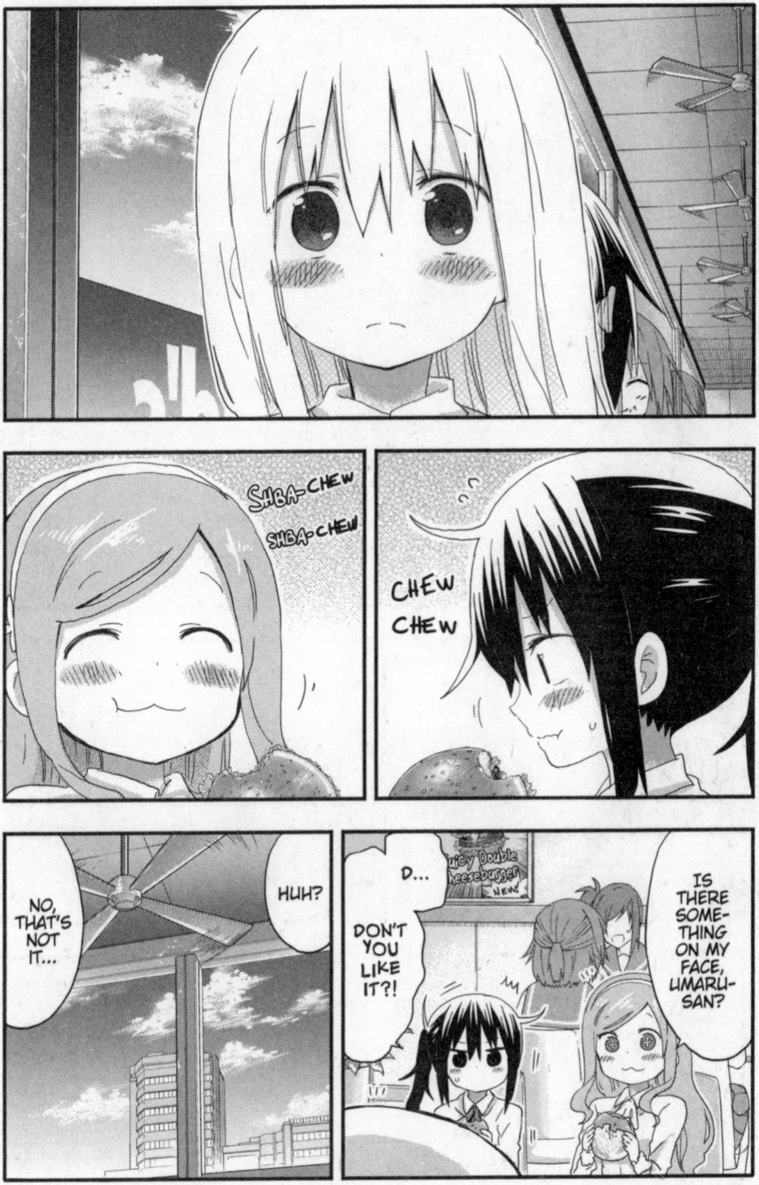
CHEW
CHEW
SHBA-CHEW
SHBA-CHEW
IS THERE SOMETHING ON MY FACE, UMARU-SAN?
uicy Double heeseburger NEW!
D...
DON'T YOU LIKE IT?!
HUH?
NO, THAT'S NOT IT...

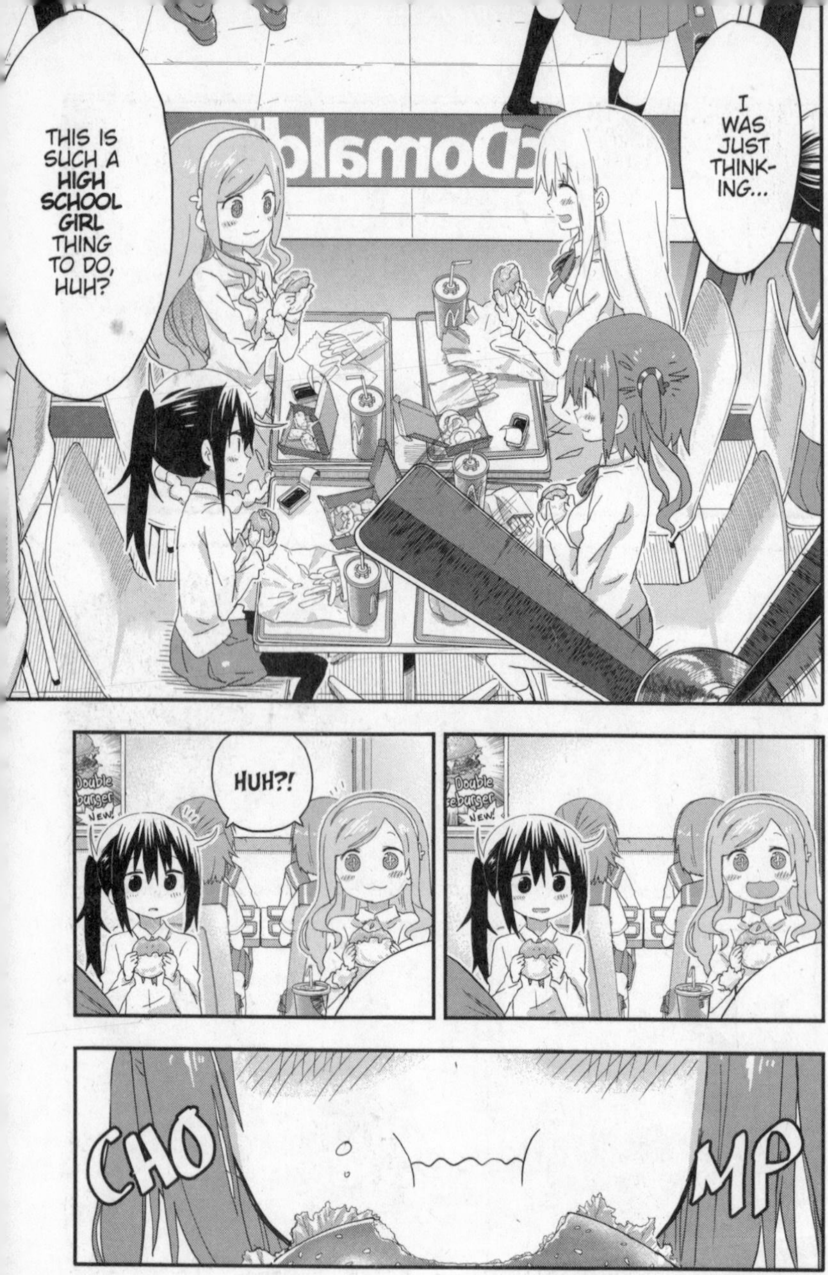
I WAS JUST THINKING...
THIS IS SUCH A HIGH SCHOOL GIRL THING TO DO, HUH?
Double
NEW!
HUH?!
Double
NEW!
CHOMP

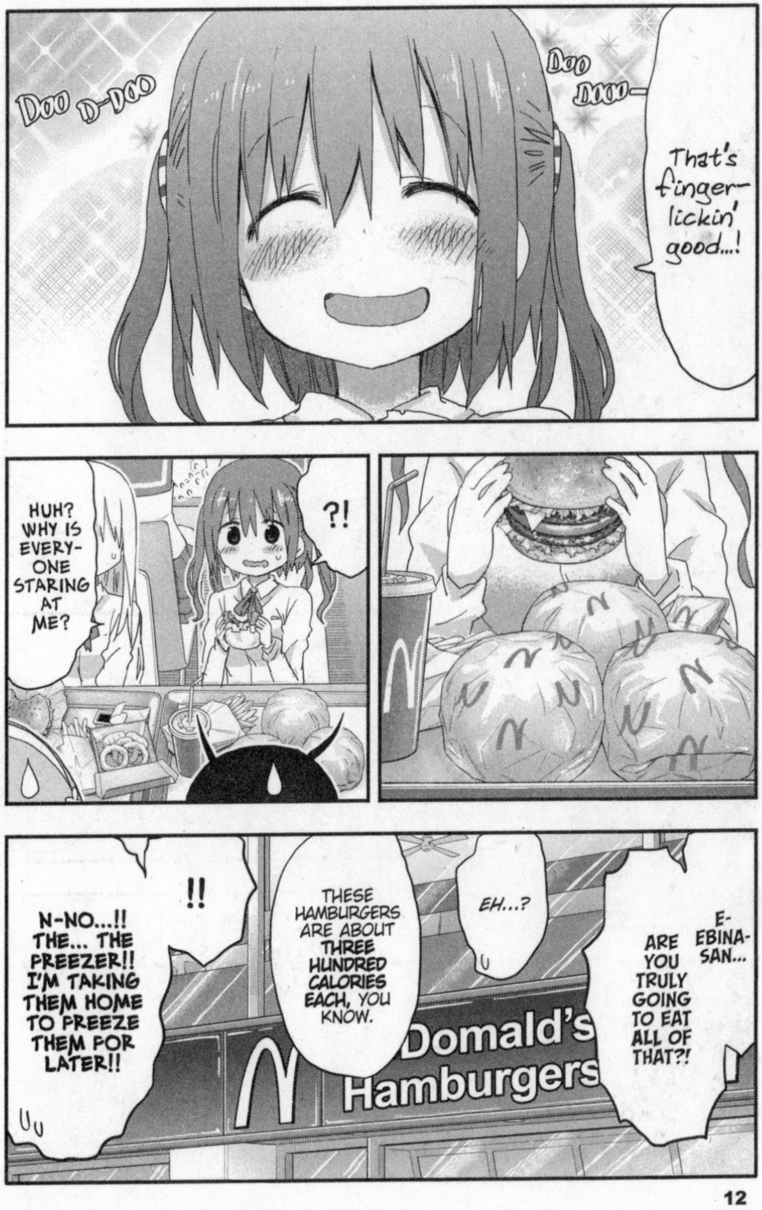

That's finger-lickin' good...!
DOO DOOO—
DOO D-DOO
?!
HUH? WHY IS EVERY-ONE STARING AT ME?
E-EBINA-SAN... ARE YOU TRULY GOING TO EAT ALL OF THAT?!
Domald's Hamburgers
EH...?
THESE HAMBURGERS ARE ABOUT THREE HUNDRED CALORIES EACH, YOU KNOW.
!!
N-NO...!! THE... THE FREEZER!! I'M TAKING THEM HOME TO FREEZE THEM FOR LATER!!

No. 109 Umaru & the Mystery Box

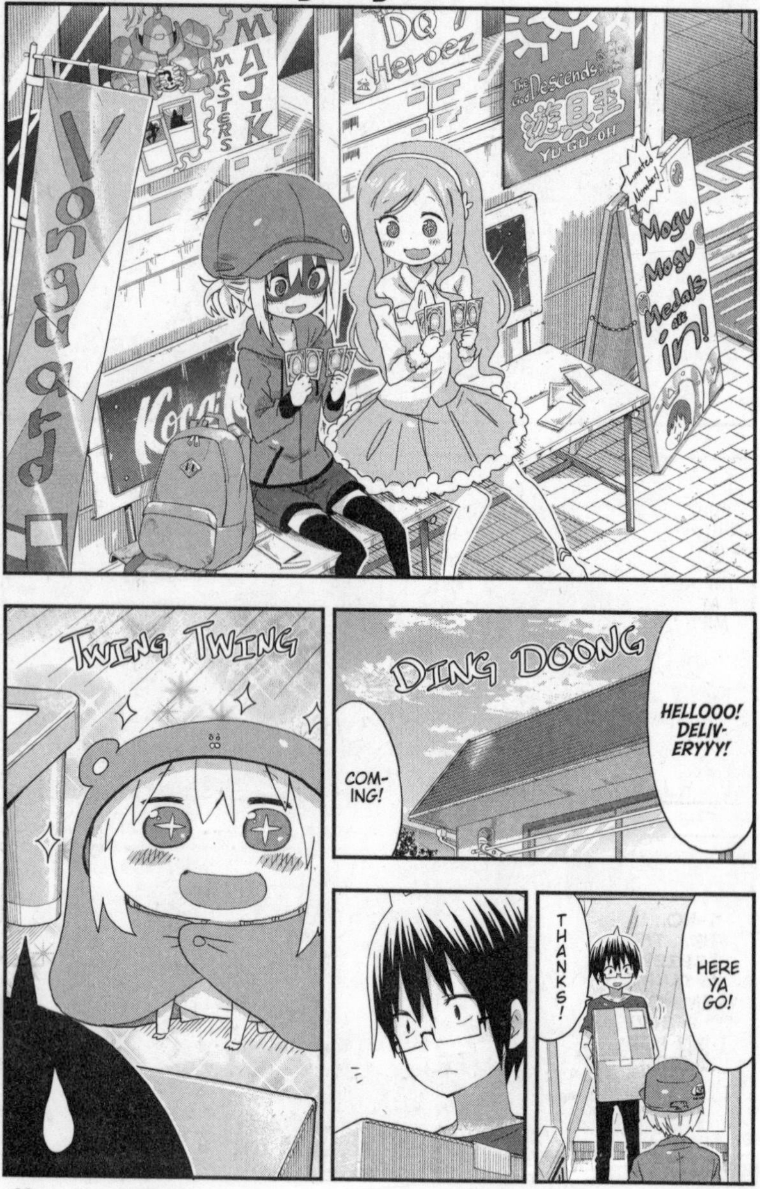
MAJIK MASTERS
DQ Heroez
The God Descends
遊具亜
YU-GU-OH
Limited Number!
Mogu Mogu Medals are in!
DING DOONG
HELLOOO! DELIV-ERYYY!
COM-ING!
HERE YA GO!
THANKS!
TWING TWING

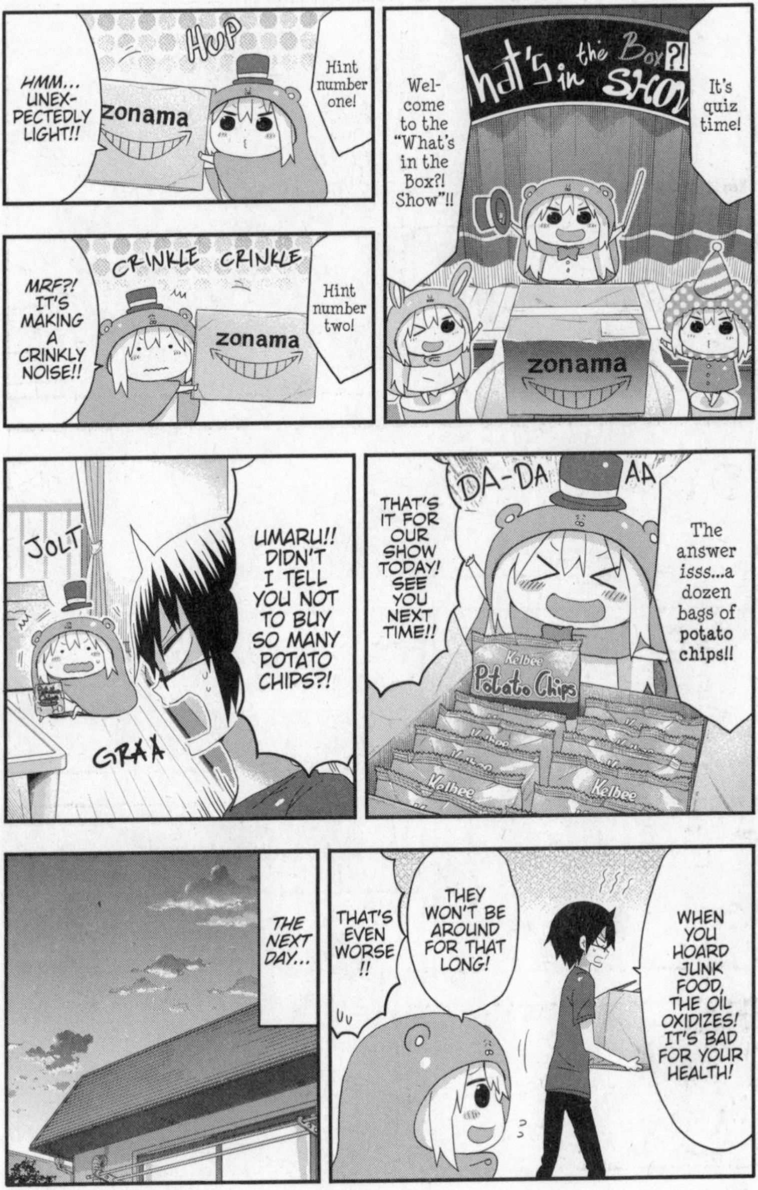
What's in the Box?! SHOW
It's quiz time!
Wel-come to the "What's in the Box?! Show"!!
zonama
Hint number one!
HUP
HMM... UNEX-PECTEDLY LIGHT!!
zonama
Hint number two!
CRINKLE CRINKLE
MRF?! IT'S MAKING A CRINKLY NOISE!!
zonama
DA-DA AA
The answer isss...a dozen bags of potato chips!!
THAT'S IT FOR OUR SHOW TODAY! SEE YOU NEXT TIME!!
Kelbee Potato Chips
UMARU!! DIDN'T I TELL YOU NOT TO BUY SO MANY POTATO CHIPS?!
JOLT
GRAA
WHEN YOU HOARD JUNK FOOD, THE OIL OXIDIZES! IT'S BAD FOR YOUR HEALTH!
THEY WON'T BE AROUND FOR THAT LONG!
THAT'S EVEN WORSE!!
THE NEXT DAY...

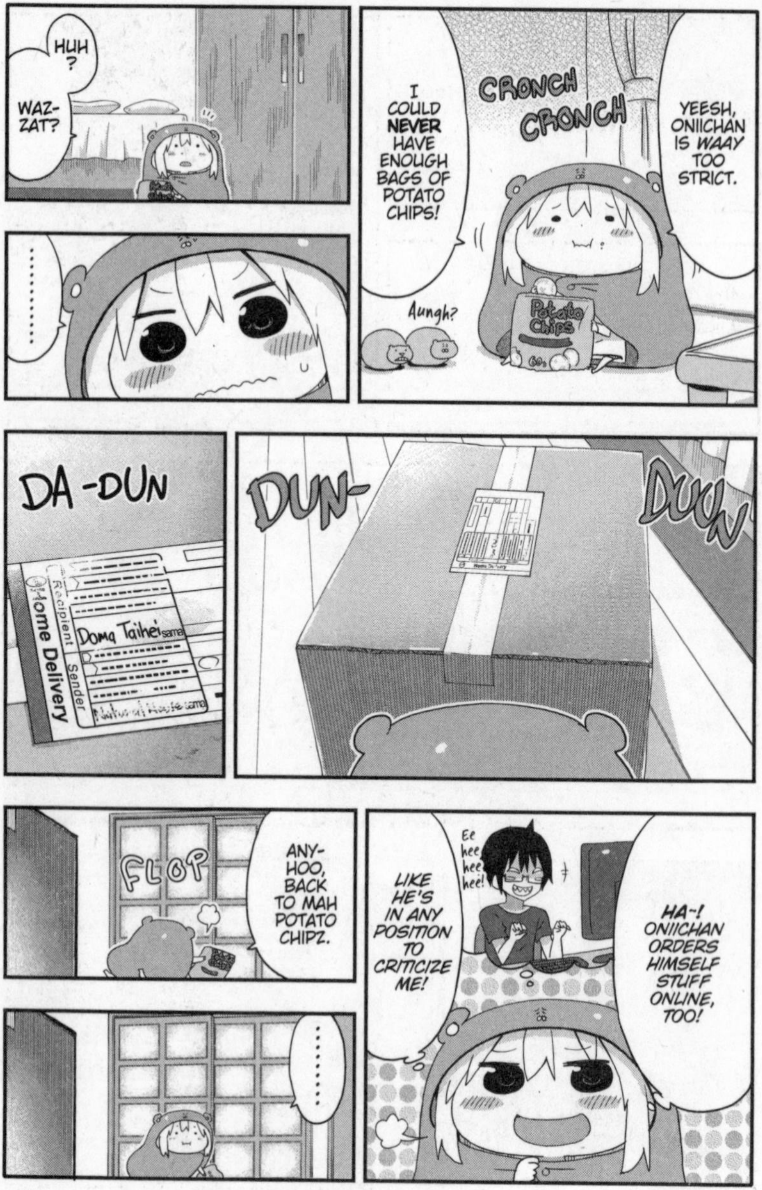
YEESH, ONIICHAN IS WAAY TOO STRICT.
CRONCH CRONCH
I COULD NEVER HAVE ENOUGH BAGS OF POTATO CHIPS!
Aungh?
Potato Chips
HUH? WAZ-ZAT?
......
DUN-DUUN
DA-DUN
Home Delivery
Recipient
Doma Taihei sama
Sender
HA~! ONIICHAN ORDERS HIMSELF STUFF ONLINE, TOO!
Ee hee hee hee!
LIKE HE'S IN ANY POSITION TO CRITICIZE ME!
ANY-HOO, BACK TO MAH POTATO CHIPZ.
FLOP
......

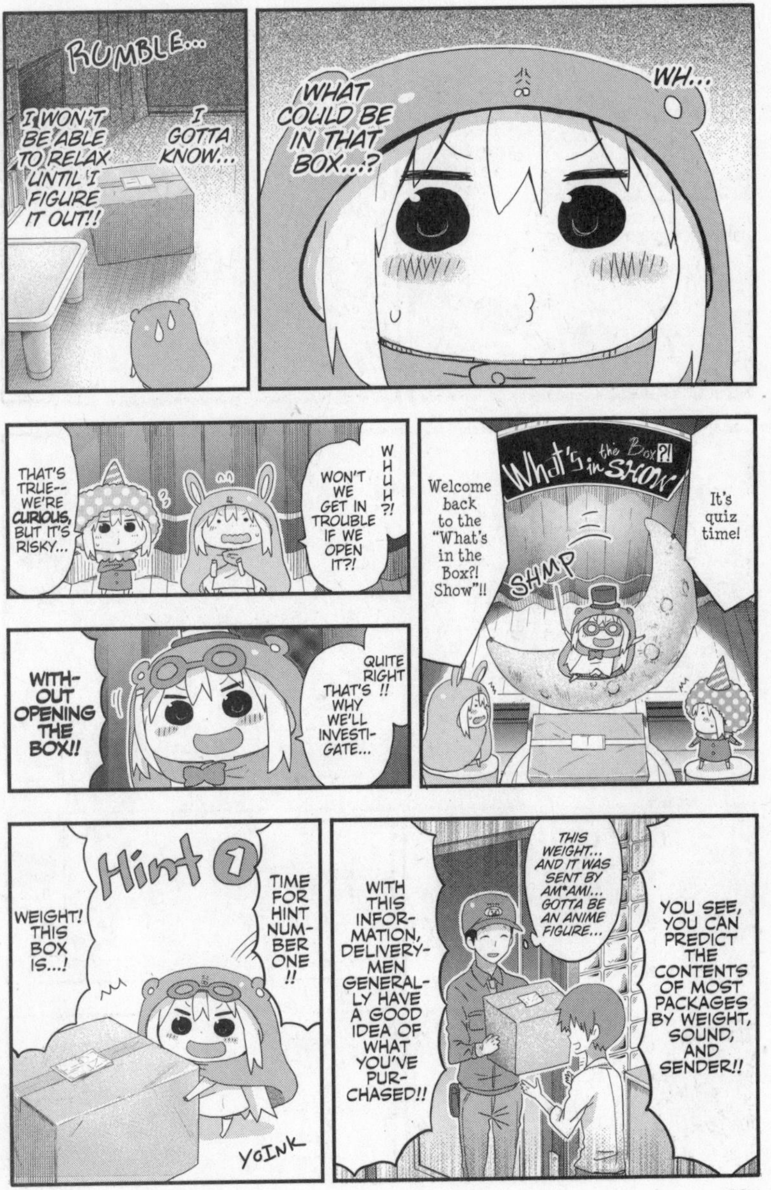
WH...
WHAT COULD BE IN THAT BOX...?
RUMBLE...
I GOTTA KNOW...
I WON'T BE ABLE TO RELAX UNTIL I FIGURE IT OUT!!
What's in the Box?! SHOW
It's quiz time!
Welcome back to the "What's in the Box?! Show"!!
SHMP
WHUH?!
WON'T WE GET IN TROUBLE IF WE OPEN IT?!
THAT'S TRUE-- WE'RE CURIOUS, BUT IT'S RISKY...
QUITE RIGHT!! THAT'S WHY WE'LL INVESTIGATE...
WITHOUT OPENING THE BOX!!
YOU SEE, YOU CAN PREDICT THE CONTENTS OF MOST PACKAGES BY WEIGHT, SOUND, AND SENDER!!
THIS WEIGHT... AND IT WAS SENT BY AM*AMI... GOTTA BE AN ANIME FIGURE...
WITH THIS INFORMATION, DELIVERYMEN GENERALLY HAVE A GOOD IDEA OF WHAT YOU'VE PURCHASED!!
TIME FOR HINT NUMBER ONE!!
Hint 1
WEIGHT! THIS BOX IS...!
YOINK

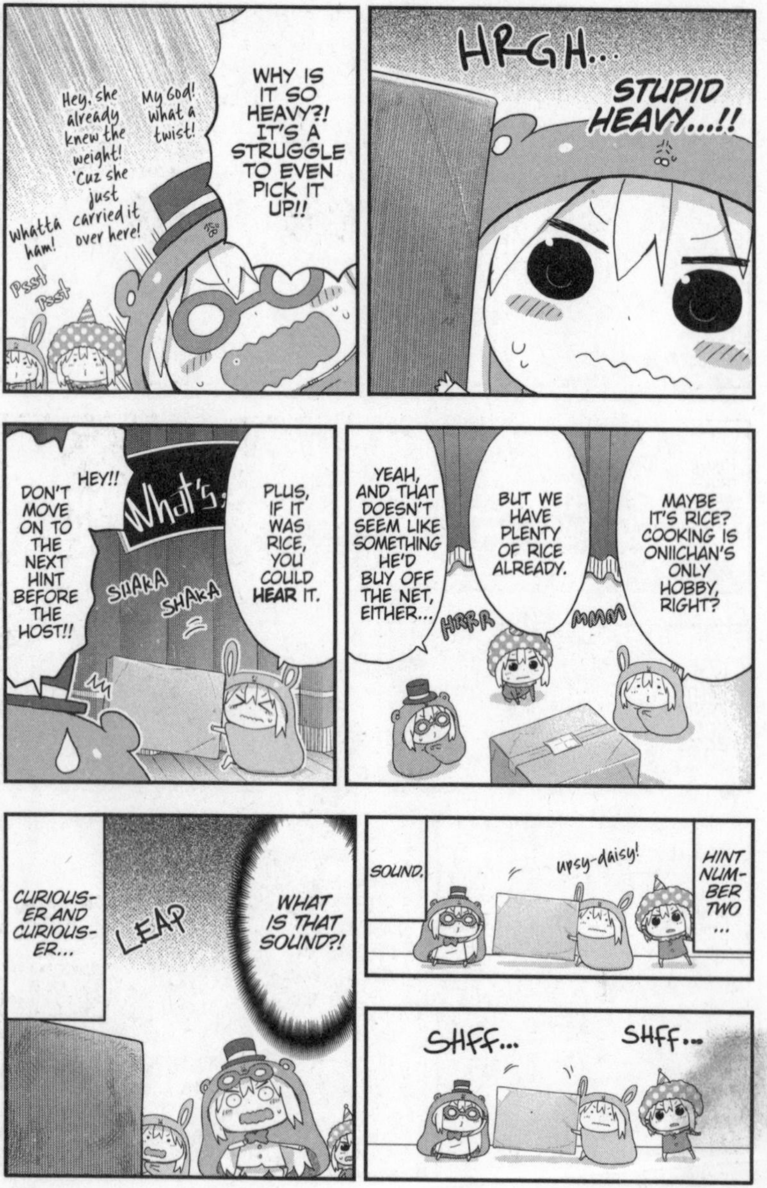

HRGH...
STUPID HEAVY...!!
WHY IS IT SO HEAVY?! IT'S A STRUGGLE TO EVEN PICK IT UP!!
My God! what a twist!
Hey, she already knew the weight! 'Cuz she just carried it over here!
Whatta ham!
Psst Psst
MAYBE IT'S RICE? COOKING IS ONIICHAN'S ONLY HOBBY, RIGHT?
BUT WE HAVE PLENTY OF RICE ALREADY.
YEAH, AND THAT DOESN'T SEEM LIKE SOMETHING HE'D BUY OFF THE NET, EITHER...
MMM
HRRR
PLUS, IF IT WAS RICE, YOU COULD **HEAR** IT.
What's
HEY!!
DON'T MOVE ON TO THE NEXT HINT BEFORE THE HOST!!
SHAKA SHAKA
HINT NUMBER TWO...
upsy-daisy!
SOUND.
SHFF... SHFF...
WHAT IS THAT SOUND?!
LEAP
CURIOUSER AND CURIOUSER...

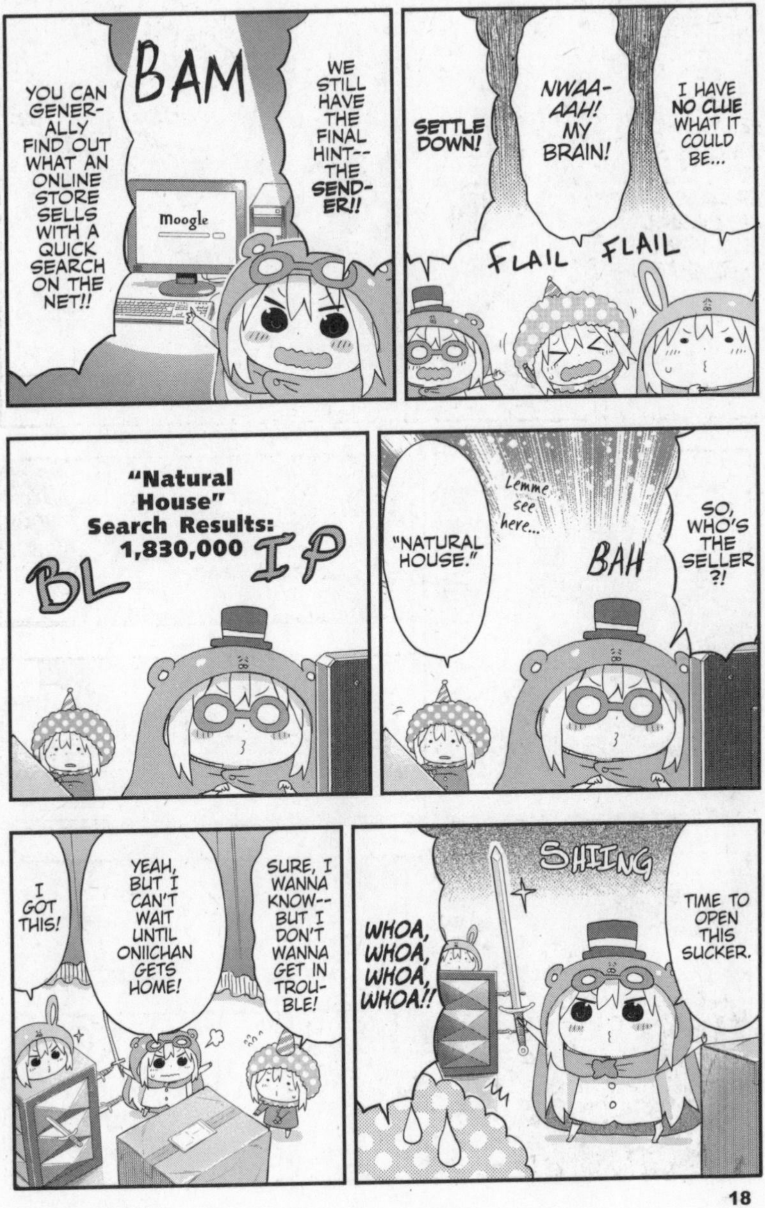
I HAVE NO CLUE WHAT IT COULD BE...
NWAA-AAH! MY BRAIN!
SETTLE DOWN!
FLAIL FLAIL
WE STILL HAVE THE FINAL HINT--THE SENDER!!
BAM
YOU CAN GENERALLY FIND OUT WHAT AN ONLINE STORE SELLS WITH A QUICK SEARCH ON THE NET!!
moogle
SO, WHO'S THE SELLER?!
BAH
Lemme see here...
"NATURAL HOUSE."
"Natural House" Search Results: 1,830,000
BLIP
TIME TO OPEN THIS SUCKER.
SHIING
WHOA, WHOA, WHOA, WHOA!!
SURE, I WANNA KNOW--BUT I DON'T WANNA GET IN TROUBLE!
YEAH, BUT I CAN'T WAIT UNTIL ONIICHAN GETS HOME!
I GOT THIS!

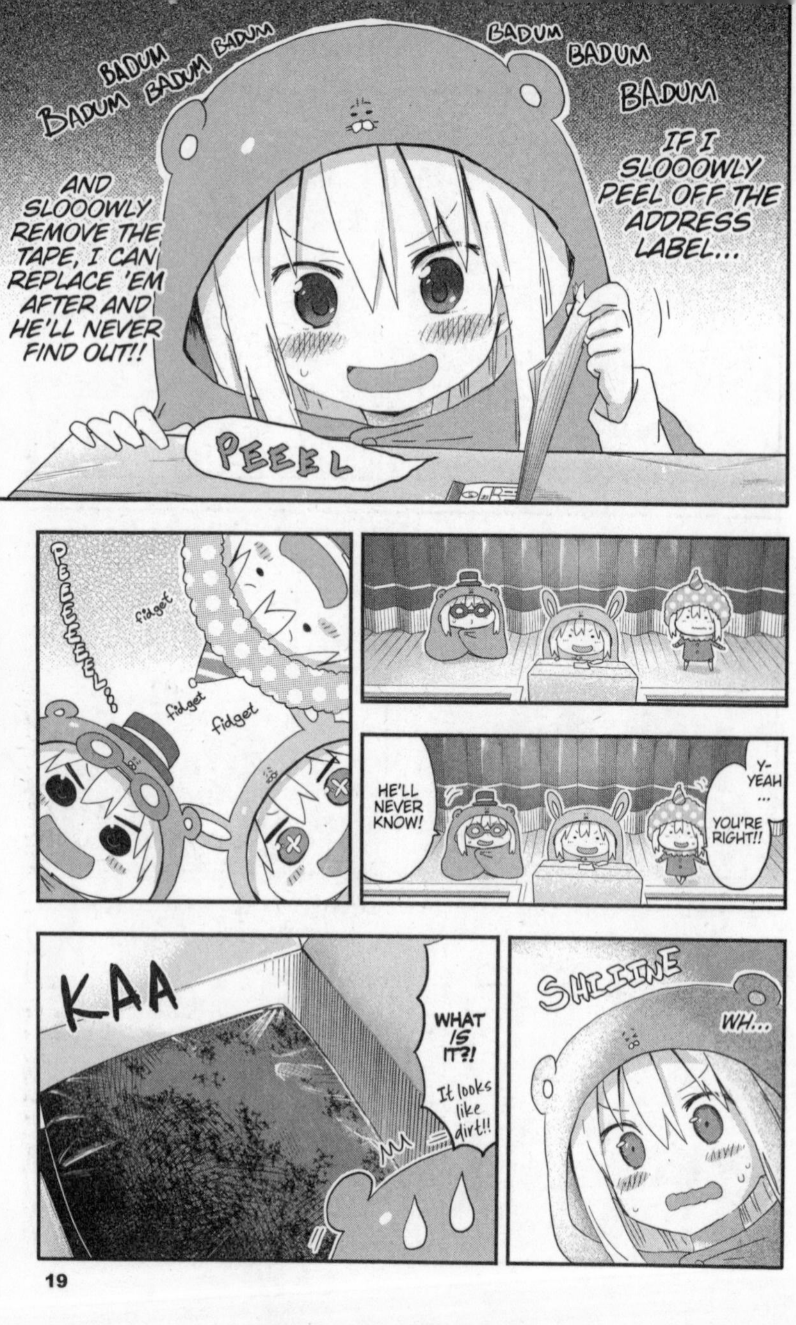
BADUM
BADUM
BADUM
IF I SLOOOWLY PEEL OFF THE ADDRESS LABEL...
BADUM BADUM BADUM
BADUM
AND SLOOOWLY REMOVE THE TAPE, I CAN REPLACE 'EM AFTER AND HE'LL NEVER FIND OUT!!
PEEEL
Y-YEAH... YOU'RE RIGHT!!
HE'LL NEVER KNOW!
PEEEEEEL...
fidget
fidget
fidget
SHIIINE
WH...
KAA
WHAT IS IT?!
It looks like dirt!!

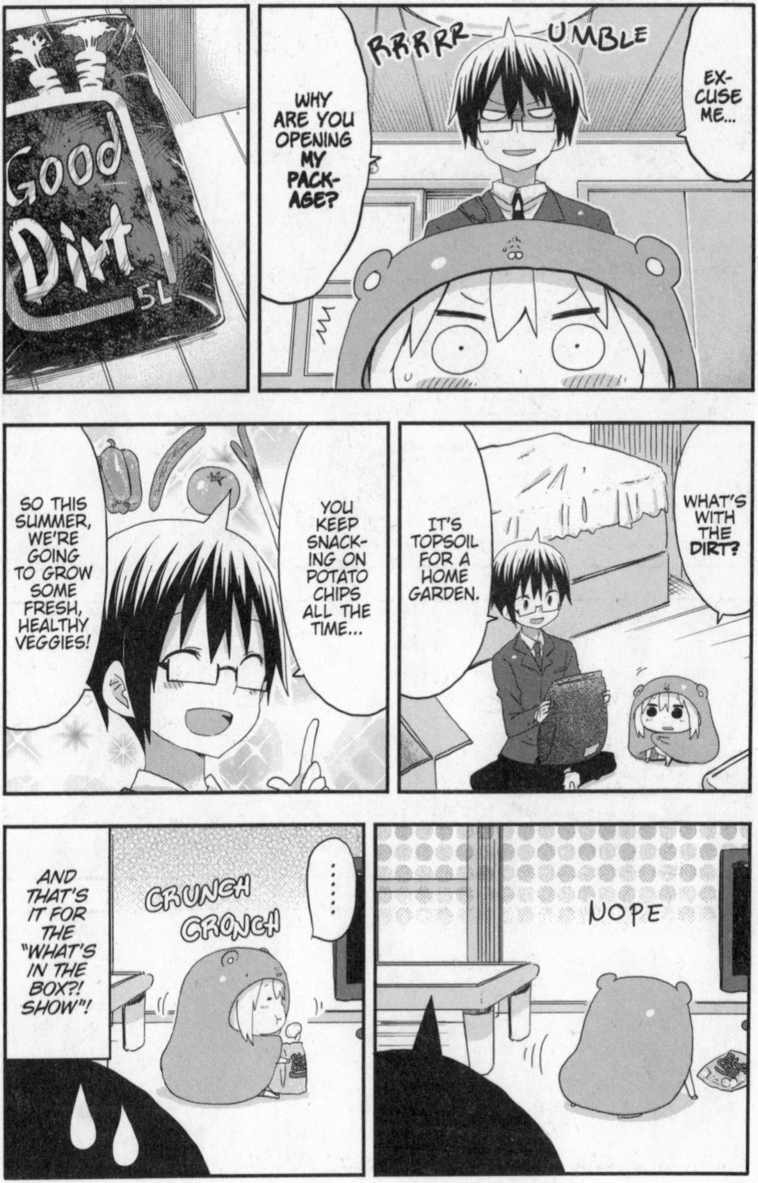
EX-CUSE ME...
RRRRR—UMBLE
WHY ARE YOU OPENING MY PACK-AGE?
Good Dirt
5L
WHAT'S WITH THE DIRT?
IT'S TOPSOIL FOR A HOME GARDEN.
YOU KEEP SNACK-ING ON POTATO CHIPS ALL THE TIME...
SO THIS SUMMER, WE'RE GOING TO GROW SOME FRESH, HEALTHY VEGGIES!
NOPE
......
CRUNCH
CRONCH
AND THAT'S IT FOR THE "WHAT'S IN THE BOX?! SHOW"!

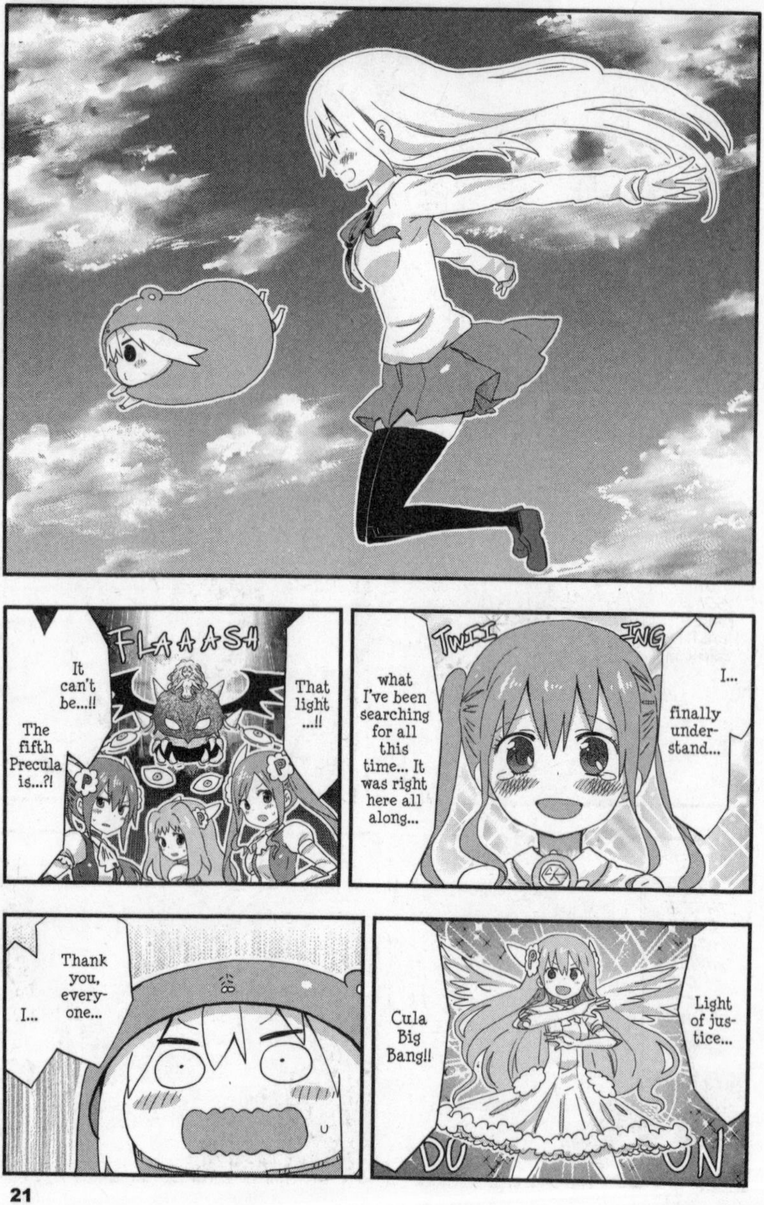
TWIIING
I...
finally understand...
what I've been searching for all this time... It was right here all along...
FLAAASH
That light...!!
It can't be...!!
The fifth Precula is...?!
Light of justice...
Cula Big Bang!!
DU UN
I...
Thank you, everyone...

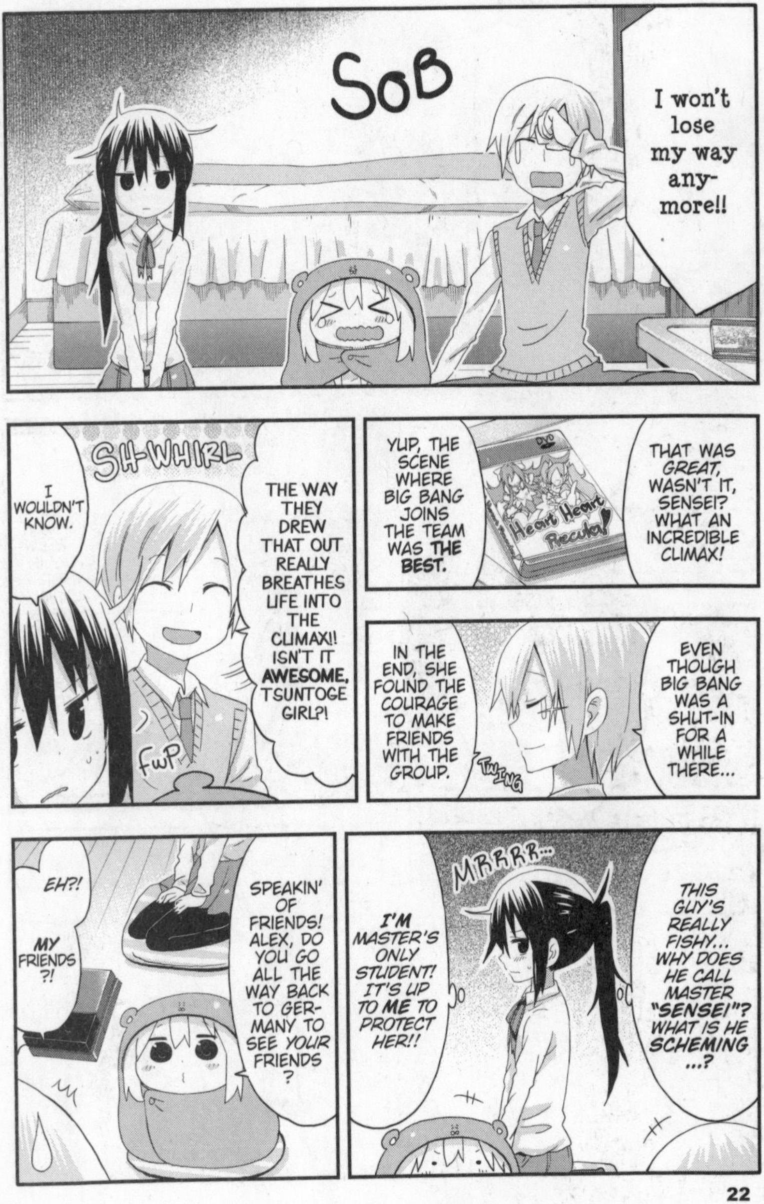

I won't lose my way any-more!!
SOB
THAT WAS GREAT, WASN'T IT, SENSEI? WHAT AN INCREDIBLE CLIMAX!
DVD
Heart Heart Precula
YUP, THE SCENE WHERE BIG BANG JOINS THE TEAM WAS THE BEST.
EVEN THOUGH BIG BANG WAS A SHUT-IN FOR A WHILE THERE...
IN THE END, SHE FOUND THE COURAGE TO MAKE FRIENDS WITH THE GROUP.
TWING
SH-WHIRL
THE WAY THEY DREW THAT OUT REALLY BREATHES LIFE INTO THE CLIMAX!! ISN'T IT AWESOME, TSUNTOGE GIRL?!
I WOULDN'T KNOW.
FWP
THIS GUY'S REALLY FISHY... WHY DOES HE CALL MASTER "SENSEI"? WHAT IS HE SCHEMING ...?
MRRRR...
I'M MASTER'S ONLY STUDENT! IT'S UP TO ME TO PROTECT HER!!
SPEAKIN' OF FRIENDS! ALEX, DO YOU GO ALL THE WAY BACK TO GER-MANY TO SEE YOUR FRIENDS ?
EH?!
MY FRIENDS ?!

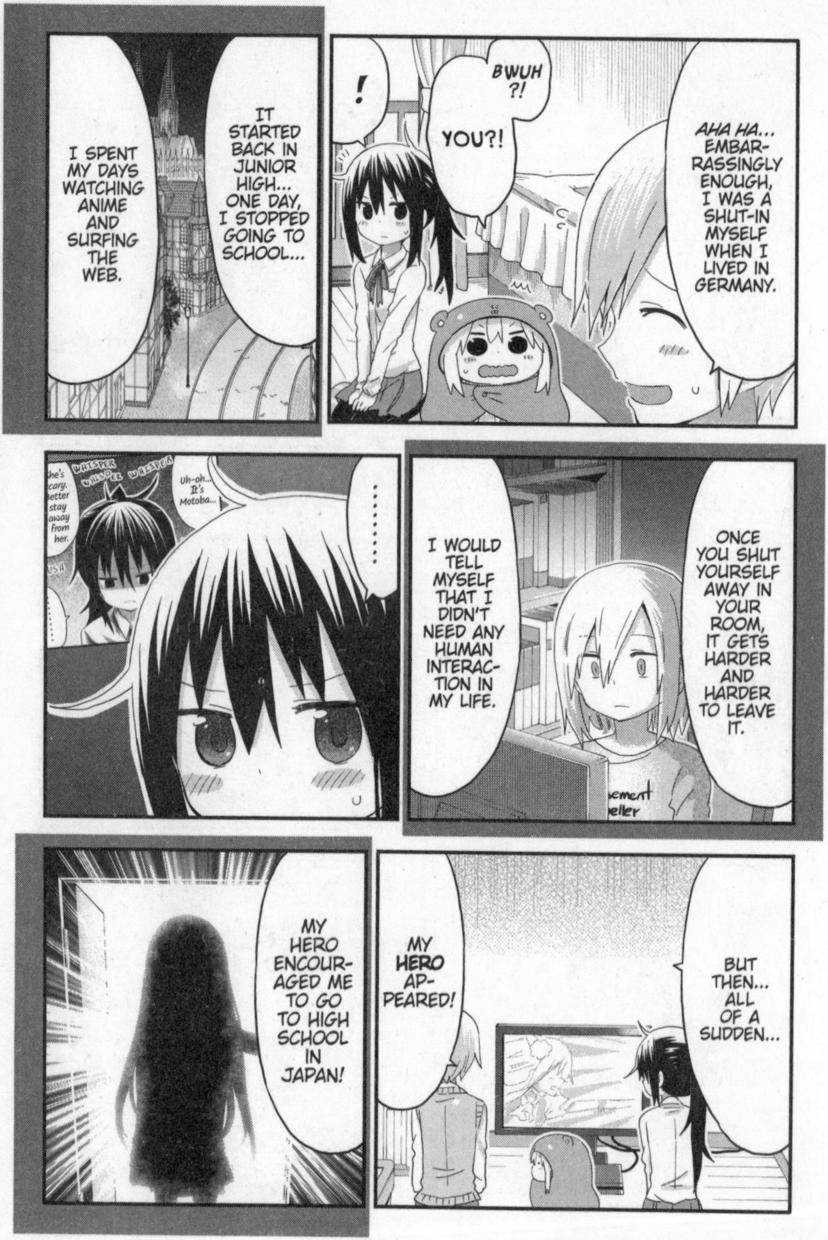
AHA HA... EMBARRASSINGLY ENOUGH, I WAS A SHUT-IN MYSELF WHEN I LIVED IN GERMANY.
BWUH ?!
YOU?!
!
IT STARTED BACK IN JUNIOR HIGH... ONE DAY, I STOPPED GOING TO SCHOOL...
I SPENT MY DAYS WATCHING ANIME AND SURFING THE WEB.
ONCE YOU SHUT YOURSELF AWAY IN YOUR ROOM, IT GETS HARDER AND HARDER TO LEAVE IT.
I WOULD TELL MYSELF THAT I DIDN'T NEED ANY HUMAN INTERACTION IN MY LIFE.
....
Uh-oh... It's Motoba...
WHISPER WHISPER WHISPER
he's cary. etter stay away from her.
BUT THEN... ALL OF A SUDDEN...
MY HERO APPEARED!
MY HERO ENCOURAGED ME TO GO TO HIGH SCHOOL IN JAPAN!

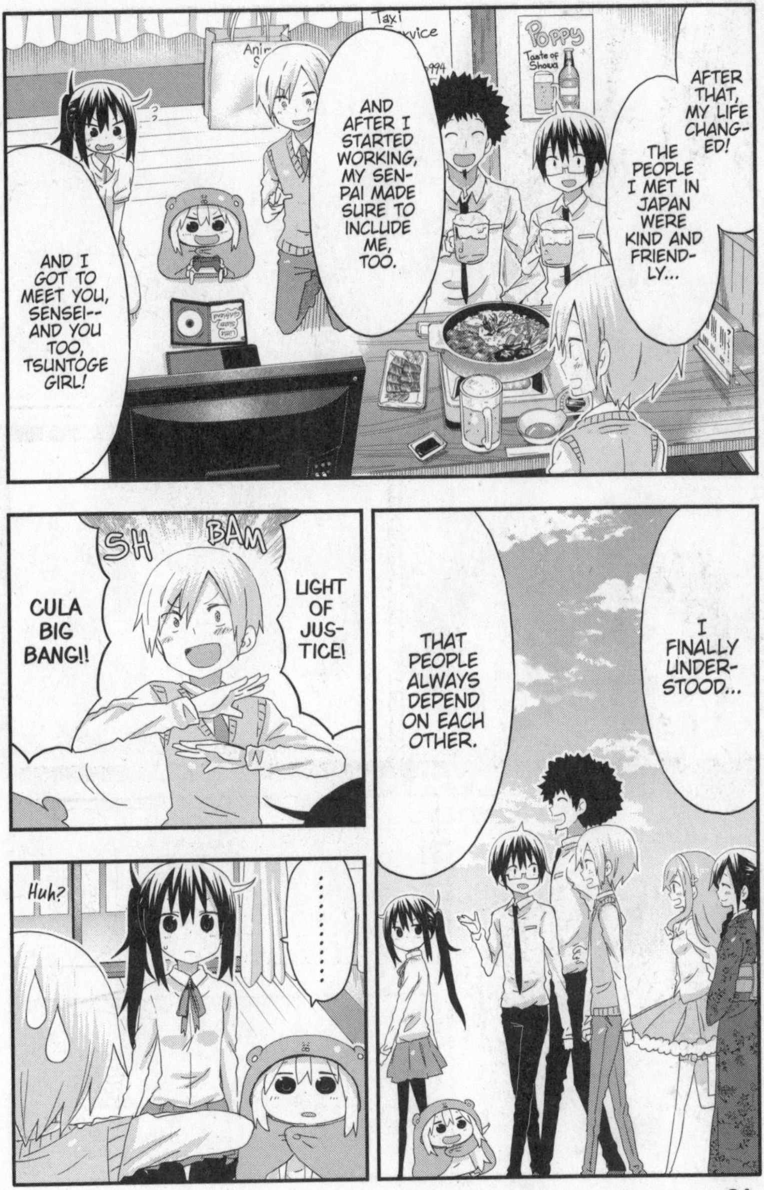
Taxi Service
Poppy
Taste of Showa
AFTER THAT, MY LIFE CHANG-ED!
THE PEOPLE I MET IN JAPAN WERE KIND AND FRIEND-LY...
AND AFTER I STARTED WORKING, MY SEN-PAI MADE SURE TO INCLUDE ME, TOO.
AND I GOT TO MEET YOU, SENSEI-- AND YOU TOO, TSUNTOGE GIRL!
I FINALLY UNDER-STOOD...
THAT PEOPLE ALWAYS DEPEND ON EACH OTHER.
SH
BAM
LIGHT OF JUS-TICE!
CULA BIG BANG!!
......
Huh?

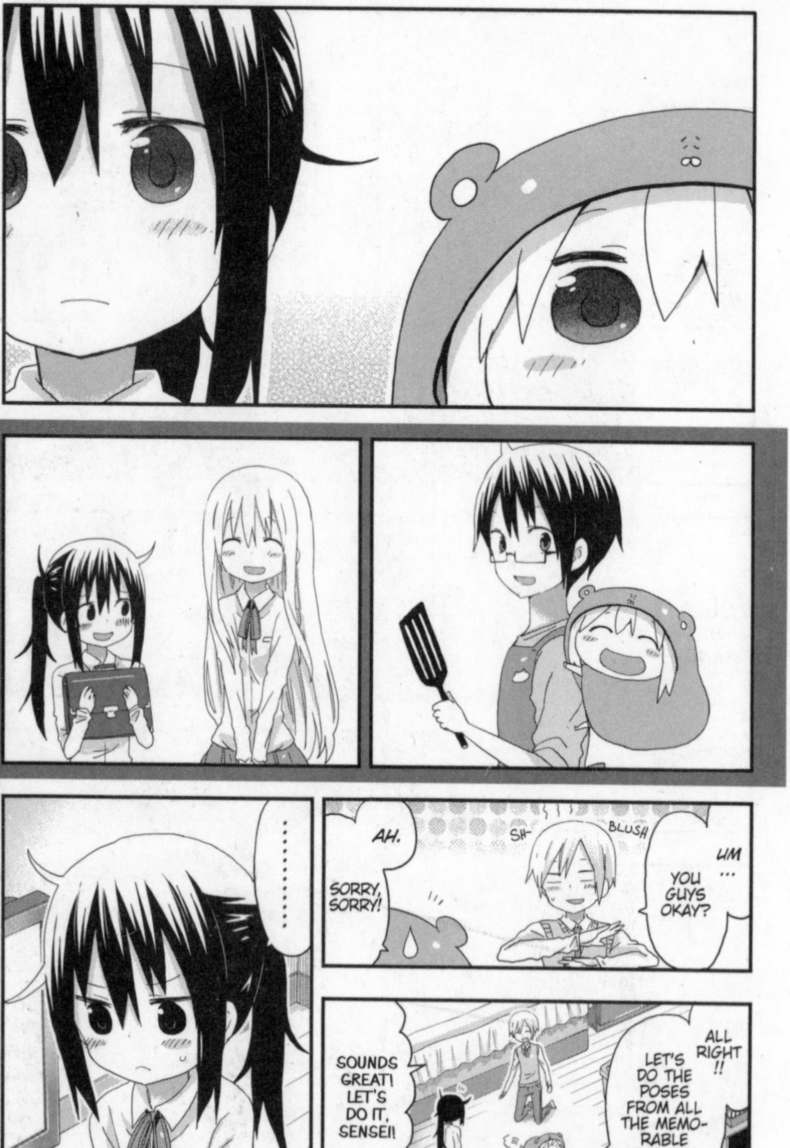

BLUSH
UM...
YOU GUYS OKAY?
SH-
AH.
SORRY, SORRY!
ALL RIGHT!!
LET'S DO THE POSES FROM ALL THE MEMO-RABLE SCENES!
SOUNDS GREAT! LET'S DO IT, SENSEI!
......

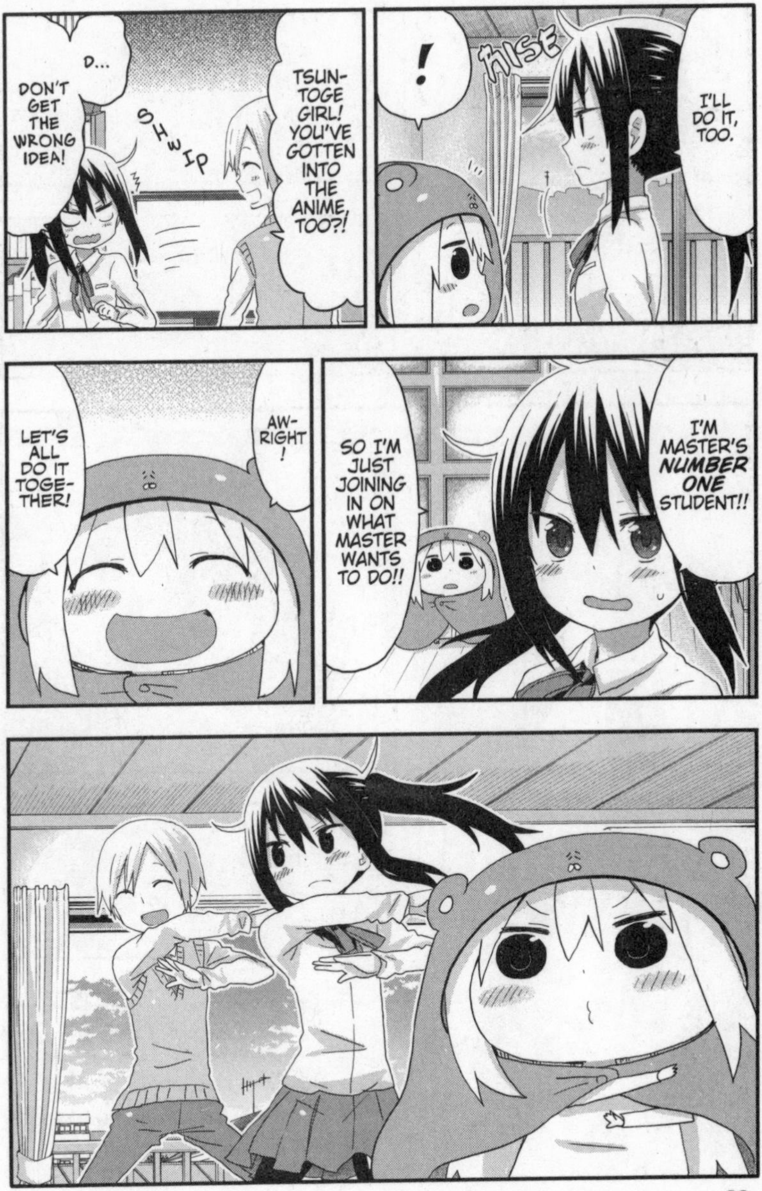
!
RISE
I'LL DO IT, TOO.
TSUN-TOGE GIRL! YOU'VE GOTTEN INTO THE ANIME, TOO?!
SHWIP
D...
DON'T GET THE WRONG IDEA!
I'M MASTER'S **NUMBER ONE** STUDENT!!
SO I'M JUST JOINING IN ON WHAT MASTER WANTS TO DO!!
AW-RIGHT!
LET'S ALL DO IT TOGE-THER!

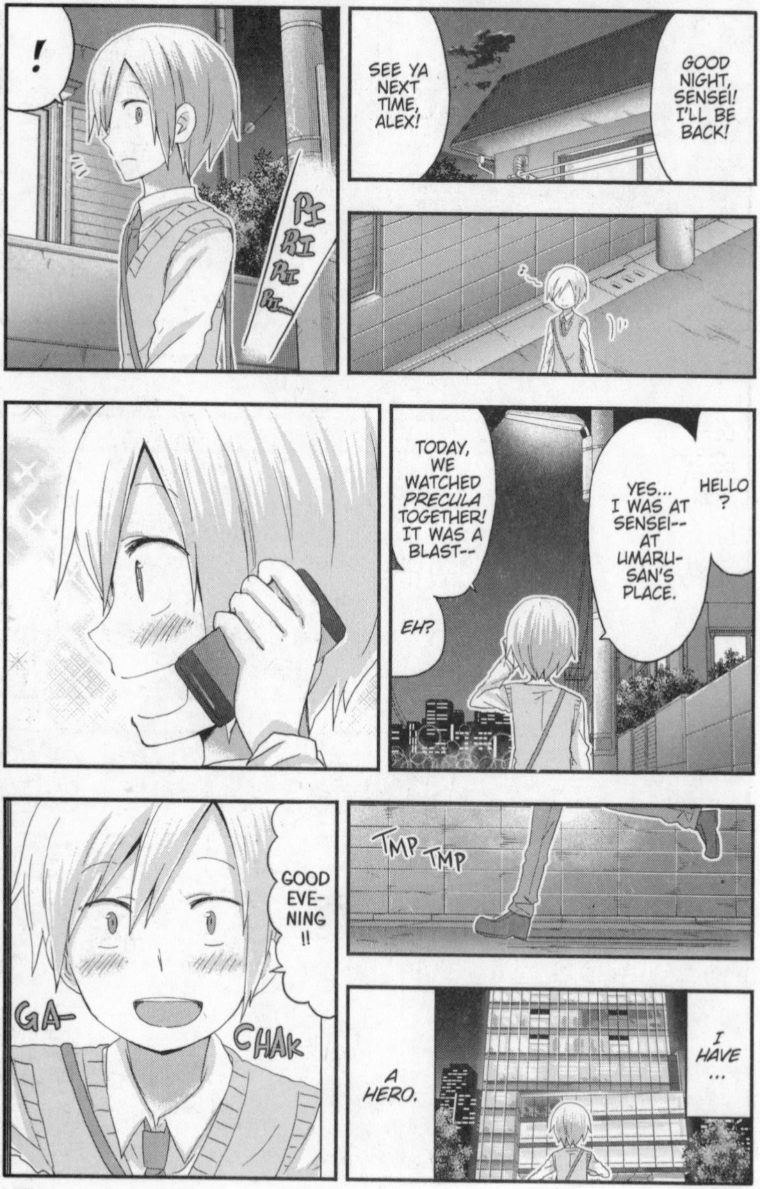
GOOD NIGHT, SENSEI! I'LL BE BACK!
SEE YA NEXT TIME, ALEX!
!
PI RI RI PI...
HELLO ?
YES... I WAS AT SENSEI-- AT UMARU-SAN'S PLACE.
TODAY, WE WATCHED *PRECULA* TOGETHER! IT WAS A BLAST--
EH?
TMP TMP
I HAVE ...
A HERO.
GOOD EVE-NING !!
GA-CHAK

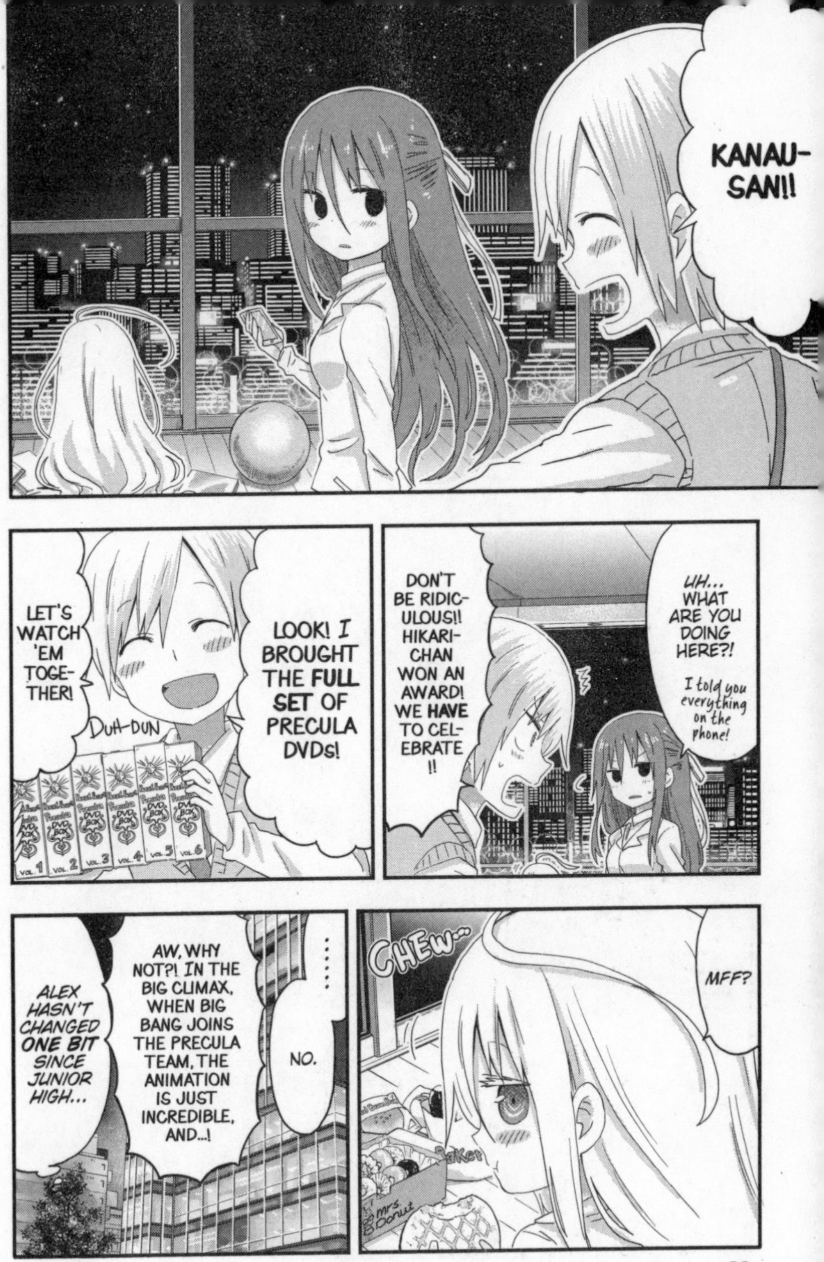
KANAU-SAN!!
UH... WHAT ARE YOU DOING HERE?!
I told you everything on the phone!
DON'T BE RIDICU-ULOUS!! HIKARI-CHAN WON AN AWARD! WE HAVE TO CEL-EBRATE!!
LOOK! I BROUGHT THE FULL SET OF PRECULA DVDs!
DUH-DUN
LET'S WATCH 'EM TOGE-THER!
CHEW...
MFF?
......
NO.
AW, WHY NOT?! IN THE BIG CLIMAX, WHEN BIG BANG JOINS THE PRECULA TEAM, THE ANIMATION IS JUST INCREDIBLE, AND...!
ALEX HASN'T CHANGED ONE BIT SINCE JUNIOR HIGH...

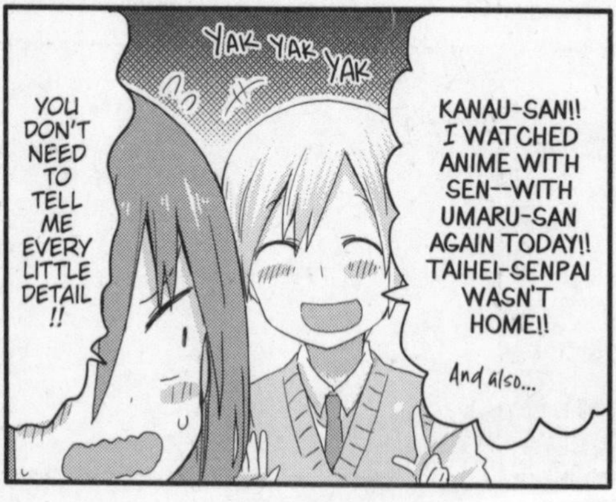
YAK YAK YAK
KANAU-SAN!! I WATCHED ANIME WITH SEN--WITH UMARU-SAN AGAIN TODAY!! TAIHEI-SENPAI WASN'T HOME!!
And also...
YOU DON'T NEED TO TELL ME EVERY LITTLE DETAIL!!

No. 111 Umaru & Capsule Toys

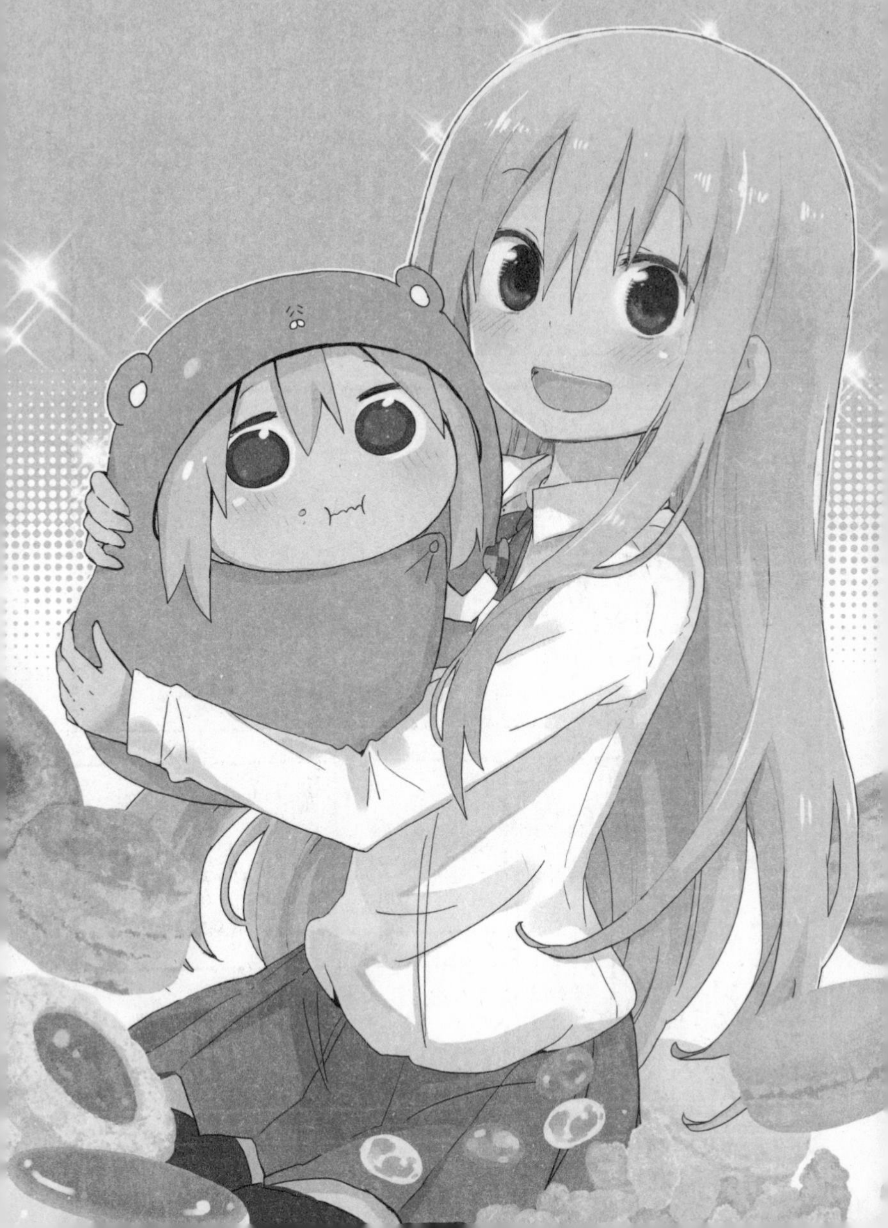

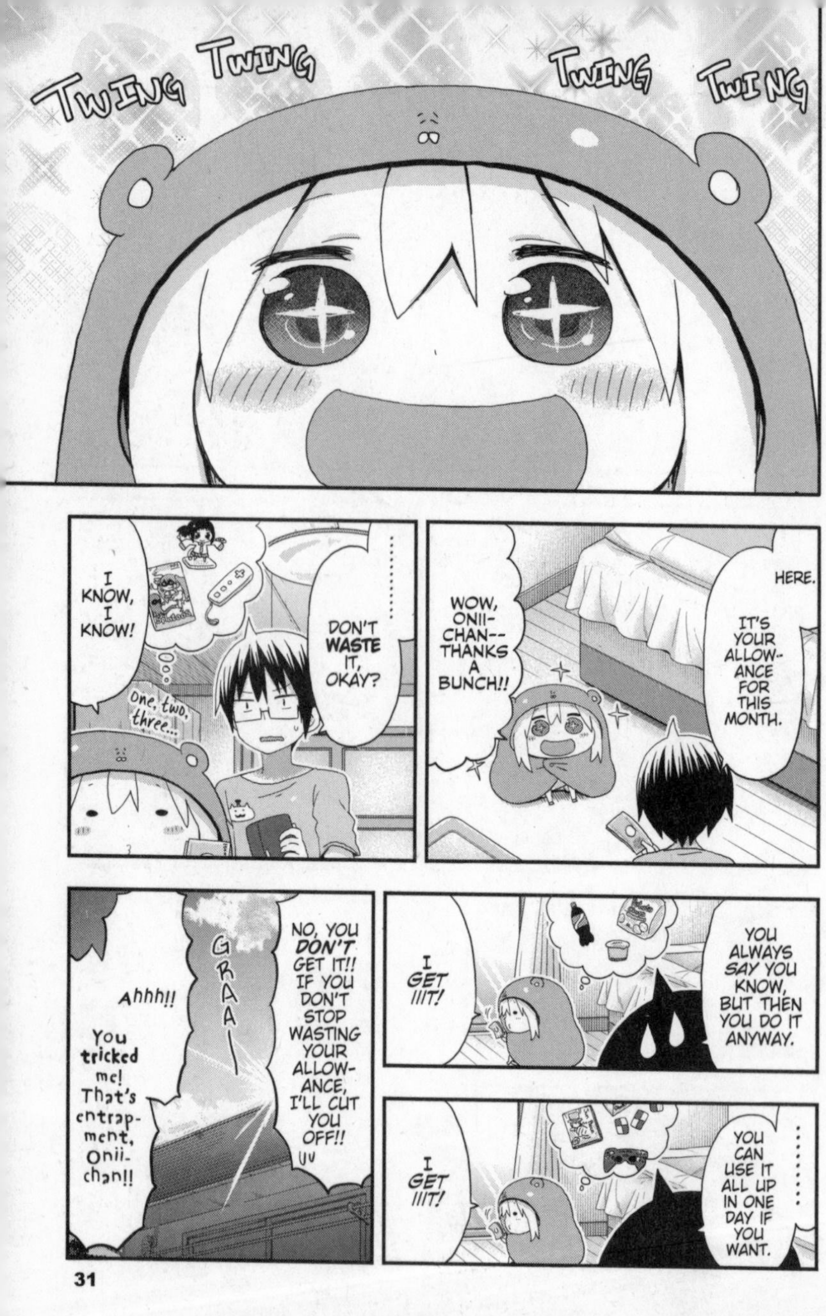
TWING
TWING
TWING
TWING
HERE.
IT'S YOUR ALLOW-ANCE FOR THIS MONTH.
WOW, ONII-CHAN--THANKS A BUNCH!!
......
DON'T WASTE IT, OKAY?
I KNOW, I KNOW!
One, two, three...
YOU ALWAYS SAY YOU KNOW, BUT THEN YOU DO IT ANYWAY.
I GET IIIT!
......
YOU CAN USE IT ALL UP IN ONE DAY IF YOU WANT.
I GET IIIT!
NO, YOU DON'T GET IT!! IF YOU DON'T STOP WASTING YOUR ALLOW-ANCE, I'LL CUT YOU OFF!!
GRAA!
Ahhh!!
You tricked me! That's entrap-ment, Onii-chan!!

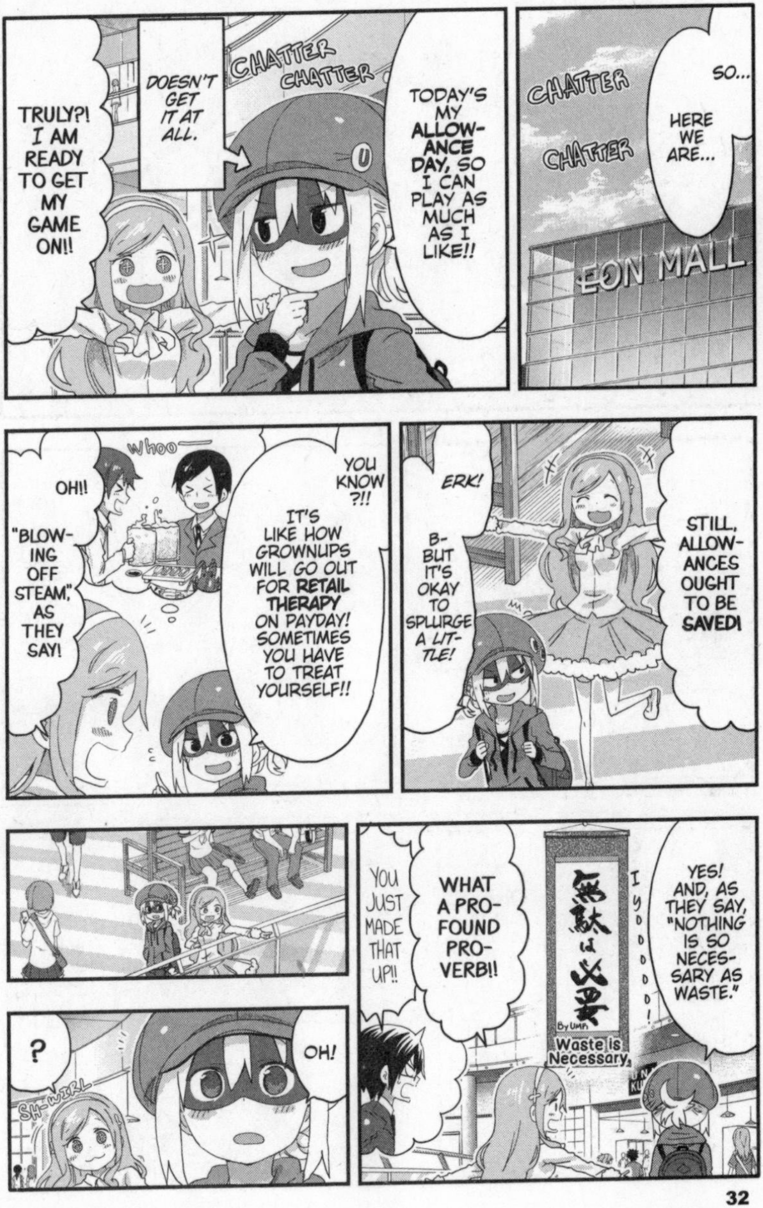
SO...
HERE WE ARE...
CHATTER
CHATTER
EON MALL
TODAY'S MY ALLOWANCE DAY, SO I CAN PLAY AS MUCH AS I LIKE!!
CHATTER CHATTER
DOESN'T GET IT AT ALL.
TRULY?! I AM READY TO GET MY GAME ON!!
STILL, ALLOWANCES OUGHT TO BE SAVED!
ERK!
B-BUT IT'S OKAY TO SPLURGE A LITTLE!
YOU KNOW?!!
IT'S LIKE HOW GROWNUPS WILL GO OUT FOR RETAIL THERAPY ON PAYDAY! SOMETIMES YOU HAVE TO TREAT YOURSELF!!
whoo—
OH!!
"BLOWING OFF STEAM," AS THEY SAY!
YES! AND, AS THEY SAY, "NOTHING IS SO NECESSARY AS WASTE."
IYODDDDD!
無駄は必要
Waste is Necessary
WHAT A PROFOUND PROVERB!!
YOU JUST MADE THAT UP!!
OH!
SH-WIRL
?

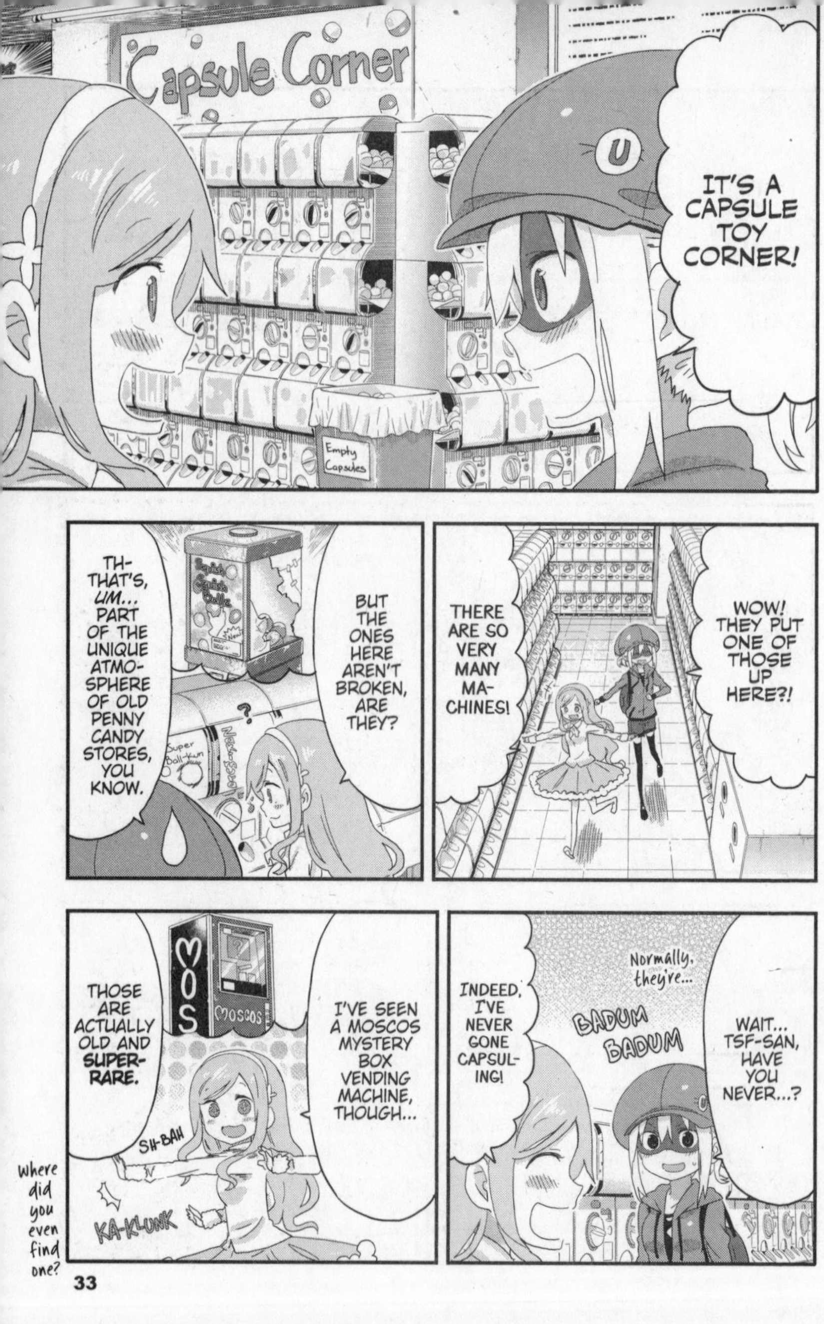
Capsule Corner
IT'S A CAPSULE TOY CORNER!
Empty Capsules
WOW! THEY PUT ONE OF THOSE UP HERE?!
THERE ARE SO VERY MANY MA-CHINES!
BUT THE ONES HERE AREN'T BROKEN, ARE THEY?
Squish Squish Balls
New
Super Ball-Kun
TH-THAT'S, UM... PART OF THE UNIQUE ATMO-SPHERE OF OLD PENNY CANDY STORES, YOU KNOW.
WAIT... TSF-SAN, HAVE YOU NEVER...?
Normally, they're...
BADUM BADUM
INDEED, I'VE NEVER GONE CAPSUL-ING!
I'VE SEEN A MOSCOS MYSTERY BOX VENDING MACHINE, THOUGH...
MOS
MOSCOS
THOSE ARE ACTUALLY OLD AND **SUPER-RARE.**
SH-BAH
KA-KLUNK
where did you even find one?

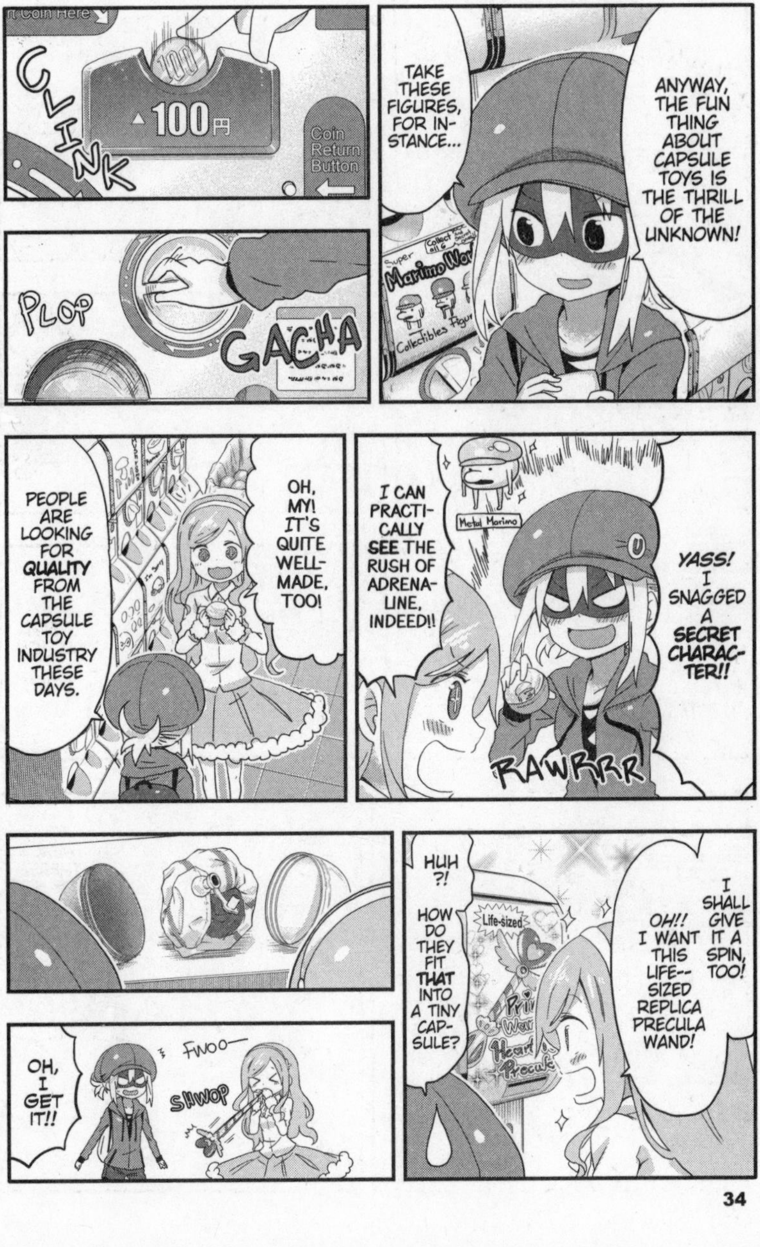
ANYWAY, THE FUN THING ABOUT CAPSULE TOYS IS THE THRILL OF THE UNKNOWN!
TAKE THESE FIGURES, FOR IN-STANCE...
Super Marimo World
Collect all 6
Collectibles Figure
Coin Here
100円
Coin Return Button
CLINK
GACHA
PLOP
YASS! I SNAGGED A SECRET CHARAC-TER!!
I CAN PRACTI-CALLY SEE THE RUSH OF ADRENA-LINE, INDEED!!
Metal Marimo
RAWRRR
OH, MY! IT'S QUITE WELL-MADE, TOO!
PEOPLE ARE LOOKING FOR QUALITY FROM THE CAPSULE TOY INDUSTRY THESE DAYS.
I SHALL GIVE IT A SPIN, TOO!
OH!! I WANT THIS LIFE--SIZED REPLICA PRECULA WAND!
HUH?!
HOW DO THEY FIT THAT INTO A TINY CAP-SULE?
Life-sized
FWOO—
OH, I GET IT!!
SHWOP

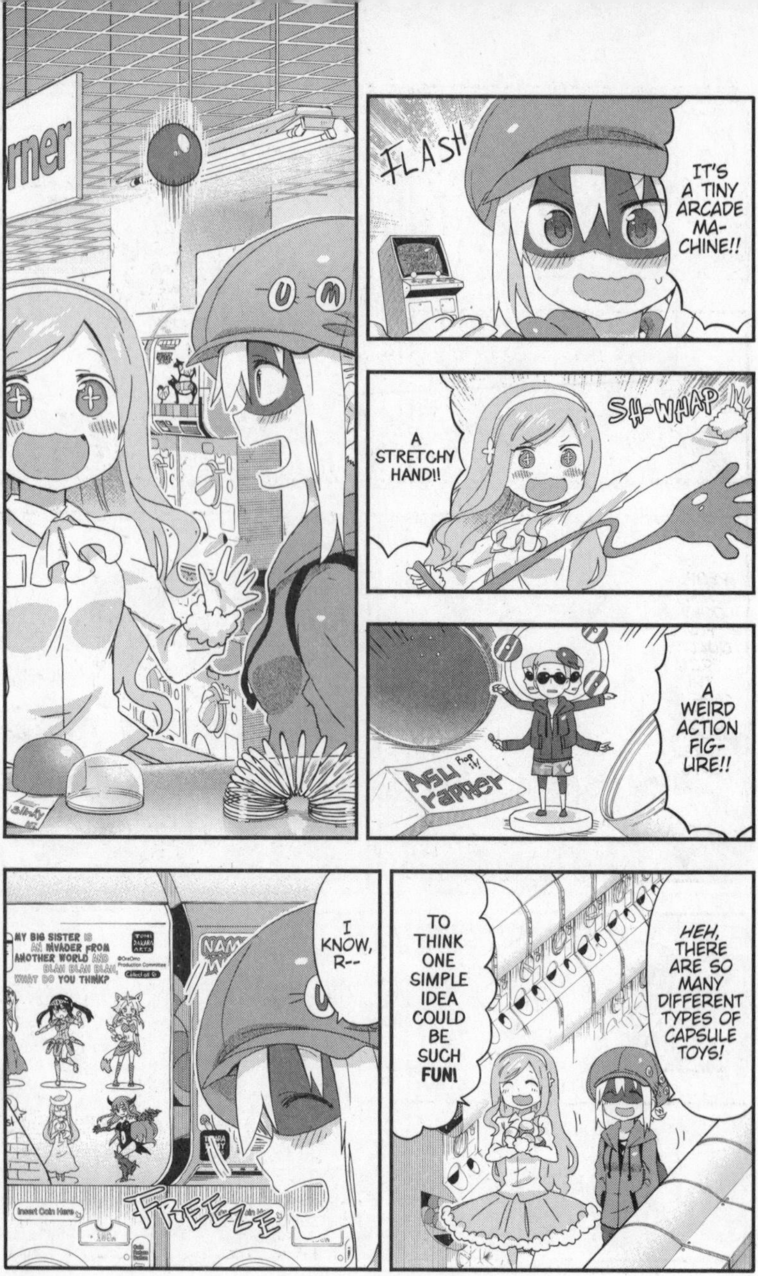
FLASH
IT'S A TINY ARCADE MA-CHINE!!
SH-WHAP
A STRETCHY HAND!!
A WEIRD ACTION FIG-URE!!
orner
HEH, THERE ARE SO MANY DIFFERENT TYPES OF CAPSULE TOYS!
TO THINK ONE SIMPLE IDEA COULD BE SUCH FUN!
I KNOW, R--
MY BIG SISTER IS AN INVADER FROM ANOTHER WORLD AND BLAH BLAH BLAH, WHAT DO YOU THINK?
Insert Coin Here
FREEZE

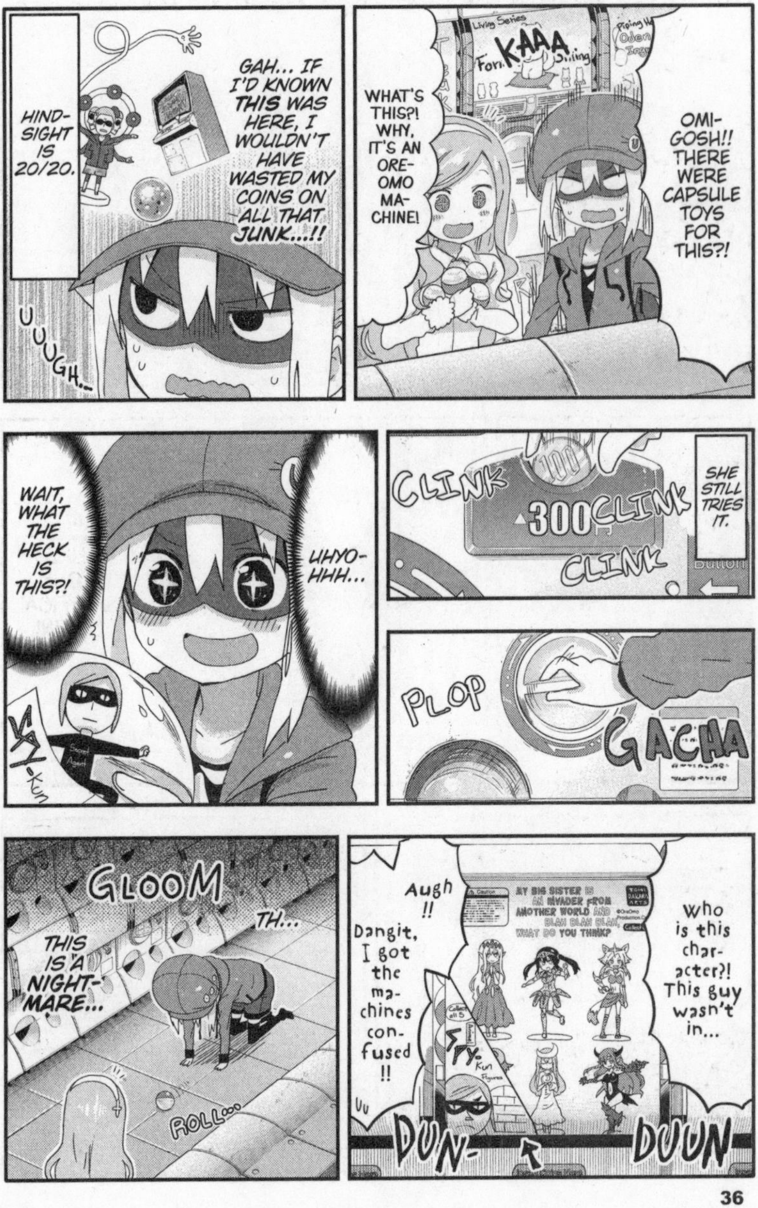
OMI-GOSH!! THERE WERE CAPSULE TOYS FOR THIS?!
KAAA
WHAT'S THIS?! WHY, IT'S AN OREOMO MACHINE!
GAH... IF I'D KNOWN THIS WAS HERE, I WOULDN'T HAVE WASTED MY COINS ON ALL THAT JUNK...!!
HINDSIGHT IS 20/20.
UUUGH...
SHE STILL TRIES IT.
CLINK
300
CLINK
CLINK
PLOP
GACHA
UHYO-HHH...
WAIT, WHAT THE HECK IS THIS?!
Who is this character?! This guy wasn't in...
MY BIG SISTER IS AN INVADER FROM ANOTHER WORLD AND BLAH BLAH BLAH, WHAT DO YOU THINK?
Augh!!
Dangit, I got the machines confused!!
Spy-Kun Figures
DUN- DUUN
GLOOM
TH...
THIS IS A NIGHTMARE...
ROLL...

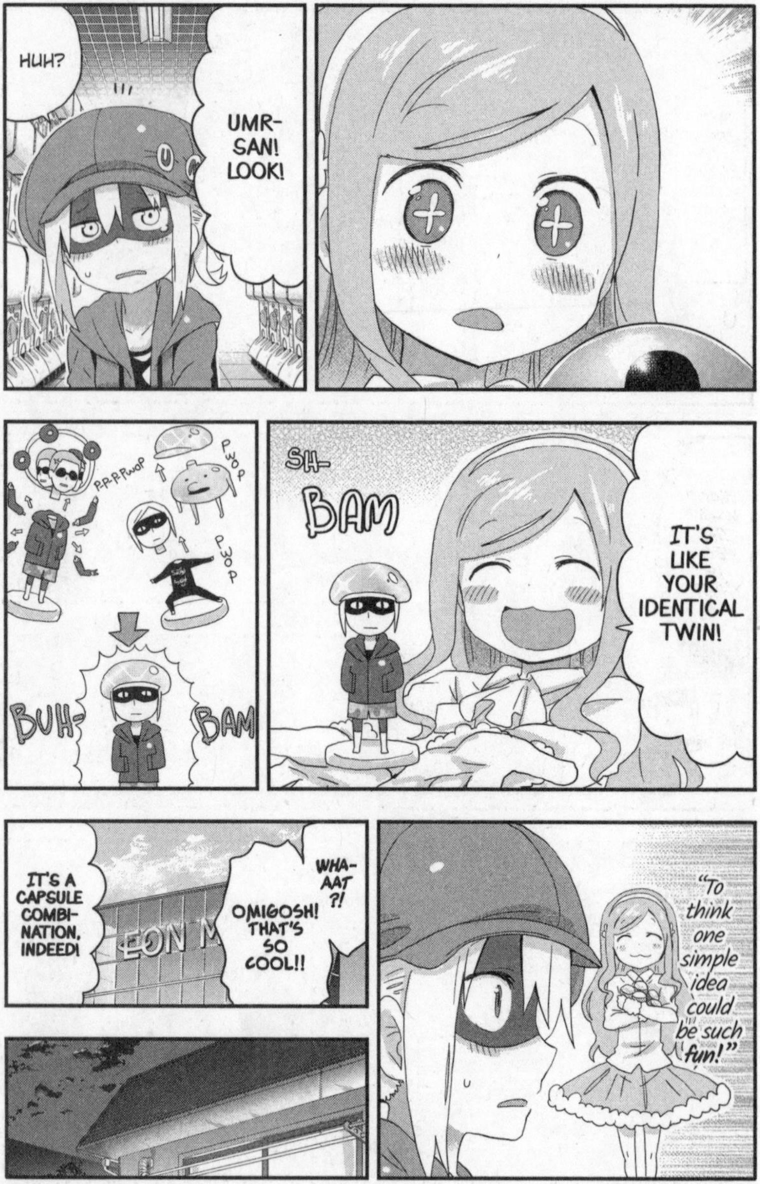
UMR-SAN! LOOK!
HUH?
IT'S LIKE YOUR IDENTICAL TWIN!
SH-BAM
P-P-P-PWOP
PWOP
PWOP
BUH-BAM
"To think one simple idea could be such fun!"
WHA-AAT?!
OMIGOSH! THAT'S SO COOL!!
IT'S A CAPSULE COMBINATION, INDEED!

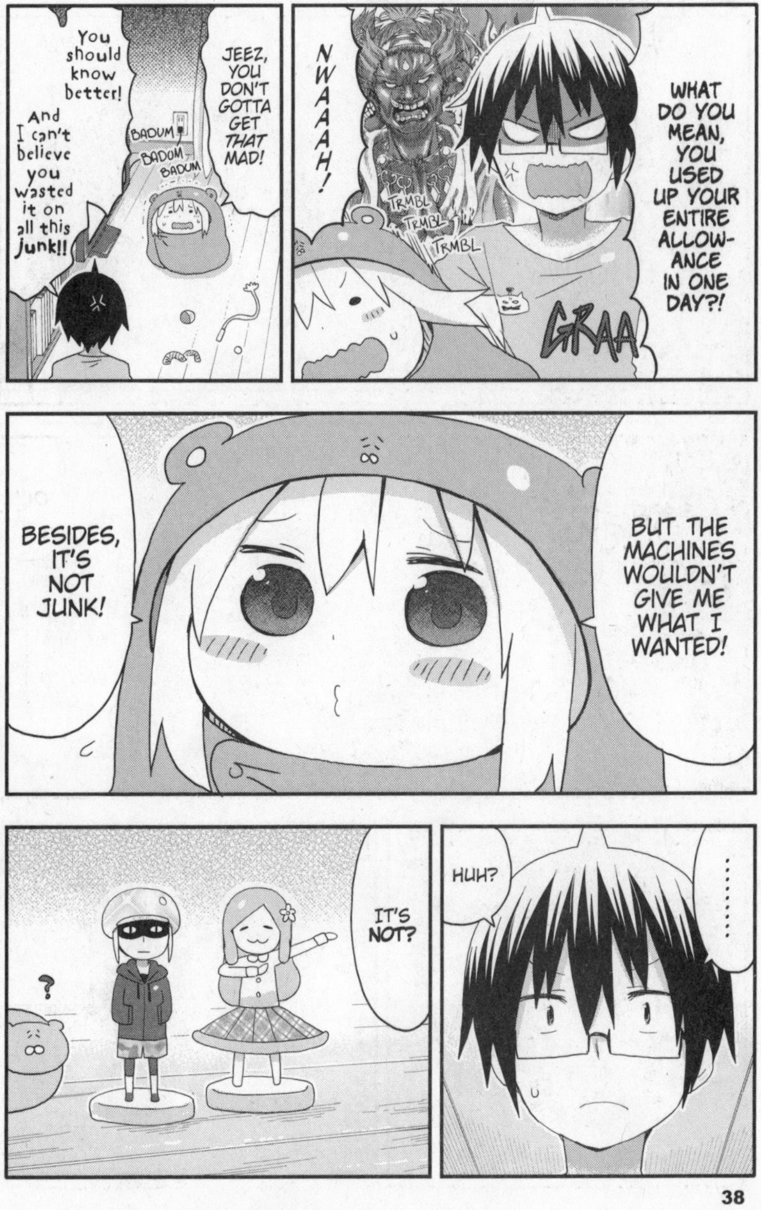
WHAT DO YOU MEAN, YOU USED UP YOUR ENTIRE ALLOW-ANCE IN ONE DAY?!
NWAAAAH!
TRMBL TRMBL TRMBL
GRAA
JEEZ, YOU DON'T GOTTA GET THAT MAD!
BADUM BADUM BADUM
You should know better!
And I can't believe you wasted it on all this junk!!
BUT THE MACHINES WOULDN'T GIVE ME WHAT I WANTED!
BESIDES, IT'S NOT JUNK!
....
HUH?
IT'S NOT?

No. 112 Umaru & the Sleepover

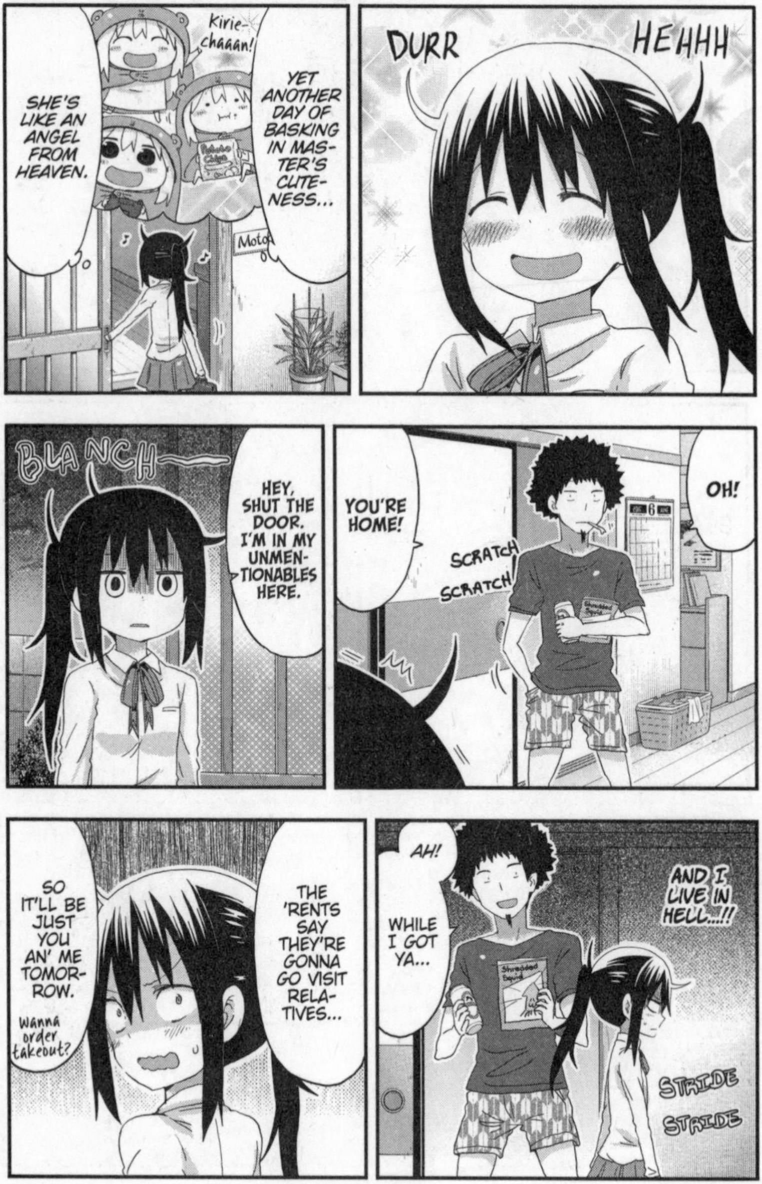

DURR
HEHHH
Kirie-chaaan!
YET ANOTHER DAY OF BASKING IN MASTER'S CUTENESS...
SHE'S LIKE AN ANGEL FROM HEAVEN.
OH!
YOU'RE HOME!
SCRATCH
SCRATCH
HEY, SHUT THE DOOR. I'M IN MY UNMENTIONABLES HERE.
BLANCH
AH!
AND I LIVE IN HELL...!!
WHILE I GOT YA...
STRIDE
STRIDE
THE 'RENTS SAY THEY'RE GONNA GO VISIT RELATIVES...
SO IT'LL BE JUST YOU AN' ME TOMORROW.
Wanna order takeout?

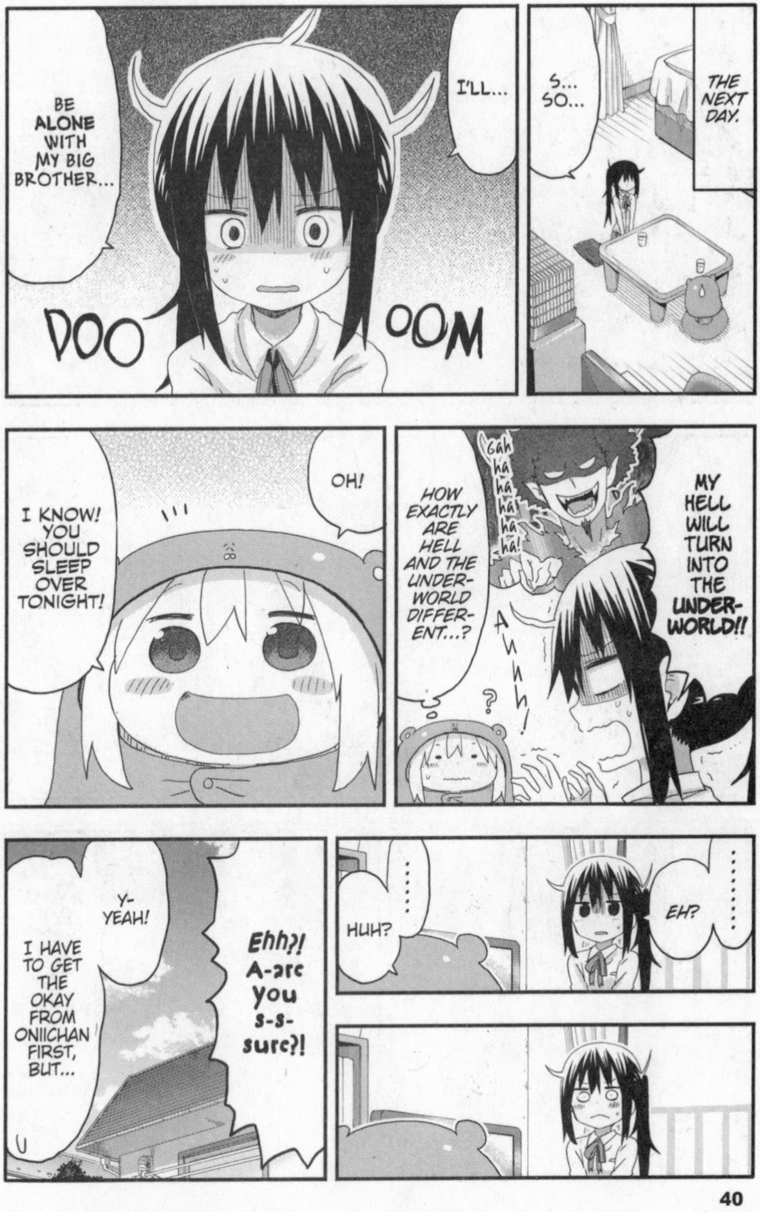
THE NEXT DAY.
S... SO...
I'LL...
BE ALONE WITH MY BIG BROTHER...
DOO OOM
MY HELL WILL TURN INTO THE UNDER-WORLD!!
Gah ha ha ha ha ha ha!
HOW EXACTLY ARE HELL AND THE UNDER-WORLD DIFFER-ENT...?
Auuhh!
?
OH!
I KNOW! YOU SHOULD SLEEP OVER TONIGHT!
......
EH?
......
HUH?
Ehh?! A-are you s-s-sure?!
Y-YEAH!
I HAVE TO GET THE OKAY FROM ONIICHAN FIRST, BUT...

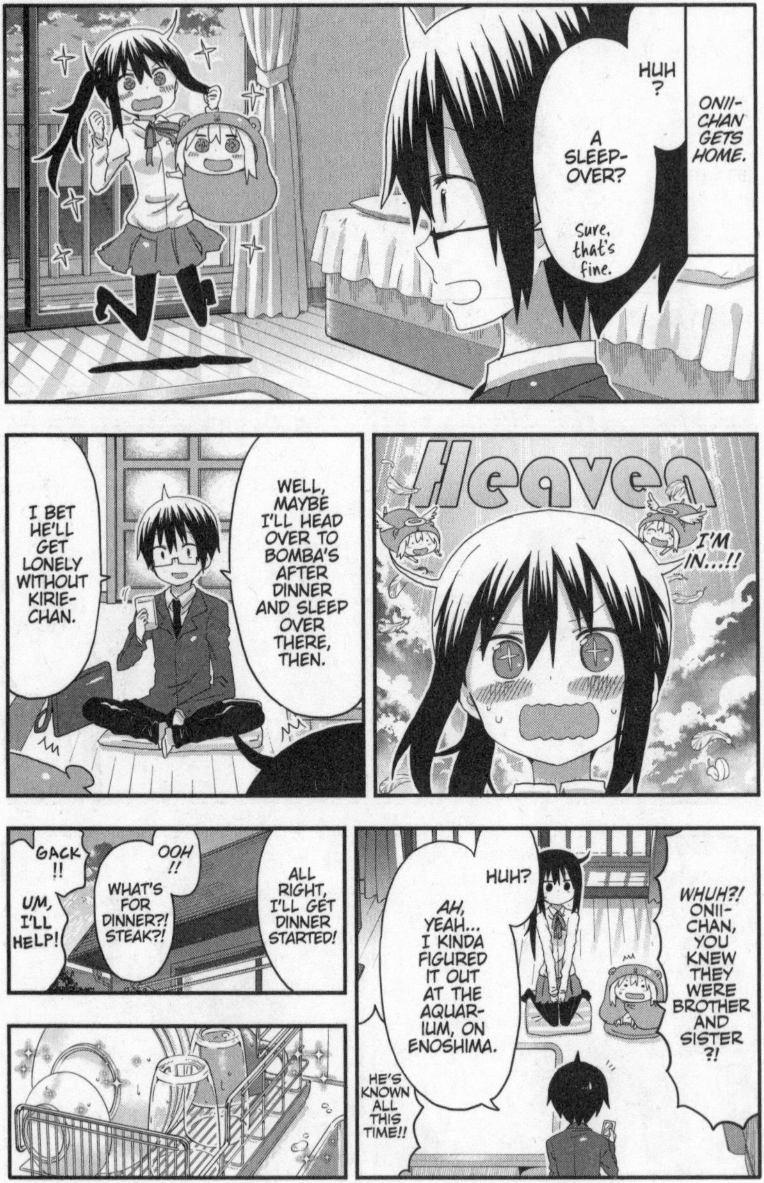
ONII-CHAN GETS HOME.
HUH? A SLEEP-OVER?
Sure, that's fine.
Heaven
I'M IN...!!
WELL, MAYBE I'LL HEAD OVER TO BOMBA'S AFTER DINNER AND SLEEP OVER THERE, THEN.
I BET HE'LL GET LONELY WITHOUT KIRIE-CHAN.
WHUH?! ONII-CHAN, YOU KNEW THEY WERE BROTHER AND SISTER?!
HUH?
AH, YEAH... I KINDA FIGURED IT OUT AT THE AQUARIUM, ON ENOSHIMA.
HE'S KNOWN ALL THIS TIME!!
ALL RIGHT, I'LL GET DINNER STARTED!
OOH!!
WHAT'S FOR DINNER?! STEAK?!
GACK!!
UM, I'LL HELP!

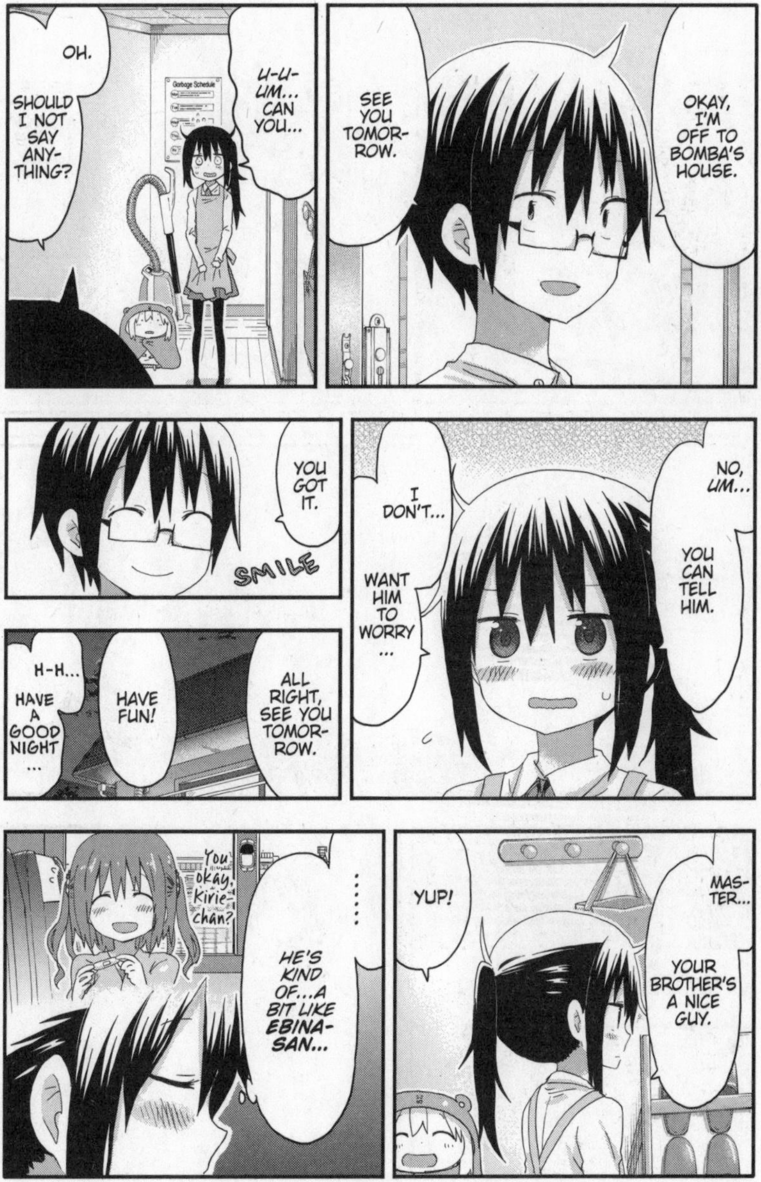
OKAY, I'M OFF TO BOMBA'S HOUSE.
SEE YOU TOMORROW.
U-U-UM... CAN YOU...
OH.
SHOULD I NOT SAY ANYTHING?
Garbage Schedule
NO, UM...
YOU CAN TELL HIM.
I DON'T...
WANT HIM TO WORRY...
YOU GOT IT.
SMILE
ALL RIGHT, SEE YOU TOMORROW.
HAVE FUN!
H-H...
HAVE A GOOD NIGHT...
MASTER...
YOUR BROTHER'S A NICE GUY.
YUP!
......
HE'S KIND OF...A BIT LIKE EBINA-SAN...
You okay, Kirie-chan?

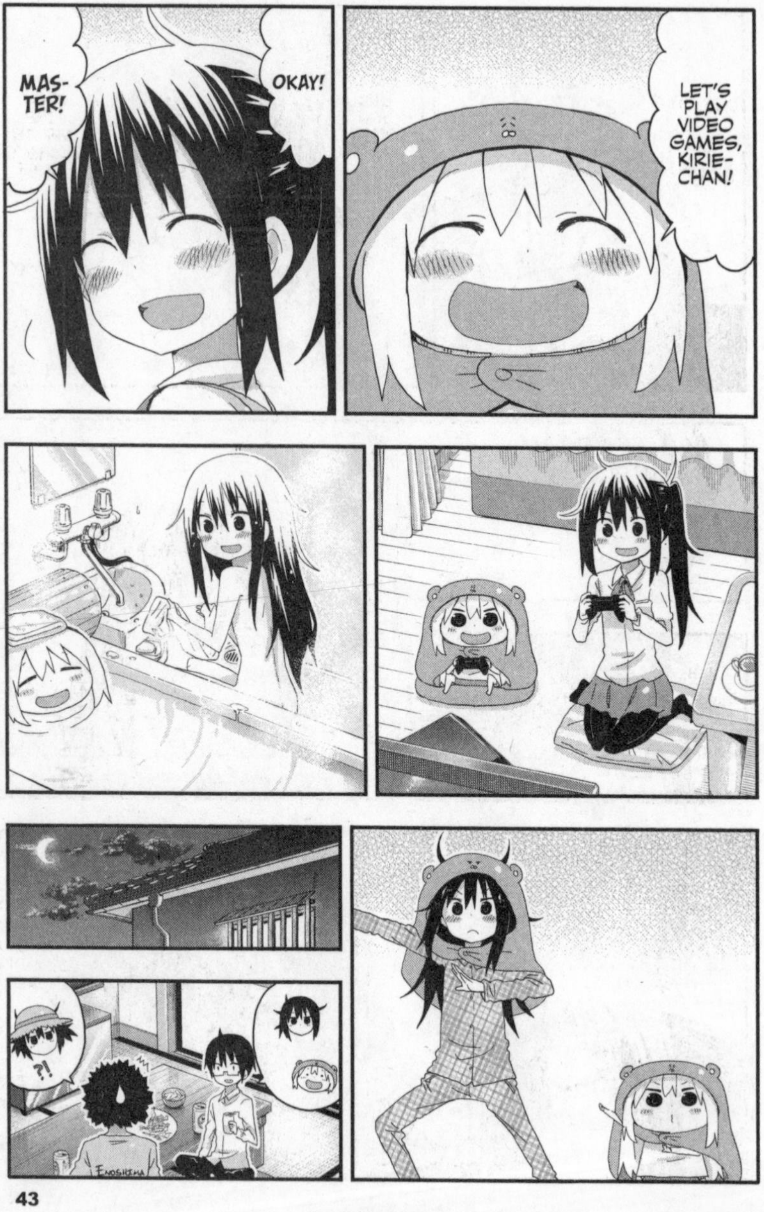
LET'S PLAY VIDEO GAMES, KIRIE-CHAN!
OKAY!
MAS-TER!
?!
ENOSHIMA

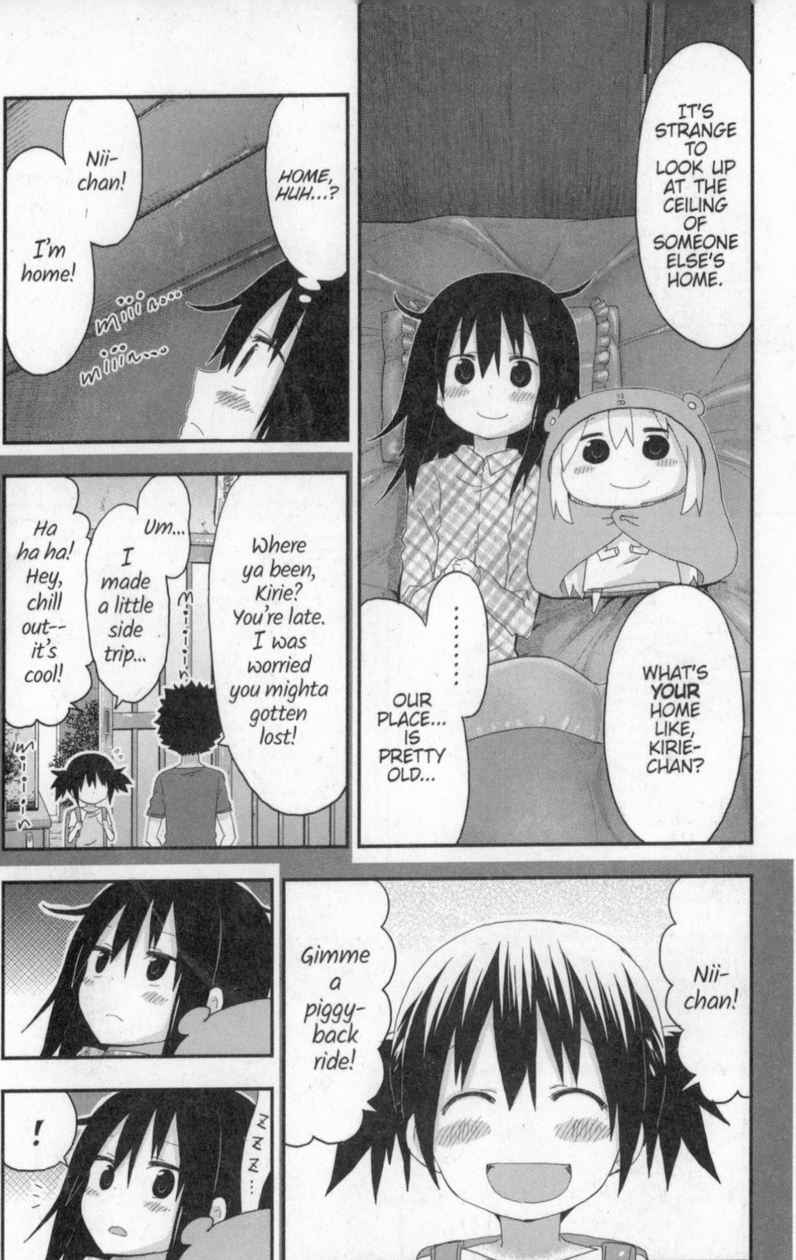
IT'S STRANGE TO LOOK UP AT THE CEILING OF SOMEONE ELSE'S HOME.
WHAT'S YOUR HOME LIKE, KIRIE-CHAN?
......
OUR PLACE... IS PRETTY OLD...
HOME, HUH...?
Nii-chan! I'm home!
miii n...
miiin...
Where ya been, Kirie? You're late. I was worried you mighta gotten lost!
Um... I made a little side trip...
Ha ha ha! Hey, chill out--it's cool!
Mi-i-i-n
Mi-i-i-n
Nii-chan!
Gimme a piggy-back ride!
!
Z Z Z...

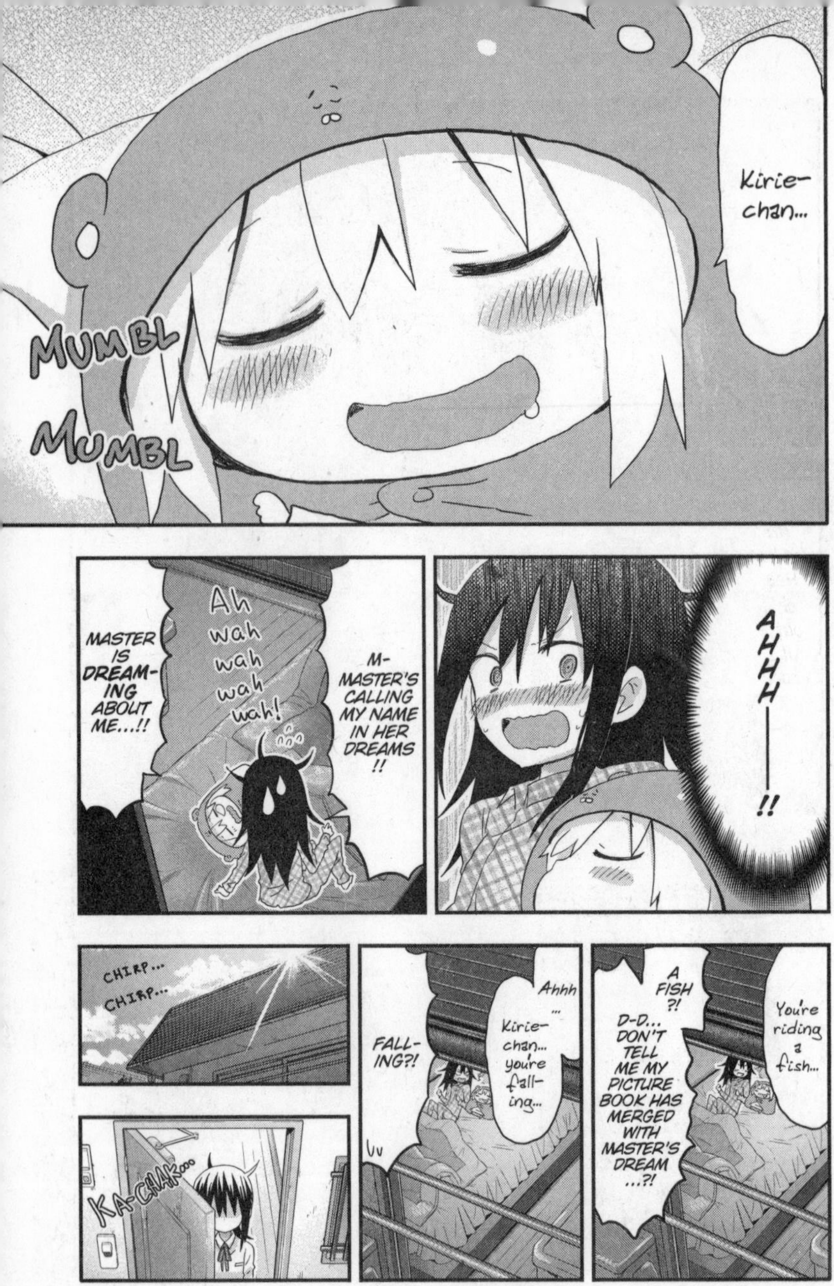

Kirie-chan...
MUMBL
MUMBL
AHHH——!!
M-MASTER'S CALLING MY NAME IN HER DREAMS!!
Ah wah wah wah wah!
MASTER IS DREAMING ABOUT ME...!!
You're riding a fish...
A FISH?!
D-D... DON'T TELL ME MY PICTURE BOOK HAS MERGED WITH MASTER'S DREAM...?!
Ahhh... Kirie-chan... you're falling...
FALLING?!
uu
CHIRP... CHIRP...
KA-CHAK...

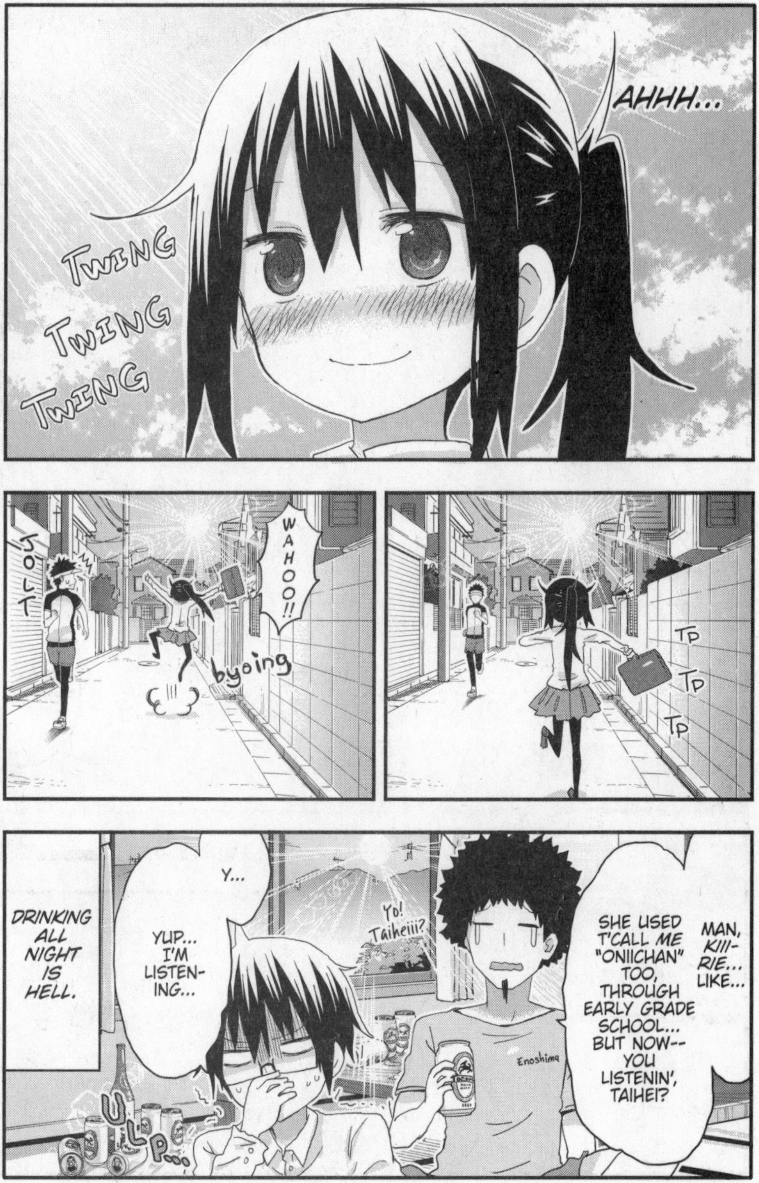
AHHH...
TWING
TWING
TWING
Tp
Tp
Tp
WAHOO!!
JOLT
byoing
MAN, KIII-RIE... LIKE...
SHE USED T'CALL ME "ONIICHAN" TOO, THROUGH EARLY GRADE SCHOOL... BUT NOW-- YOU LISTENIN', TAIHEI?
Enoshima
Yo! Taiheiii?
Y...
YUP... I'M LISTEN-ING...
DRINKING ALL NIGHT IS HELL.
ULP...

No. 113 Umaru & the Camera

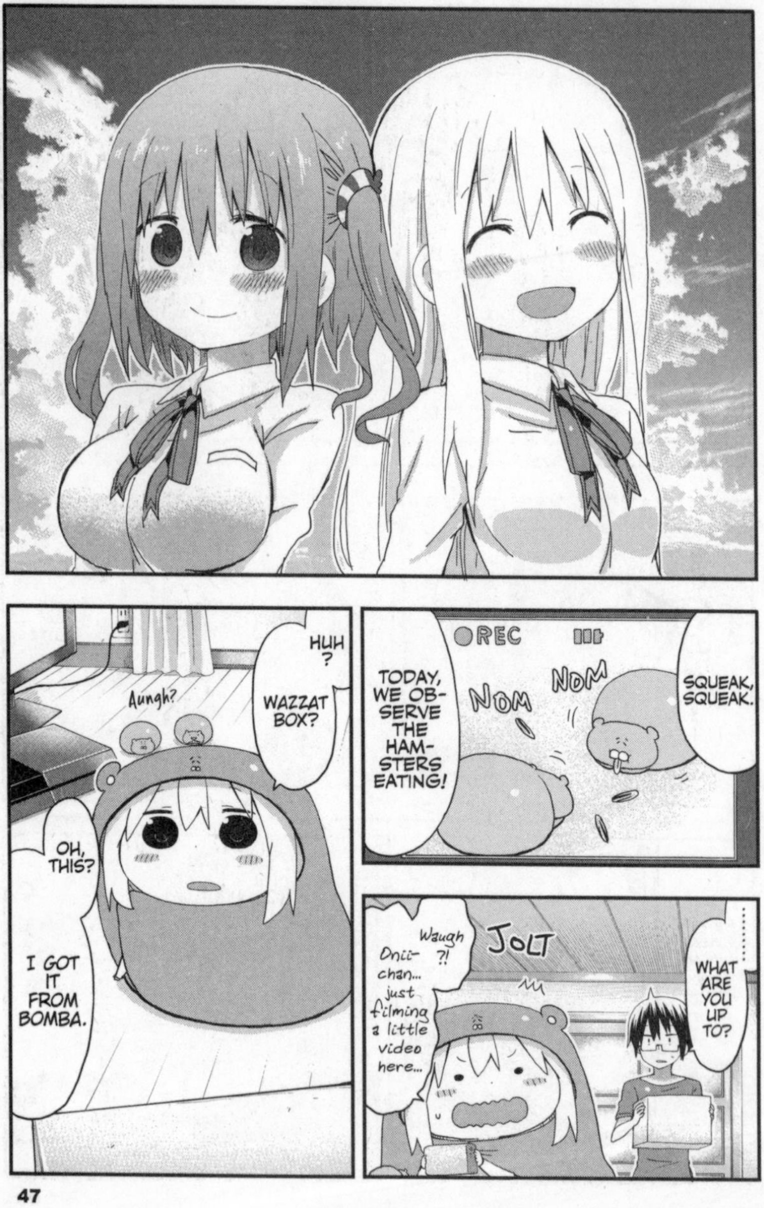
SQUEAK, SQUEAK.
REC
NOM
NOM
TODAY, WE OBSERVE THE HAMSTERS EATING!
......
WHAT ARE YOU UP TO?
JOLT
Waugh ?!
Onii-chan... just filming a little video here...
HUH? WAZZAT BOX?
Aungh?
OH, THIS?
I GOT IT FROM BOMBA.

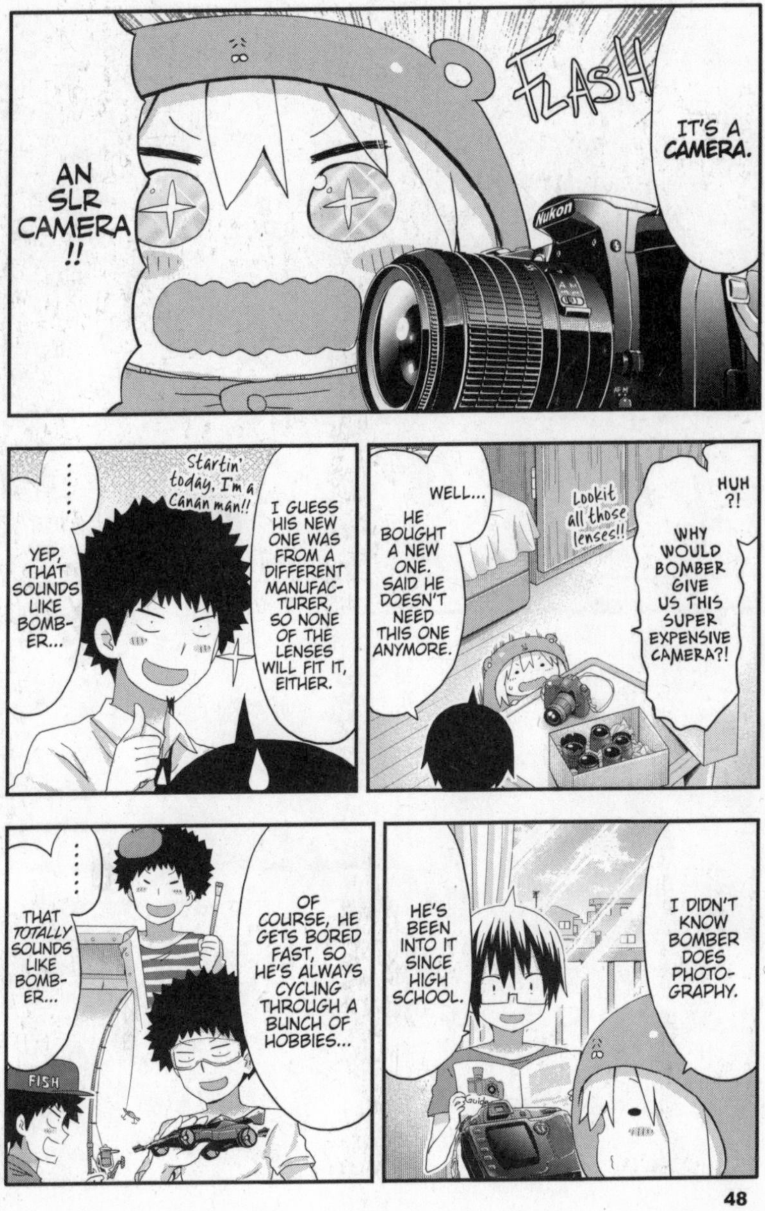
FLASH
IT'S A CAMERA.
Nukon
AN SLR CAMERA!!
HUH?!
WHY WOULD BOMBER GIVE US THIS SUPER EXPENSIVE CAMERA?!
Lookit all those lenses!!
WELL...
HE BOUGHT A NEW ONE. SAID HE DOESN'T NEED THIS ONE ANYMORE.
I GUESS HIS NEW ONE WAS FROM A DIFFERENT MANUFAC-TURER, SO NONE OF THE LENSES WILL FIT IT, EITHER.
Startin' today. I'm a Canan man!!
......
YEP, THAT SOUNDS LIKE BOMB-ER...
I DIDN'T KNOW BOMBER DOES PHOTO-GRAPHY.
HE'S BEEN INTO IT SINCE HIGH SCHOOL.
Guide
OF COURSE, HE GETS BORED FAST, SO HE'S ALWAYS CYCLING THROUGH A BUNCH OF HOBBIES...
......
THAT *TOTALLY* SOUNDS LIKE BOMB-ER...
FISH

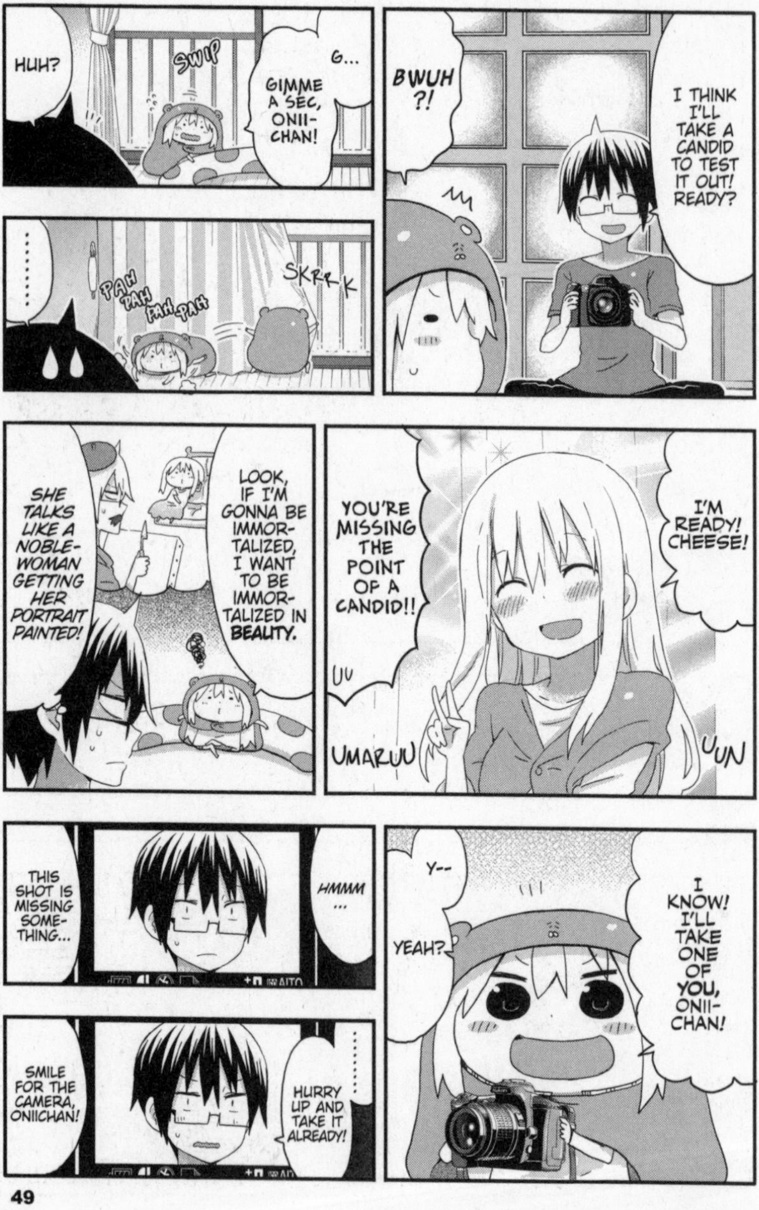
I THINK I'LL TAKE A CANDID TO TEST IT OUT! READY?
BWUH?!
G...
GIMME A SEC, ONII-CHAN!
SWIP
HUH?
SKRRK
PAH PAH PAH PAH
......
I'M READY! CHEESE!
UUN
YOU'RE MISSING THE POINT OF A CANDID!!
UU
UMARUU
LOOK, IF I'M GONNA BE IMMORTALIZED, I WANT TO BE IMMORTALIZED IN BEAUTY.
SHE TALKS LIKE A NOBLEWOMAN GETTING HER PORTRAIT PAINTED!
I KNOW! I'LL TAKE ONE OF YOU, ONII-CHAN!
Y--
YEAH?
HMMM...
THIS SHOT IS MISSING SOMETHING...
......
HURRY UP AND TAKE IT ALREADY!
SMILE FOR THE CAMERA, ONIICHAN!

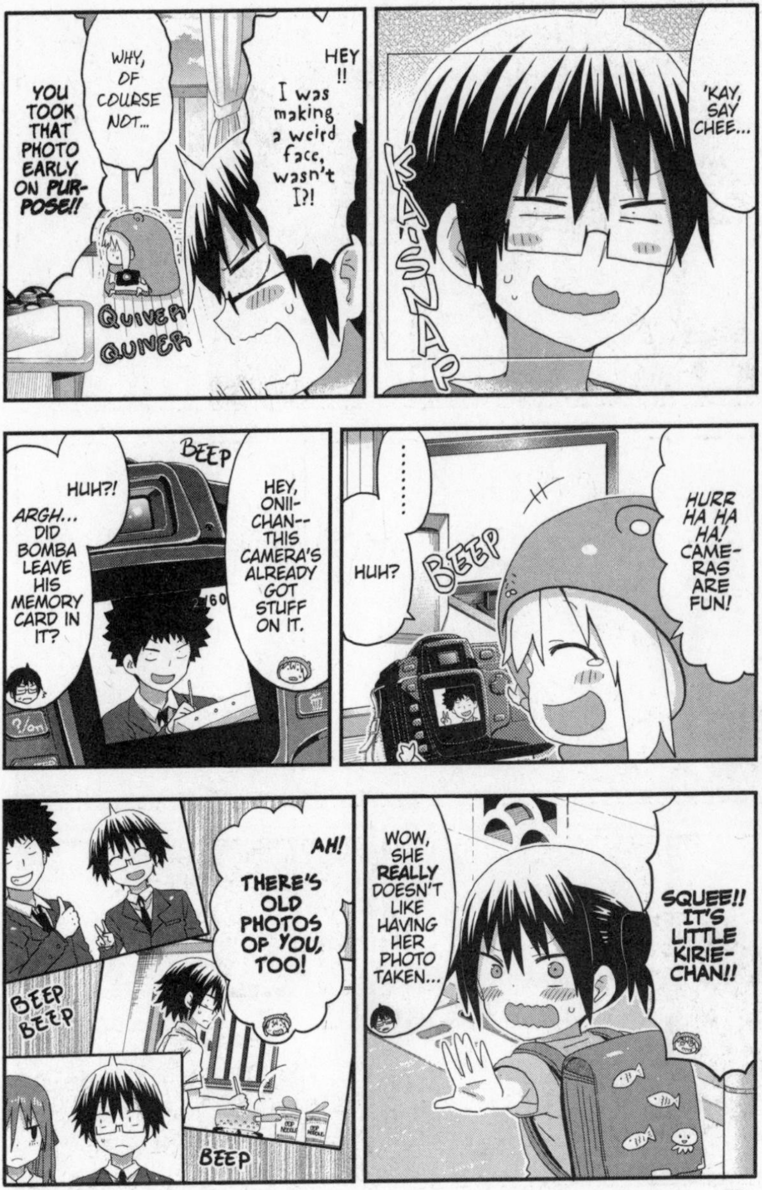
'KAY, SAY CHEE...
KA-SNAP
HEY!!
I was making a weird face, wasn't I?!
WHY, OF COURSE NOT...
YOU TOOK THAT PHOTO EARLY ON PURPOSE!!
QUIVER QUIVER
HURR HA HA HA! CAMERAS ARE FUN!
BEEP
HUH?
......
HEY, ONII-CHAN-- THIS CAMERA'S ALREADY GOT STUFF ON IT.
BEEP
HUH?! ARGH... DID BOMBA LEAVE HIS MEMORY CARD IN IT?
SQUEE!! IT'S LITTLE KIRIE-CHAN!!
WOW, SHE REALLY DOESN'T LIKE HAVING HER PHOTO TAKEN...
AH! THERE'S OLD PHOTOS OF YOU, TOO!
BEEP BEEP
BEEP

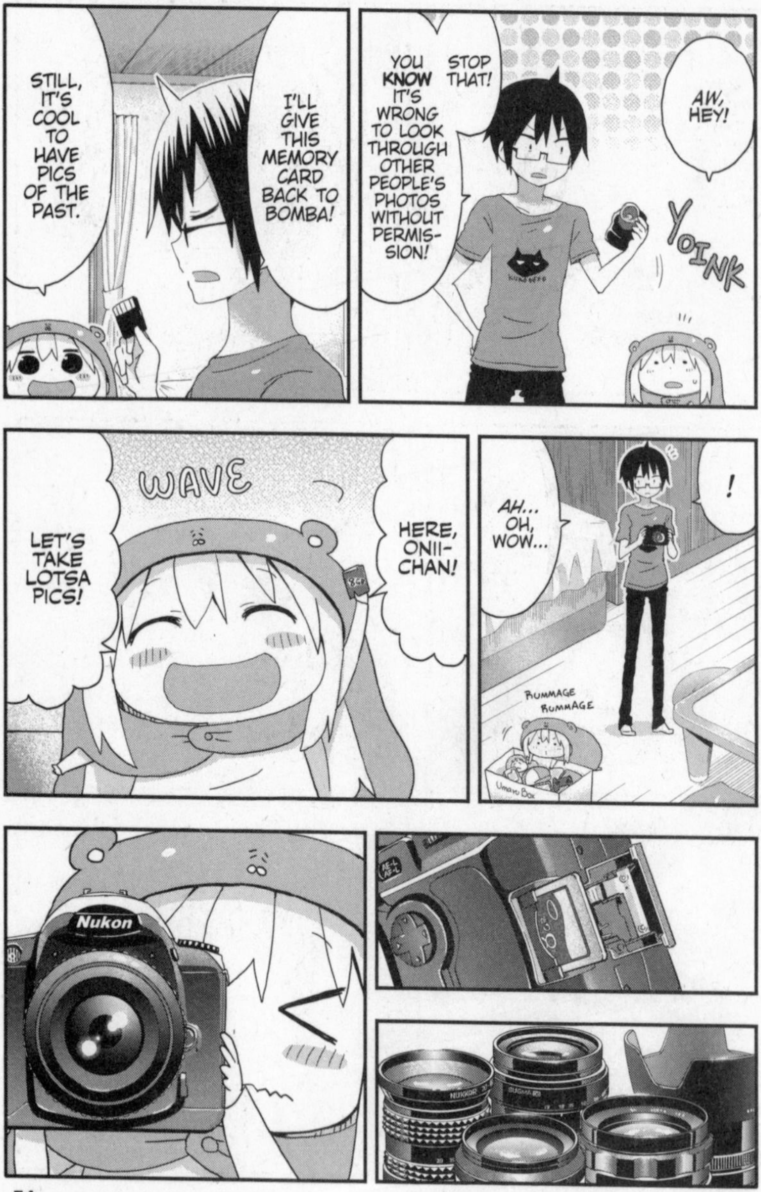
AW, HEY!
STOP THAT! YOU KNOW IT'S WRONG TO LOOK THROUGH OTHER PEOPLE'S PHOTOS WITHOUT PERMISSION!
YOINK
I'LL GIVE THIS MEMORY CARD BACK TO BOMBA!
STILL, IT'S COOL TO HAVE PICS OF THE PAST.
!
AH... OH, WOW...
RUMMAGE RUMMAGE
Umaru Box
HERE, ONII-CHAN!
WAVE
LET'S TAKE LOTSA PICS!
Nukon

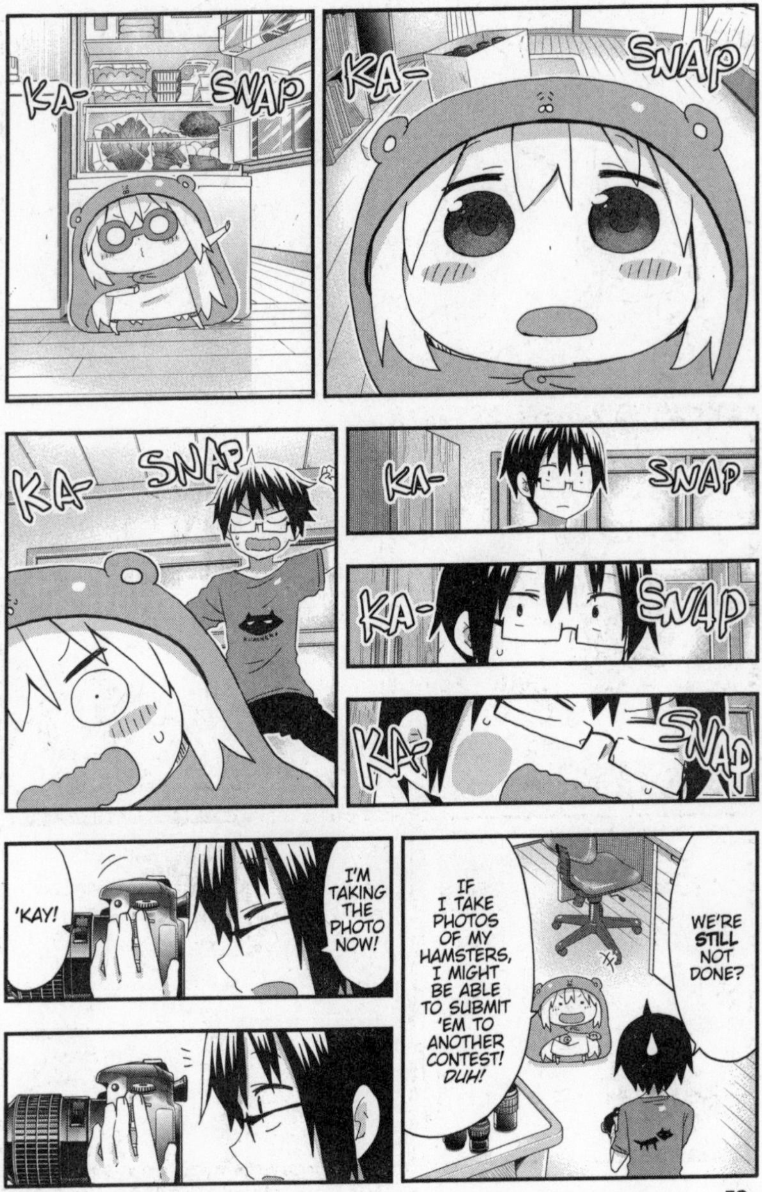
KA-
SNAP
KA-
SNAP
KA-
SNAP
KA-
SNAP
KA-
SNAP
KA-
SNAP
WE'RE STILL NOT DONE?
IF I TAKE PHOTOS OF MY HAMSTERS, I MIGHT BE ABLE TO SUBMIT 'EM TO ANOTHER CONTEST! DUH!
I'M TAKING THE PHOTO NOW!
'KAY!

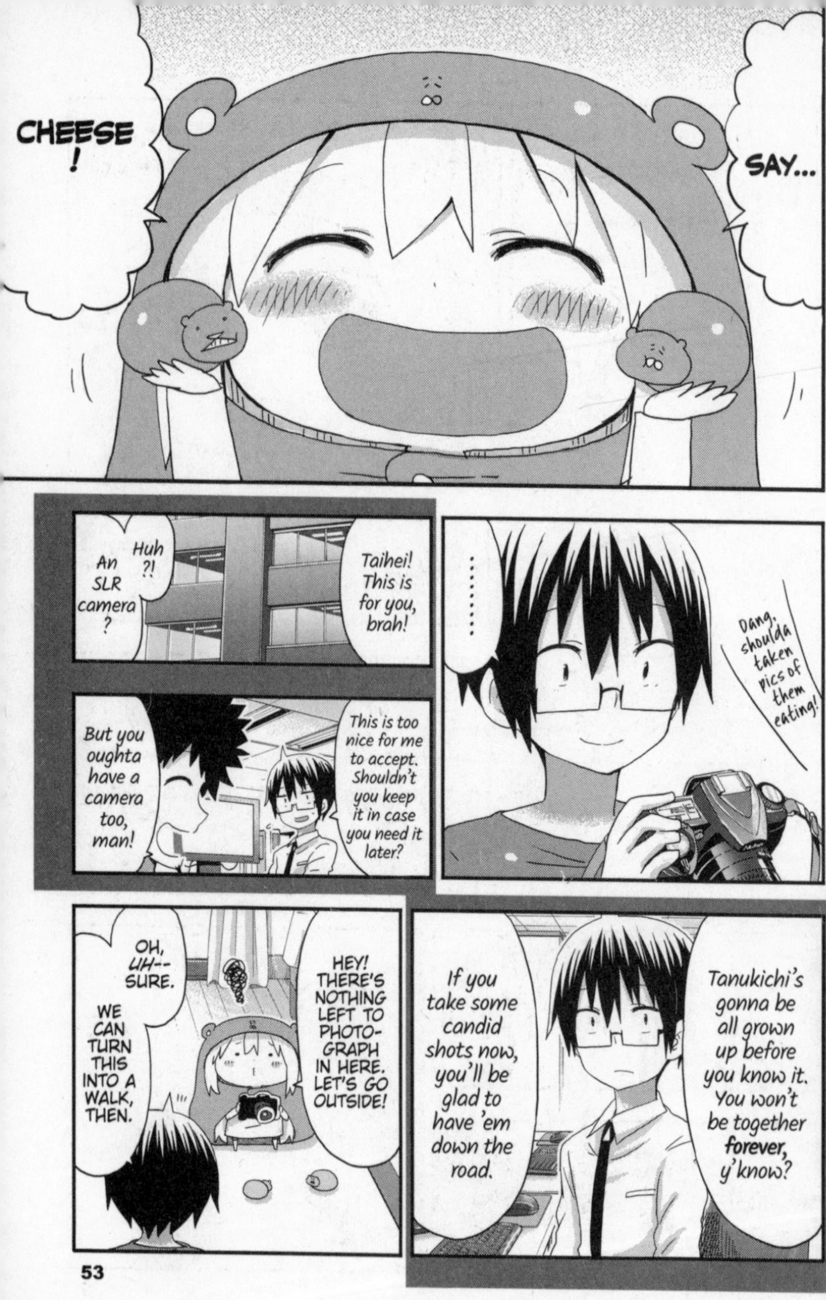
SAY...
CHEESE!
......
Dang, shoulda taken pics of them eating!
Taihei! This is for you, brah!
Huh?!
An SLR camera?
This is too nice for me to accept. Shouldn't you keep it in case you need it later?
But you oughta have a camera too, man!
Tanukichi's gonna be all grown up before you know it. You won't be together **forever**, y'know?
If you take some candid shots now, you'll be glad to have 'em down the road.
HEY! THERE'S NOTHING LEFT TO PHOTOGRAPH IN HERE. LET'S GO OUTSIDE!
OH, UH-- SURE.
WE CAN TURN THIS INTO A WALK, THEN.

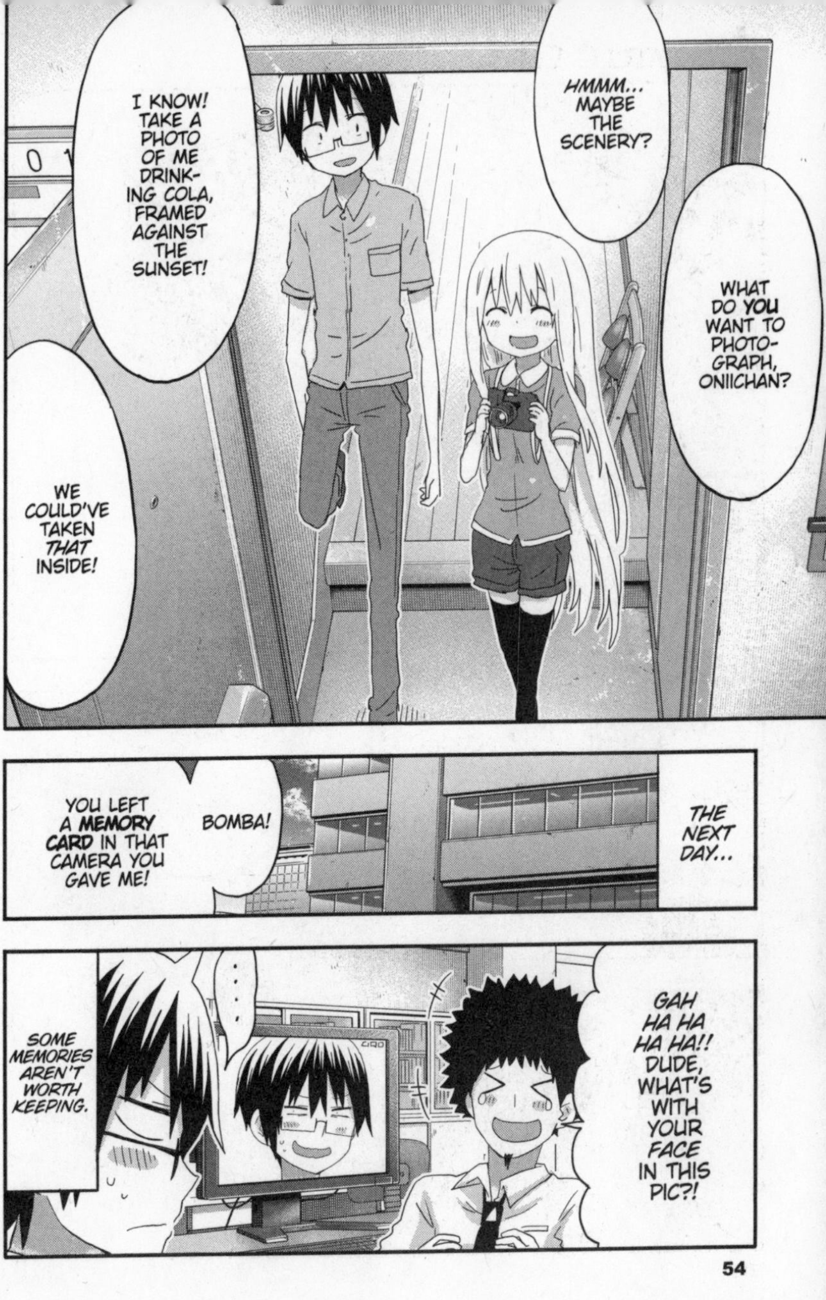

WHAT DO YOU WANT TO PHOTOGRAPH, ONIICHAN?
HMMM... MAYBE THE SCENERY?
I KNOW! TAKE A PHOTO OF ME DRINKING COLA, FRAMED AGAINST THE SUNSET!
WE COULD'VE TAKEN THAT INSIDE!
THE NEXT DAY...
BOMBA!
YOU LEFT A MEMORY CARD IN THAT CAMERA YOU GAVE ME!
GAH HA HA HA HA!! DUDE, WHAT'S WITH YOUR FACE IN THIS PIC?!
...
SOME MEMORIES AREN'T WORTH KEEPING.

No. 114 Umaru & Love

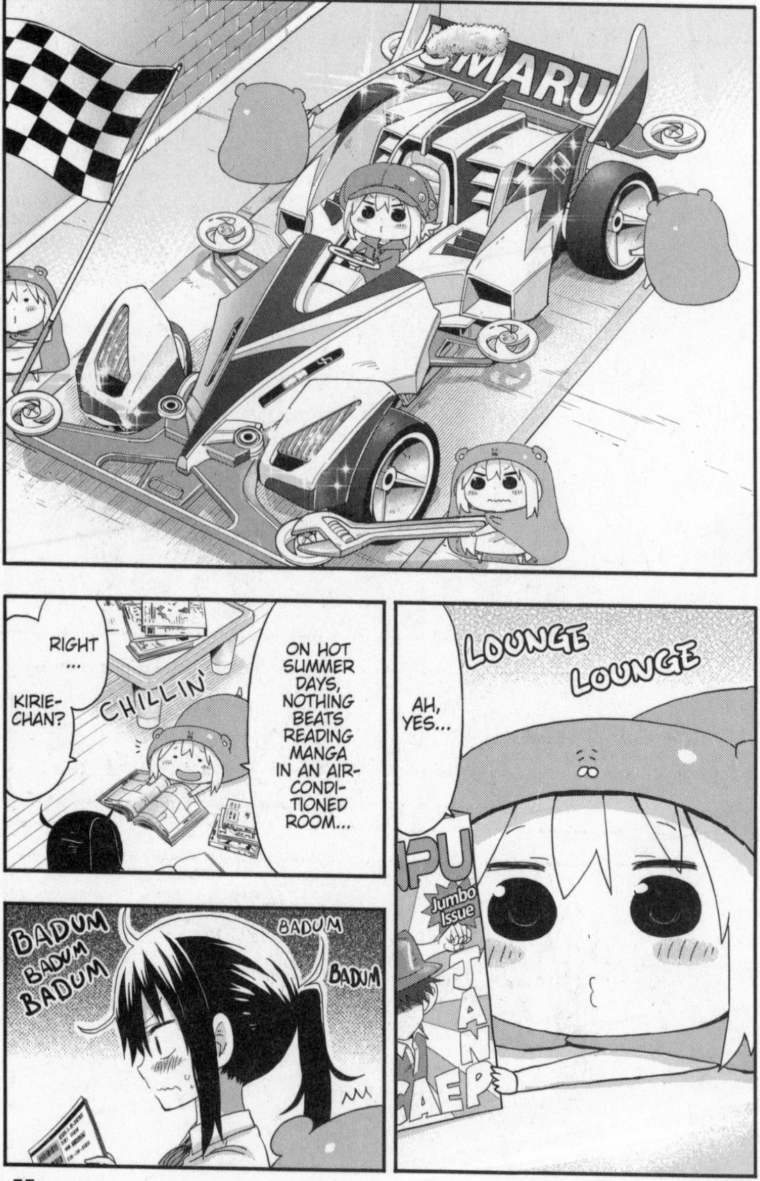

UMARU
LOUNGE LOUNGE
AH, YES...
Jumbo Issue
ON HOT SUMMER DAYS, NOTHING BEATS READING MANGA IN AN AIR-CONDITIONED ROOM...
CHILLIN'
RIGHT... KIRIE-CHAN?
BADUM BADUM BADUM
BADUM
BADUM

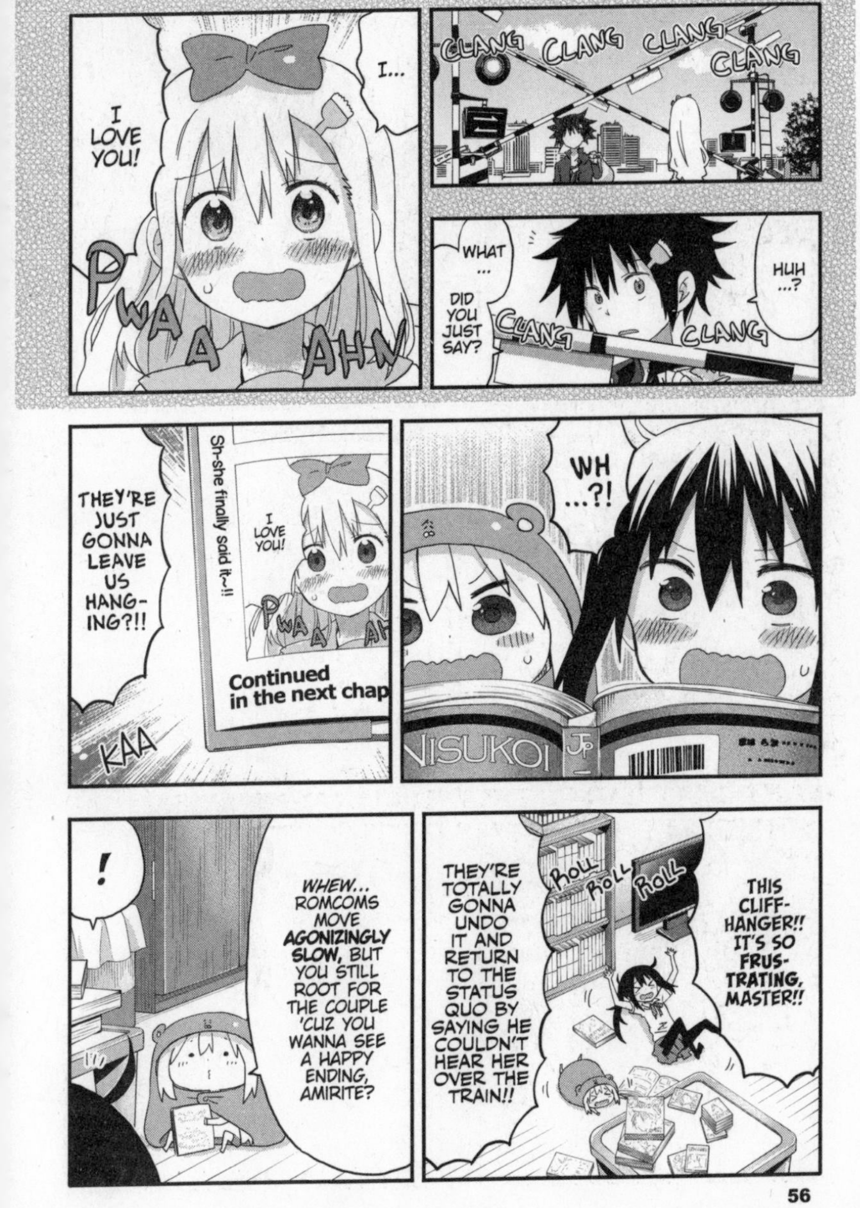
CLANG CLANG CLANG CLANG
HUH ...?
WHAT ... DID YOU JUST SAY?
CLANG CLANG
I...
I LOVE YOU!
PWAAAAHN
WH ...?!
NISUKOI
Sh-she finally said it~!!
I LOVE YOU!
Continued in the next chap
THEY'RE JUST GONNA LEAVE US HANGING?!!
KAA
THIS CLIFF-HANGER!! IT'S SO FRUSTRATING, MASTER!!
ROLL ROLL ROLL
THEY'RE TOTALLY GONNA UNDO IT AND RETURN TO THE STATUS QUO BY SAYING HE COULDN'T HEAR HER OVER THE TRAIN!!
WHEW... ROMCOMS MOVE AGONIZINGLY SLOW, BUT YOU STILL ROOT FOR THE COUPLE 'CUZ YOU WANNA SEE A HAPPY ENDING, AMIRITE?
!

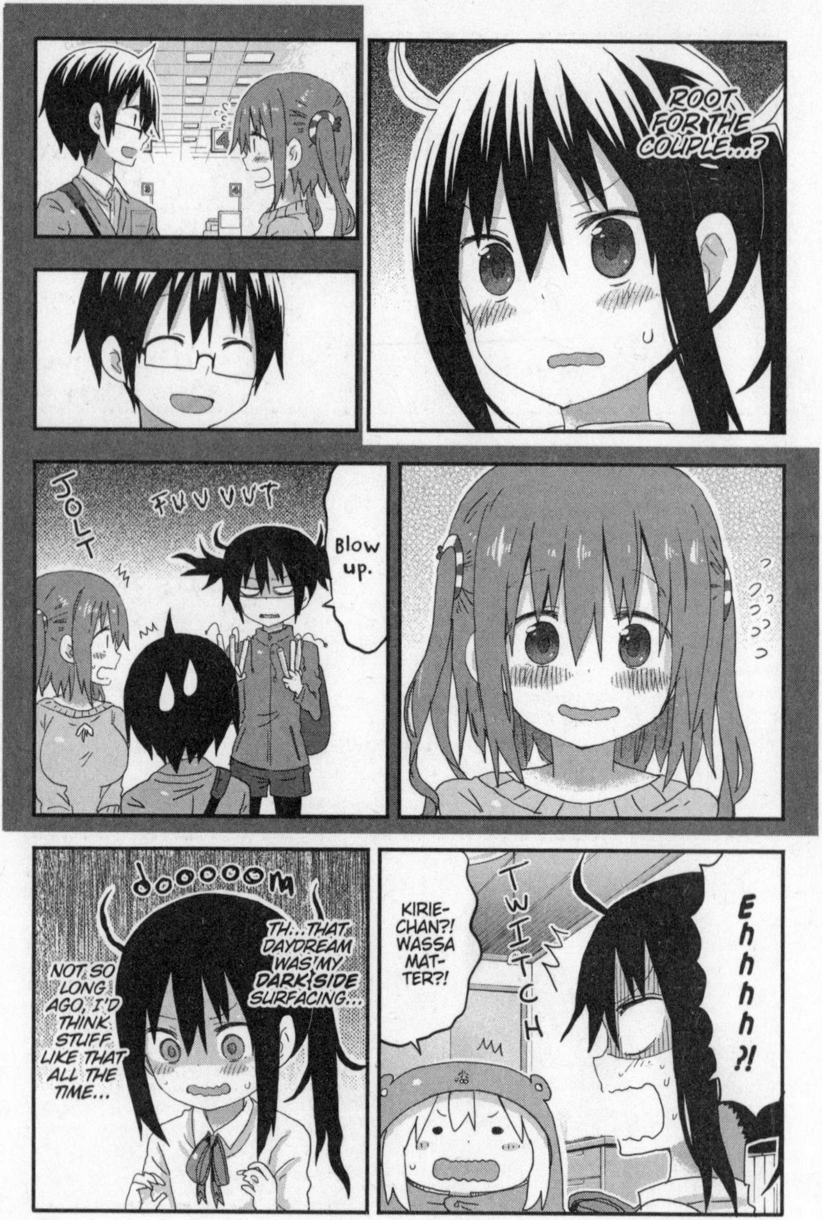
ROOT FOR THE COUPLE...?
JOLT
FUVVVT
Blow up.
Ehhhhh?!
TWITCH
KIRIE-CHAN?! WASSA MATTER?!
doooooom
TH...THAT DAYDREAM WAS MY DARK SIDE SURFACING...
NOT SO LONG AGO, I'D THINK STUFF LIKE THAT ALL THE TIME...

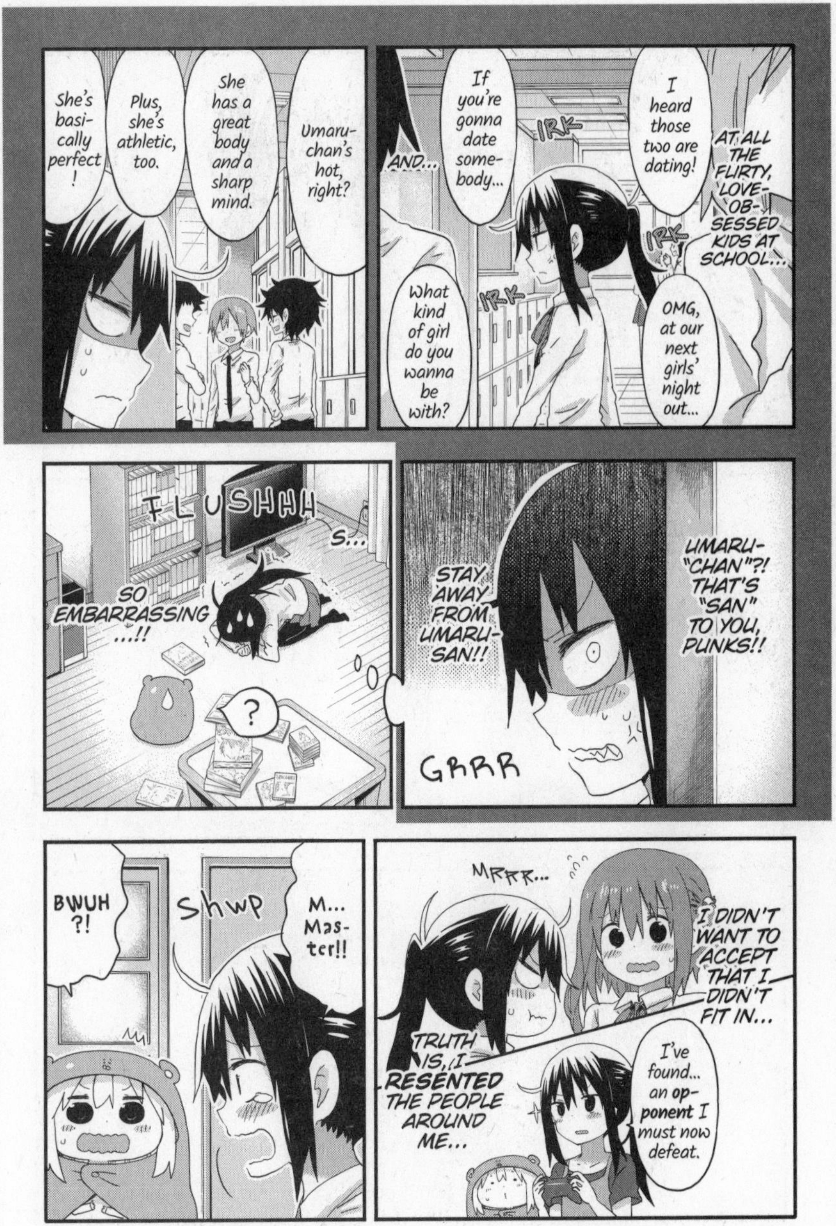
I heard those two are dating!
AT ALL THE FLIRTY, LOVE-OBSESSED KIDS AT SCHOOL...
OMG, at our next girls' night out...
IRK
IRK
If you're gonna date somebody...
IRK
What kind of girl do you wanna be with?
AND...
Umaru-chan's hot, right?
She has a great body and a sharp mind.
Plus, she's athletic, too.
She's basically perfect!
UMARU-"CHAN"?! THAT'S "SAN" TO YOU, PUNKS!!
STAY AWAY FROM UMARU-SAN!!
GRRR
FLUSHHHS...
SO EMBARRASSING...!!
?
I DIDN'T WANT TO ACCEPT THAT I DIDN'T FIT IN...
MRRR...
TRUTH IS, I RESENTED THE PEOPLE AROUND ME...
I've found... an **opponent** I must now defeat.
M... Master!!
Shwp
BWUH?!

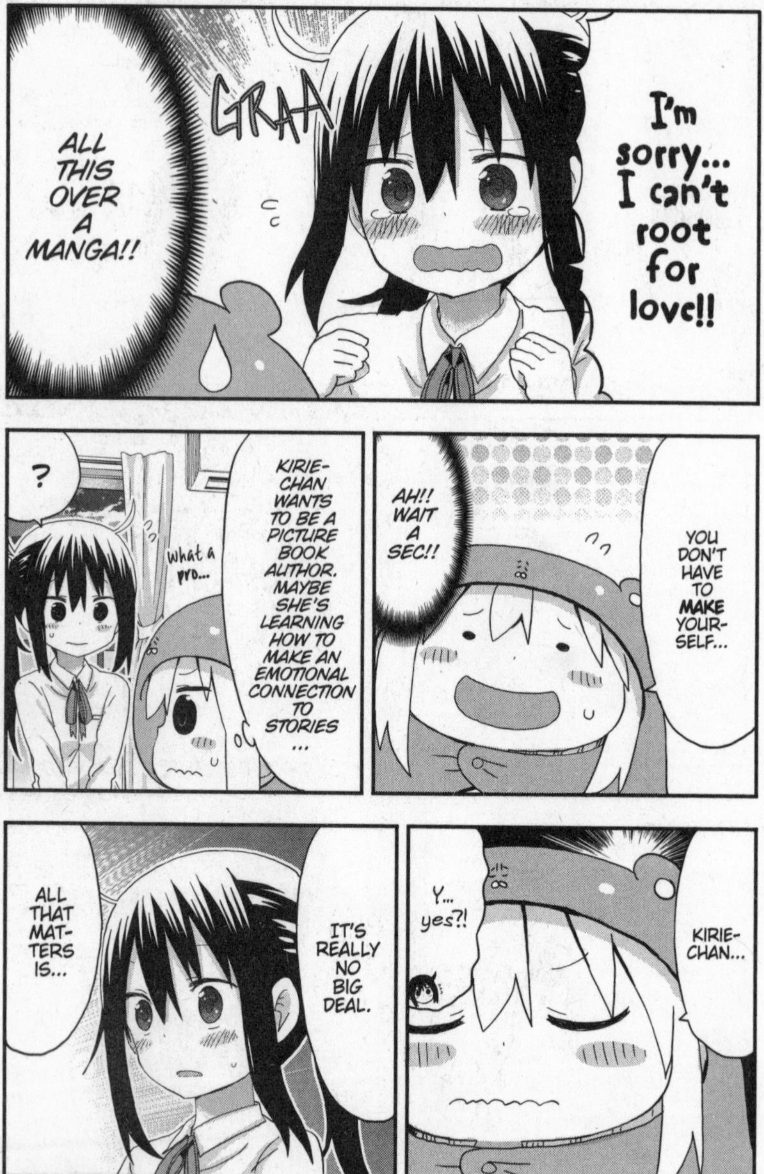
I'm sorry... I can't root for love!!
GRAA
ALL THIS OVER A MANGA!!
YOU DON'T HAVE TO MAKE YOURSELF...
AH!! WAIT A SEC!!
KIRIE-CHAN WANTS TO BE A PICTURE BOOK AUTHOR. MAYBE SHE'S LEARNING HOW TO MAKE AN EMOTIONAL CONNECTION TO STORIES...
what a pro...
?
KIRIE-CHAN...
Y... yes?!
IT'S REALLY NO BIG DEAL.
ALL THAT MATTERS IS...

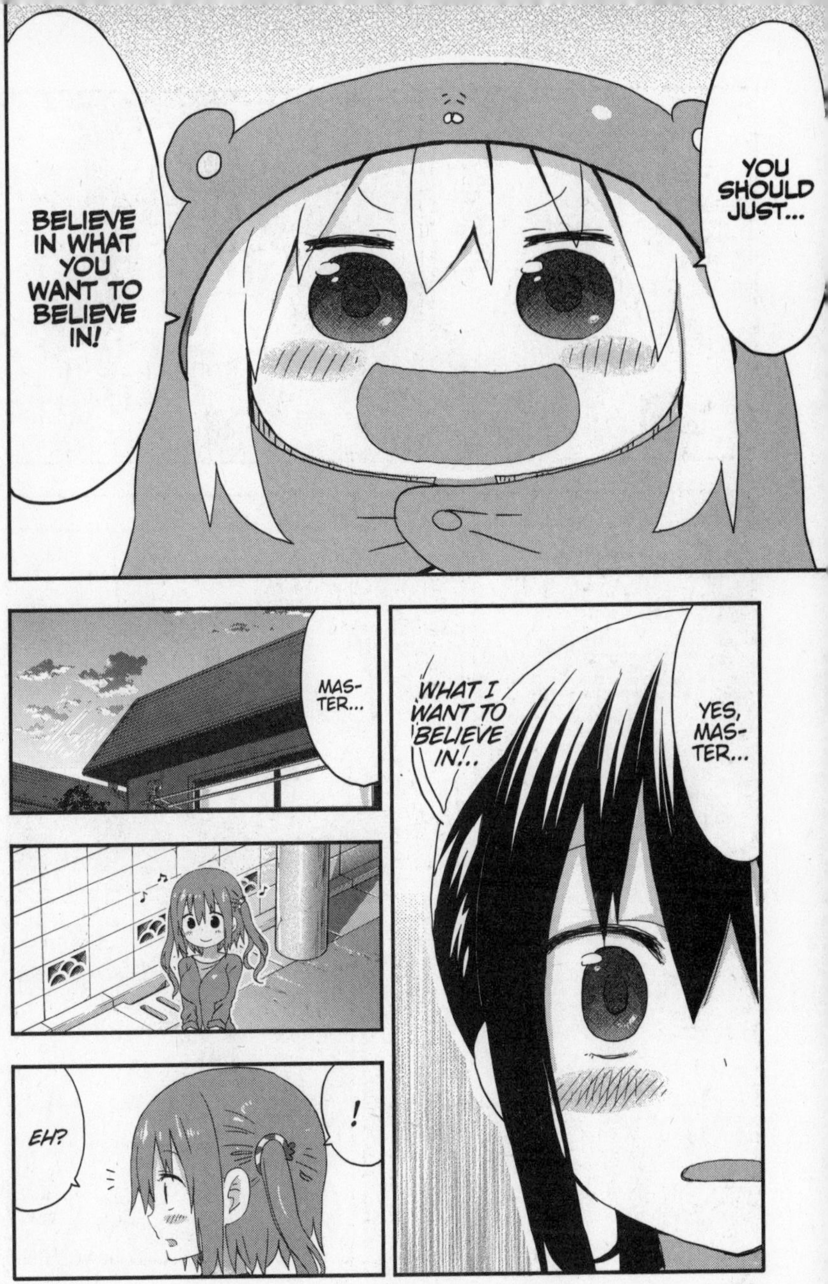
YOU SHOULD JUST...
BELIEVE IN WHAT YOU WANT TO BELIEVE IN!
YES, MASTER...
WHAT I WANT TO BELIEVE IN!...
MASTER...
!
EH?

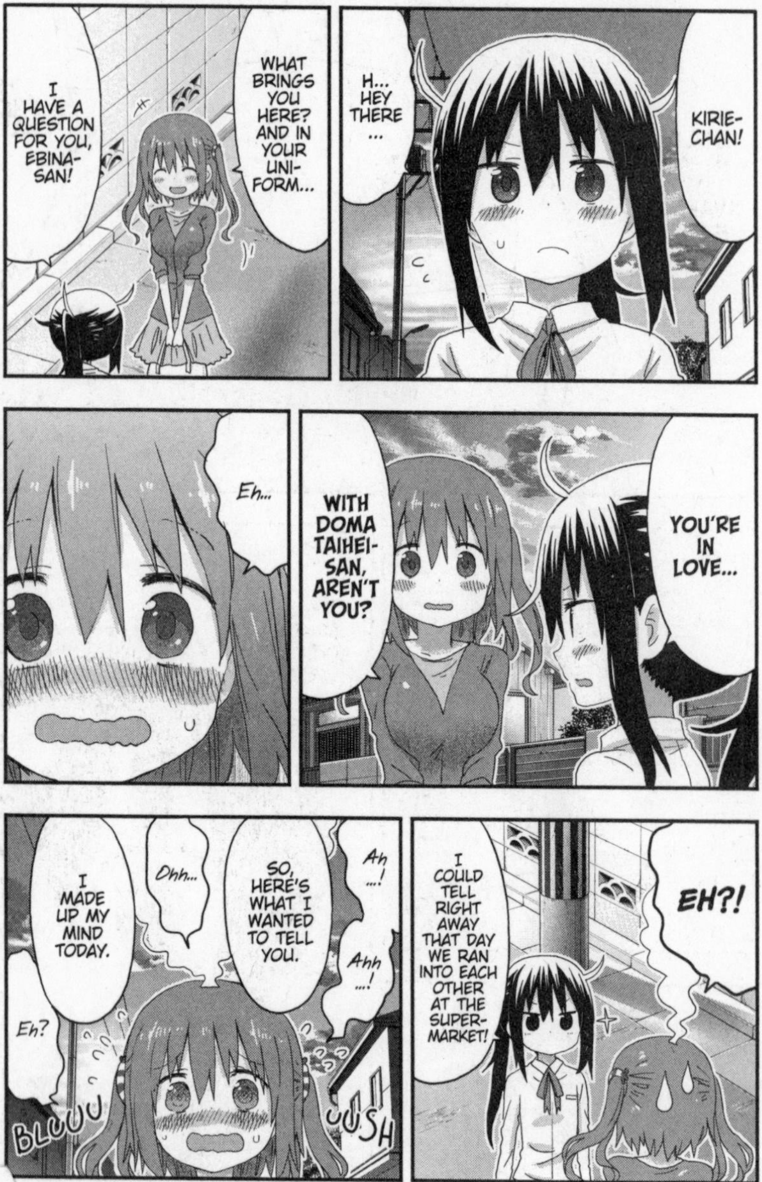
KIRIE-CHAN!
H... HEY THERE ...
WHAT BRINGS YOU HERE? AND IN YOUR UNIFORM...
I HAVE A QUESTION FOR YOU, EBINA-SAN!
YOU'RE IN LOVE...
WITH DOMA TAIHEI-SAN, AREN'T YOU?
Eh...
EH?!
I COULD TELL RIGHT AWAY THAT DAY WE RAN INTO EACH OTHER AT THE SUPERMARKET!
Ah ...!
Ahh ...!
SO, HERE'S WHAT I WANTED TO TELL YOU.
Ohh...
I MADE UP MY MIND TODAY.
Eh?
BLUUU
UUSH

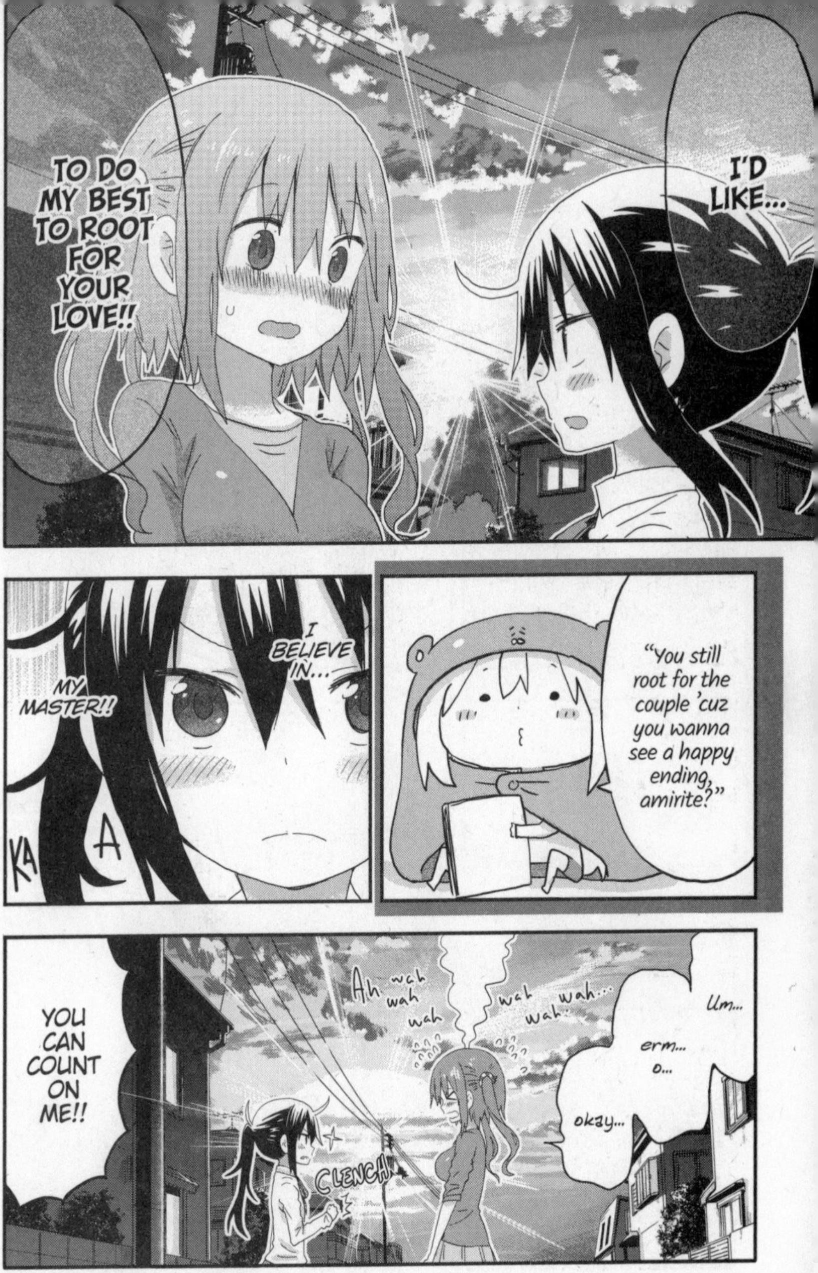
I'D LIKE...
TO DO MY BEST TO ROOT FOR YOUR LOVE!!
"You still root for the couple 'cuz you wanna see a happy ending, amirite?"
I BELIEVE IN...
MY MASTER!!
KA A
Um... erm... o... okay...
wah wah...
Ah wah wah wah
CLENCH
YOU CAN COUNT ON ME!!

No. 115 Umaru & Summer Vacation

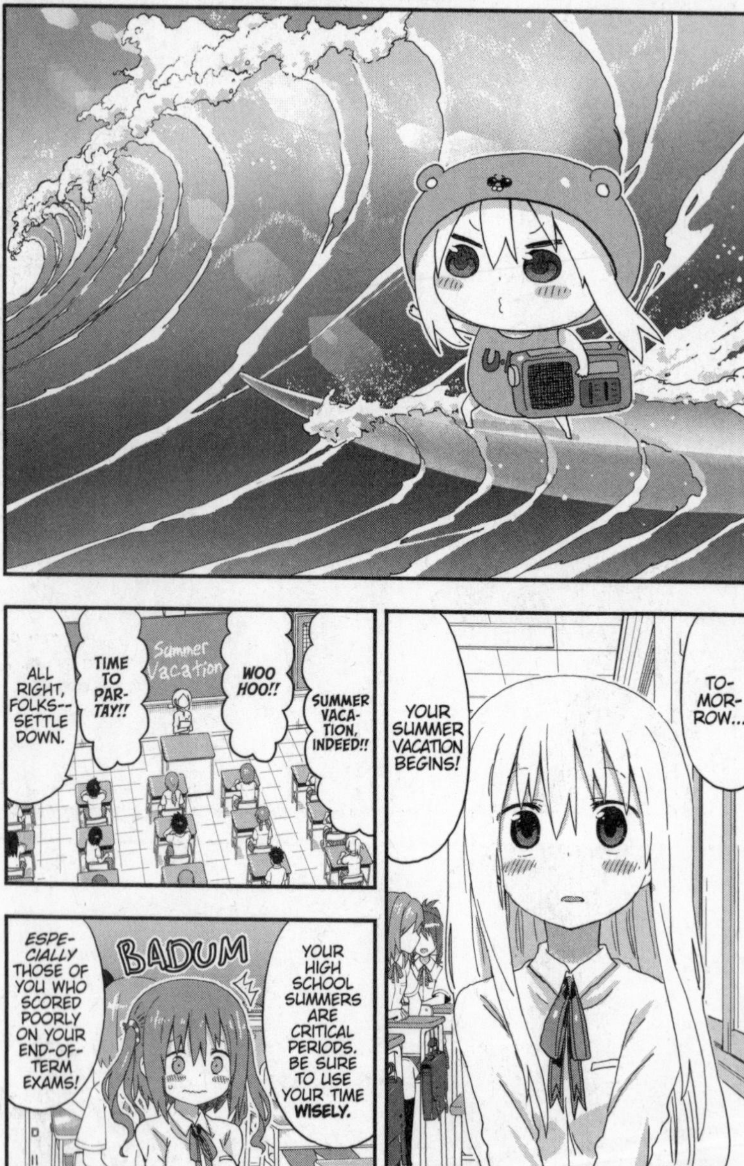
TO-MORROW...
YOUR SUMMER VACATION BEGINS!
SUMMER VACATION, INDEED!!
WOO HOO!!
Summer Vacation
TIME TO PARTAY!!
ALL RIGHT, FOLKS--SETTLE DOWN.
YOUR HIGH SCHOOL SUMMERS ARE CRITICAL PERIODS. BE SURE TO USE YOUR TIME **WISELY.**
BADUM
ESPECIALLY THOSE OF YOU WHO SCORED POORLY ON YOUR END-OF-TERM EXAMS!

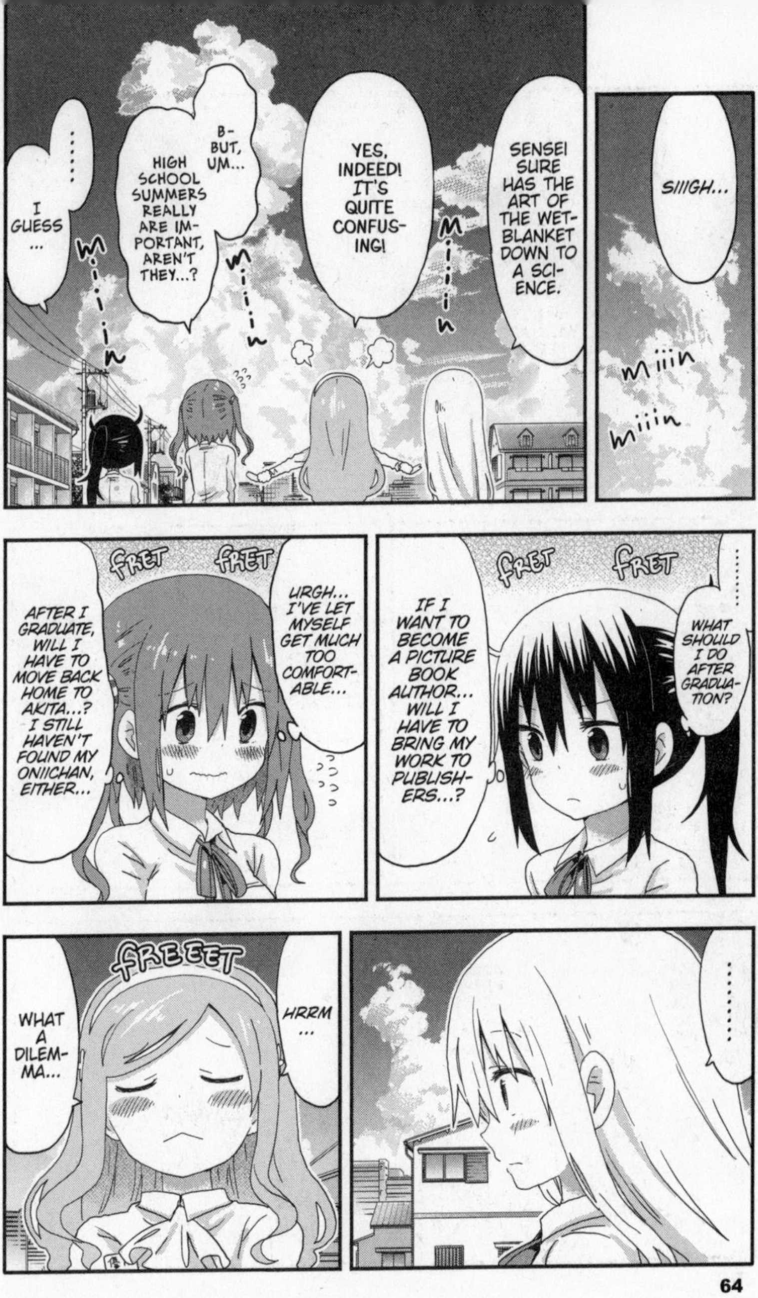
SIIIGH...
Miiin
Miiin
SENSEI SURE HAS THE ART OF THE WET-BLANKET DOWN TO A SCIENCE.
Miiin
YES, INDEED! IT'S QUITE CONFUSING!
Miiin
B-BUT, UM... HIGH SCHOOL SUMMERS REALLY ARE IMPORTANT, AREN'T THEY...?
Miiin
......
I GUESS...
......
WHAT SHOULD I DO AFTER GRADUATION?
FRET FRET
IF I WANT TO BECOME A PICTURE BOOK AUTHOR... WILL I HAVE TO BRING MY WORK TO PUBLISHERS...?
URGH... I'VE LET MYSELF GET MUCH TOO COMFORTABLE...
FRET FRET
AFTER I GRADUATE, WILL I HAVE TO MOVE BACK HOME TO AKITA...? I STILL HAVEN'T FOUND MY ONIICHAN, EITHER...
......
FREEEET
HRRM...
WHAT A DILEMMA...

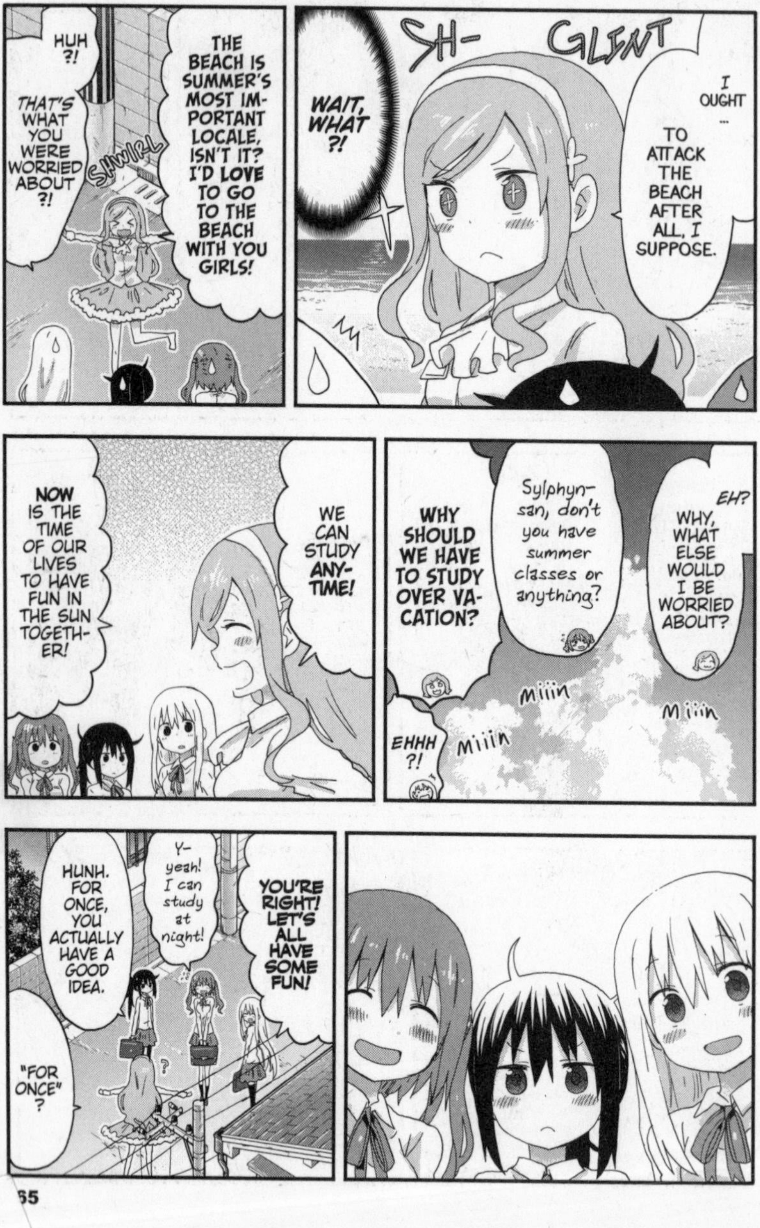
SH- GLINT
I OUGHT ... TO ATTACK THE BEACH AFTER ALL, I SUPPOSE.
WAIT, WHAT ?!
THE BEACH IS SUMMER'S MOST IMPORTANT LOCALE, ISN'T IT? I'D LOVE TO GO TO THE BEACH WITH YOU GIRLS!
SWIRL
HUH ?! THAT'S WHAT YOU WERE WORRIED ABOUT ?!
EH? WHY, WHAT ELSE WOULD I BE WORRIED ABOUT?
Sylphyn-san, don't you have summer classes or anything?
WHY SHOULD WE HAVE TO STUDY OVER VACATION?
Miiin
miiin
Miiin
EHHH ?!
WE CAN STUDY ANYTIME!
NOW IS THE TIME OF OUR LIVES TO HAVE FUN IN THE SUN TOGETHER!
YOU'RE RIGHT! LET'S ALL HAVE SOME FUN!
Y-yeah! I can study at night!
HUNH. FOR ONCE, YOU ACTUALLY HAVE A GOOD IDEA.
"FOR ONCE"?

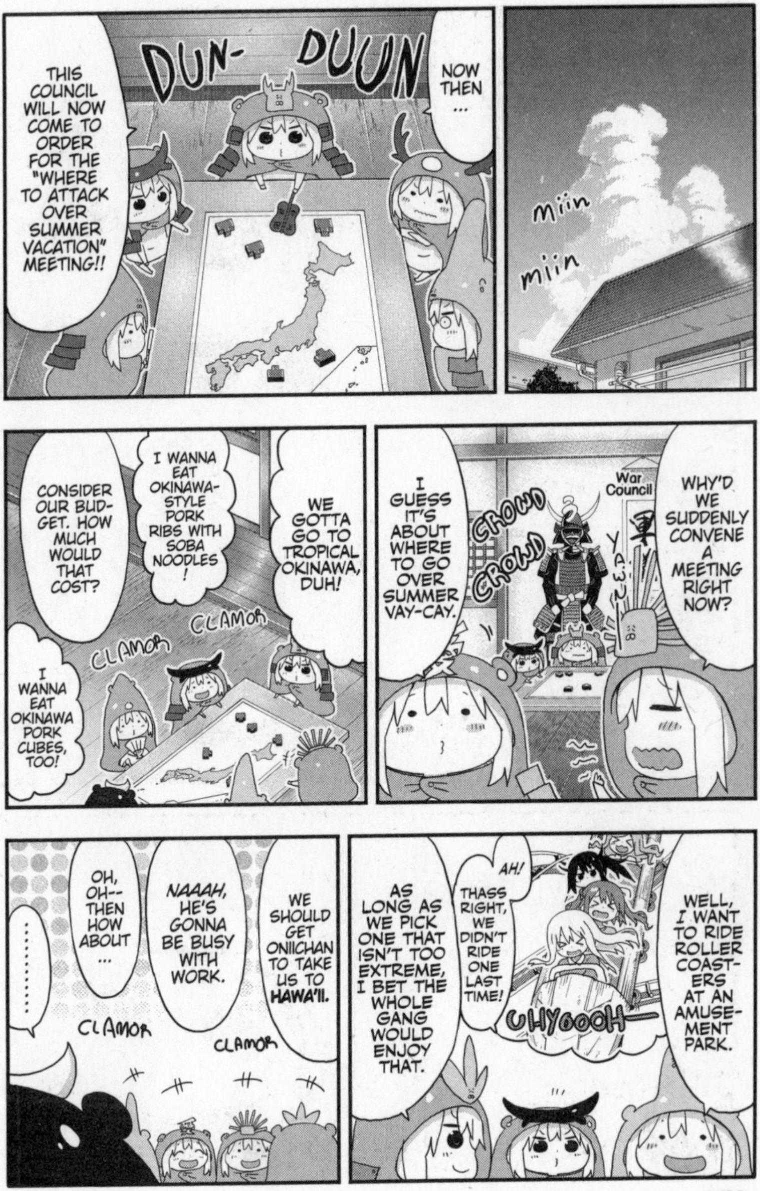
Miin
miin
NOW THEN ...
DUN- DUUN
THIS COUNCIL WILL NOW COME TO ORDER FOR THE "WHERE TO ATTACK OVER SUMMER VACATION" MEETING!!
WHY'D WE SUDDENLY CONVENE A MEETING RIGHT NOW?
War Council
YAWN
CROWD CROWD
I GUESS IT'S ABOUT WHERE TO GO OVER SUMMER VAY-CAY.
WE GOTTA GO TO TROPICAL OKINAWA, DUH!
I WANNA EAT OKINAWA-STYLE PORK RIBS WITH SOBA NOODLES!
CONSIDER OUR BUD-GET. HOW MUCH WOULD THAT COST?
CLAMOR
CLAMOR
I WANNA EAT OKINAWA PORK CUBES, TOO!
WELL, I WANT TO RIDE ROLLER COAST-ERS AT AN AMUSE-MENT PARK.
AH! THASS RIGHT, WE DIDN'T RIDE ONE LAST TIME!
UHYOOOH—
AS LONG AS WE PICK ONE THAT ISN'T TOO EXTREME, I BET THE WHOLE GANG WOULD ENJOY THAT.
WE SHOULD GET ONIICHAN TO TAKE US TO HAWA'II.
NAAAH, HE'S GONNA BE BUSY WITH WORK.
OH, OH-- THEN HOW ABOUT ...
....
CLAMOR
CLAMOR

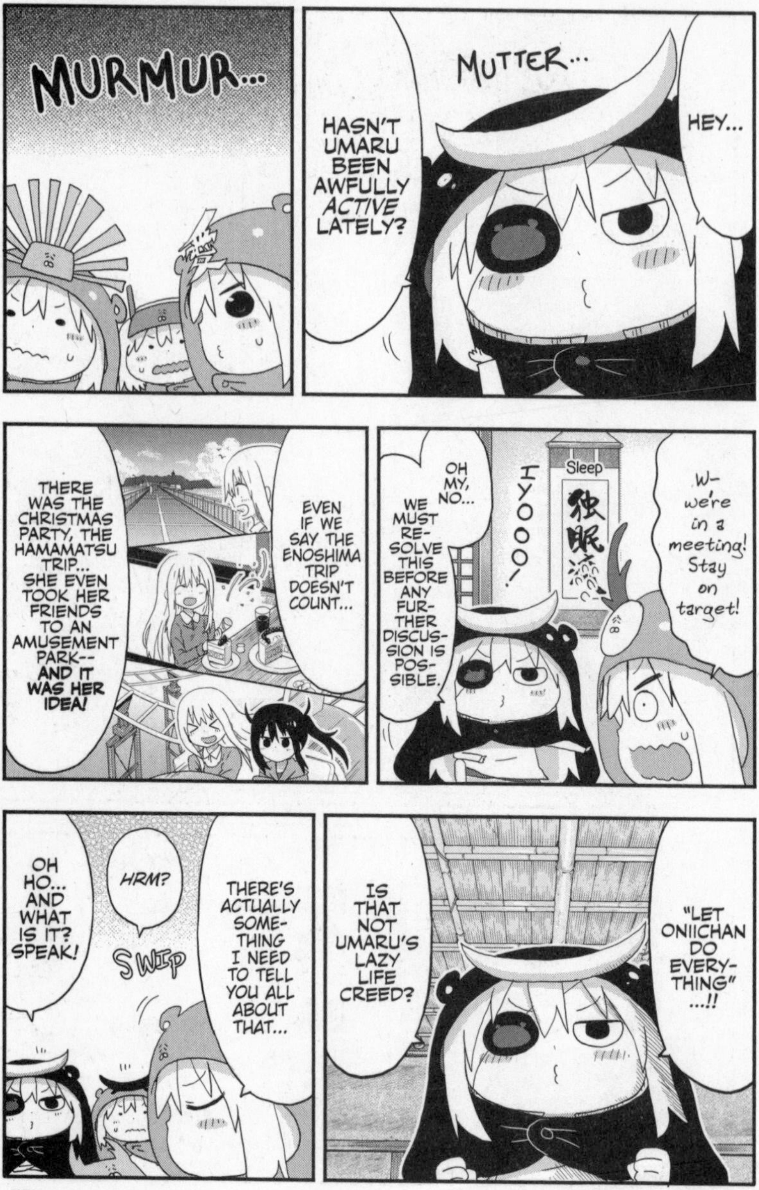
MUTTER...
HEY...
HASN'T UMARU BEEN AWFULLY *ACTIVE* LATELY?
MURMUR...
W-we're in a meeting! Stay on target!
Sleep
独眠
IYOOOO!
OH MY, NO... WE MUST RE-SOLVE THIS BEFORE ANY FUR-THER DISCUS-SION IS POS-SIBLE.
EVEN IF WE SAY THE ENOSHIMA TRIP DOESN'T COUNT...
THERE WAS THE CHRISTMAS PARTY, THE HAMAMATSU TRIP... SHE EVEN TOOK HER FRIENDS TO AN AMUSEMENT PARK-- **AND IT WAS HER IDEA!**
"LET ONIICHAN DO EVERY-THING" ...!!
IS THAT NOT UMARU'S LAZY LIFE CREED?
THERE'S ACTUALLY SOME-THING I NEED TO TELL YOU ALL ABOUT THAT...
HRM?
SWIP
OH HO... AND WHAT IS IT? SPEAK!

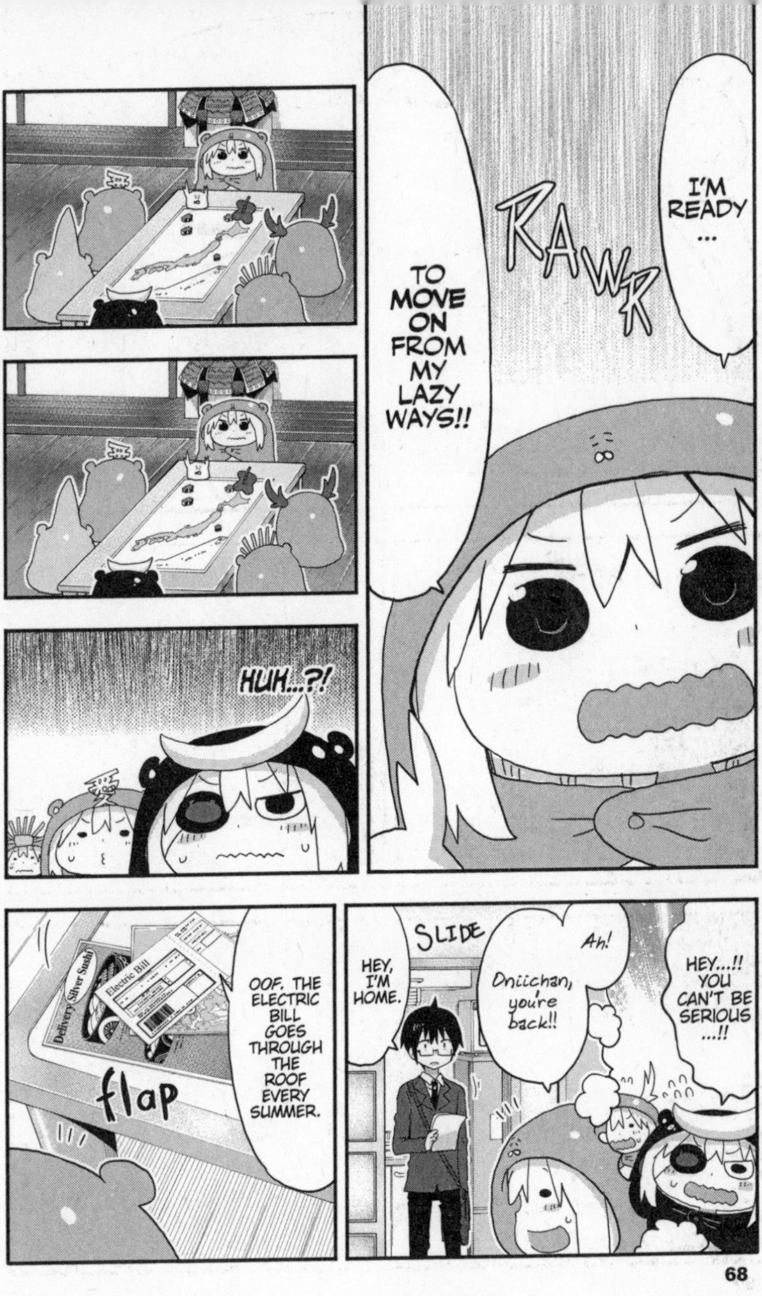
I'M READY ...
TO MOVE ON FROM MY LAZY WAYS!!
RAWR
HUH...?!
SLIDE
HEY, I'M HOME.
Ah! Oniichan, you're back!!
HEY...!! YOU CAN'T BE SERIOUS ...!!
OOF. THE ELECTRIC BILL GOES THROUGH THE ROOF EVERY SUMMER.
flap
Delivery Silver Sushi
Electric Bill

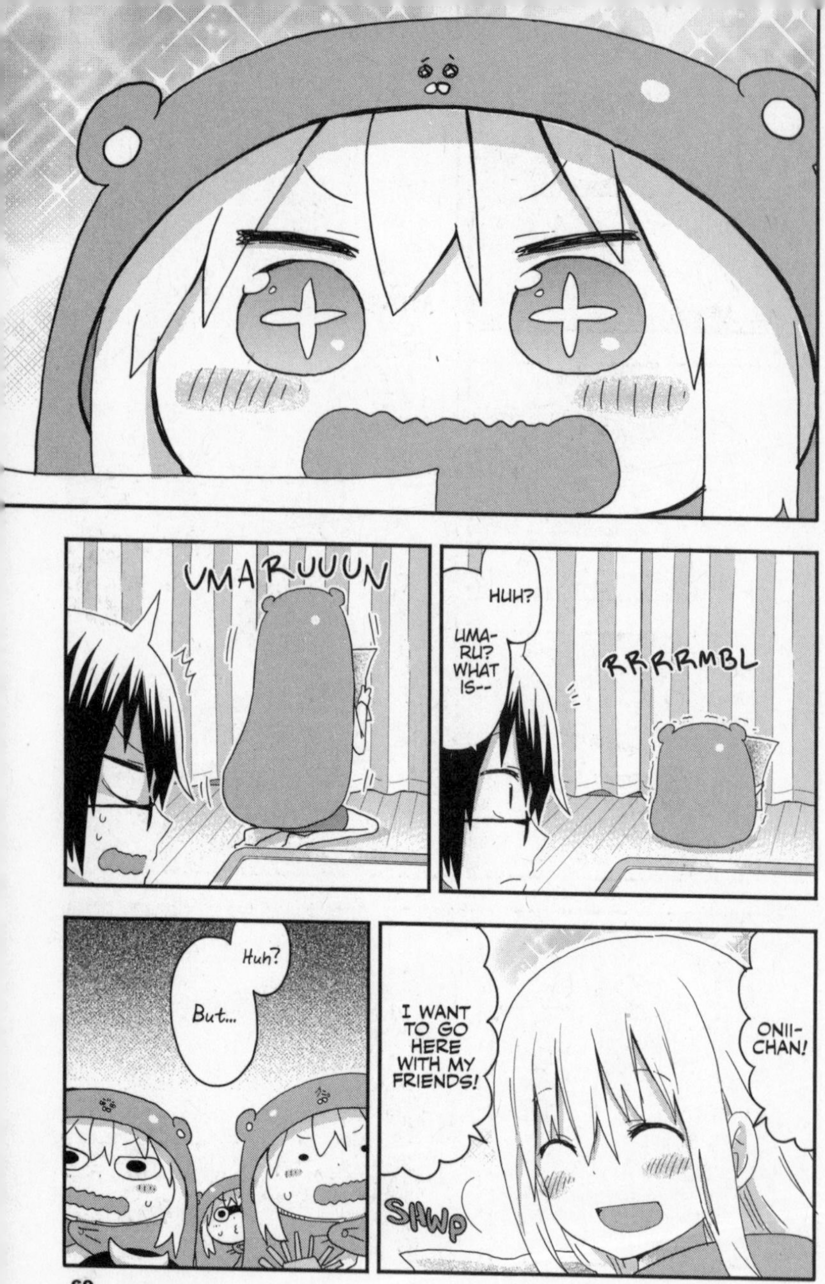

HUH?
UMA-RU? WHAT IS--
RRRRMBL
UMARUUUN
ONII-CHAN!
I WANT TO GO HERE WITH MY FRIENDS!
SHWP
Huh?
But...

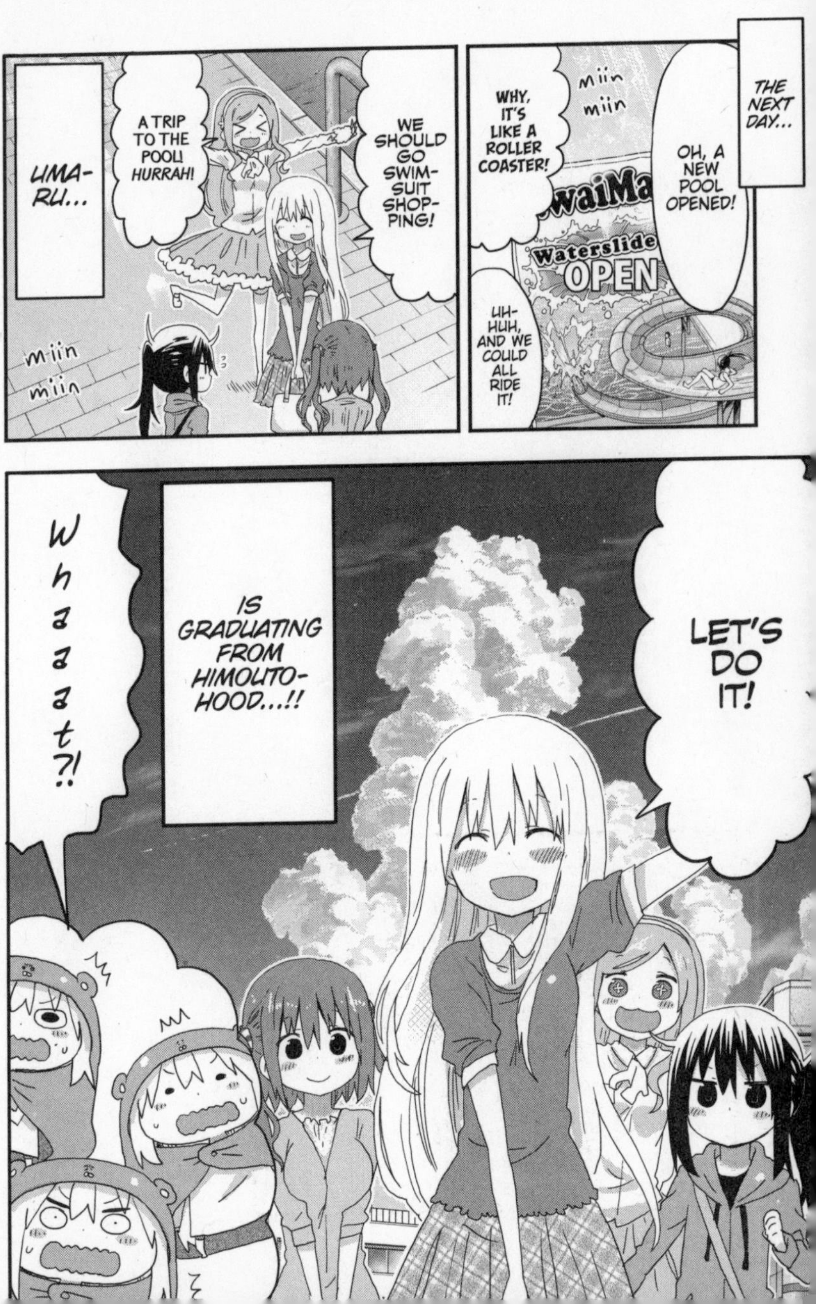
THE NEXT DAY...
OH, A NEW POOL OPENED!
miin miin
Waterslide OPEN
WHY, IT'S LIKE A ROLLER COASTER!
UH-HUH, AND WE COULD ALL RIDE IT!
WE SHOULD GO SWIMSUIT SHOPPING!
A TRIP TO THE POOL! HURRAH!
UMARU...
miin miin
LET'S DO IT!
IS GRADUATING FROM HIMOUTO-HOOD...!!
Whaaat?!

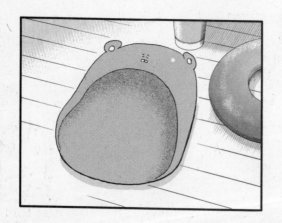

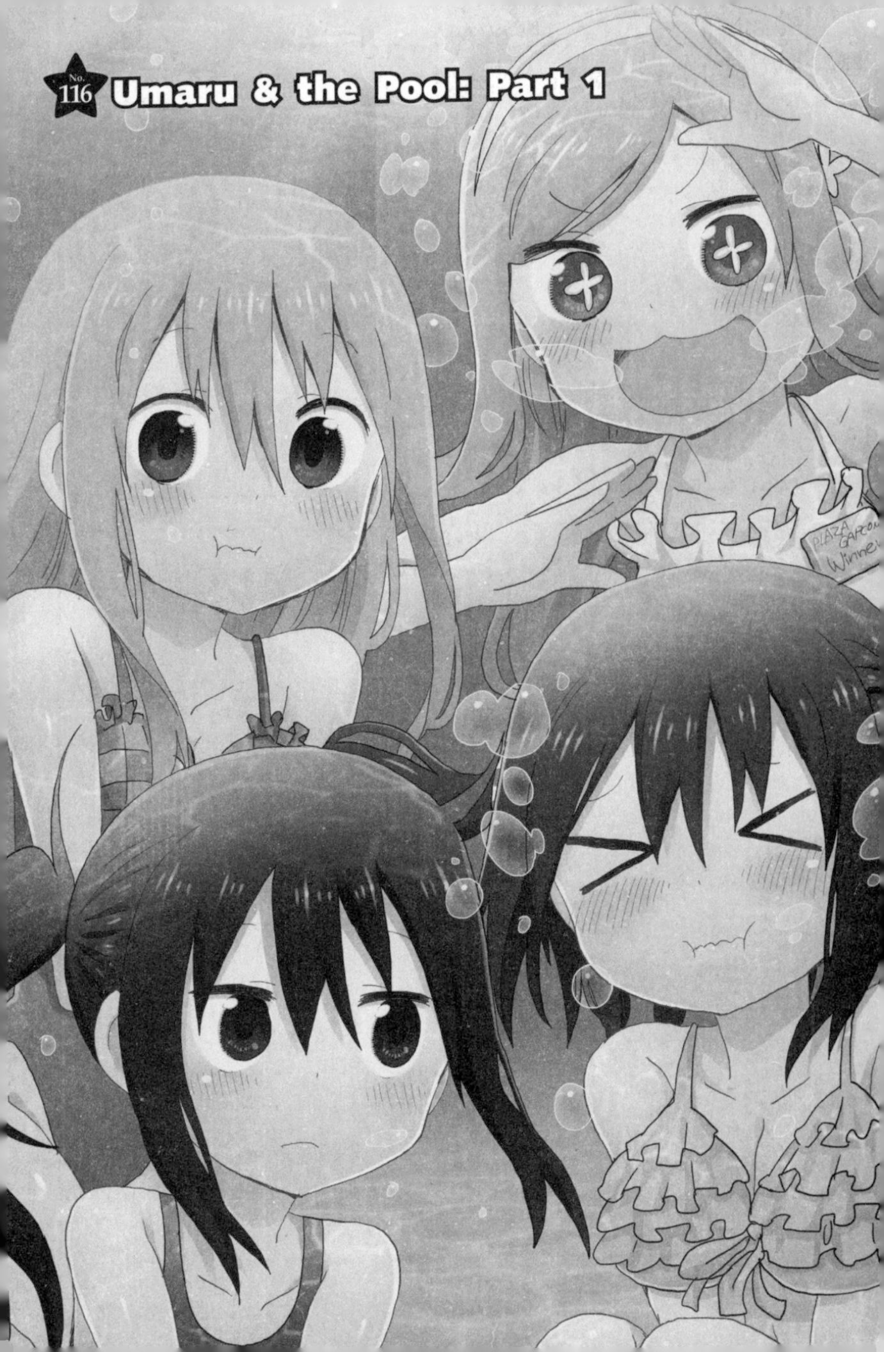
No. 116 Umaru & the Pool: Part 1

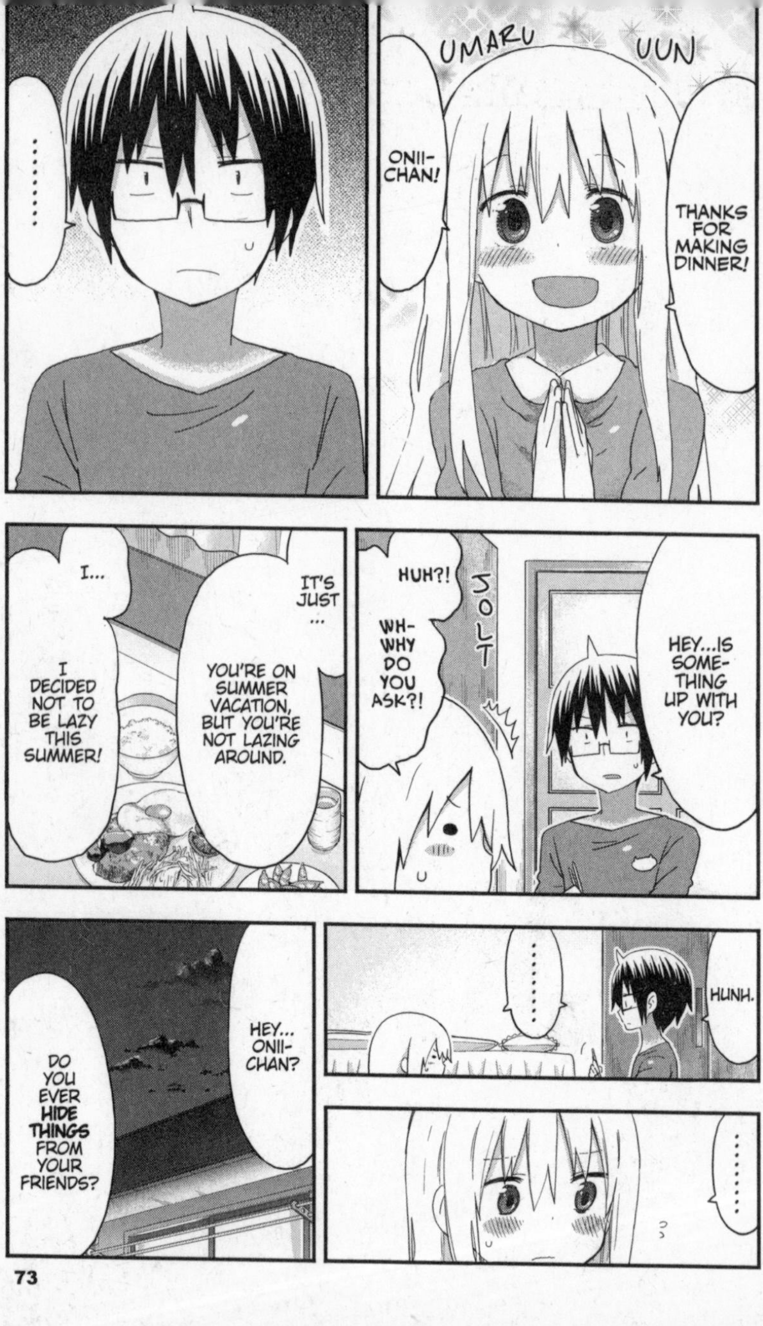
UMARU UUN
ONII-CHAN!
THANKS FOR MAKING DINNER!
......
HEY...IS SOME-THING UP WITH YOU?
JOLT
HUH?!
WH-WHY DO YOU ASK?!
IT'S JUST ...
YOU'RE ON SUMMER VACATION, BUT YOU'RE NOT LAZING AROUND.
I...
I DECIDED NOT TO BE LAZY THIS SUMMER!
HUNH.
......
......
HEY... ONII-CHAN?
DO YOU EVER **HIDE THINGS** FROM YOUR FRIENDS?

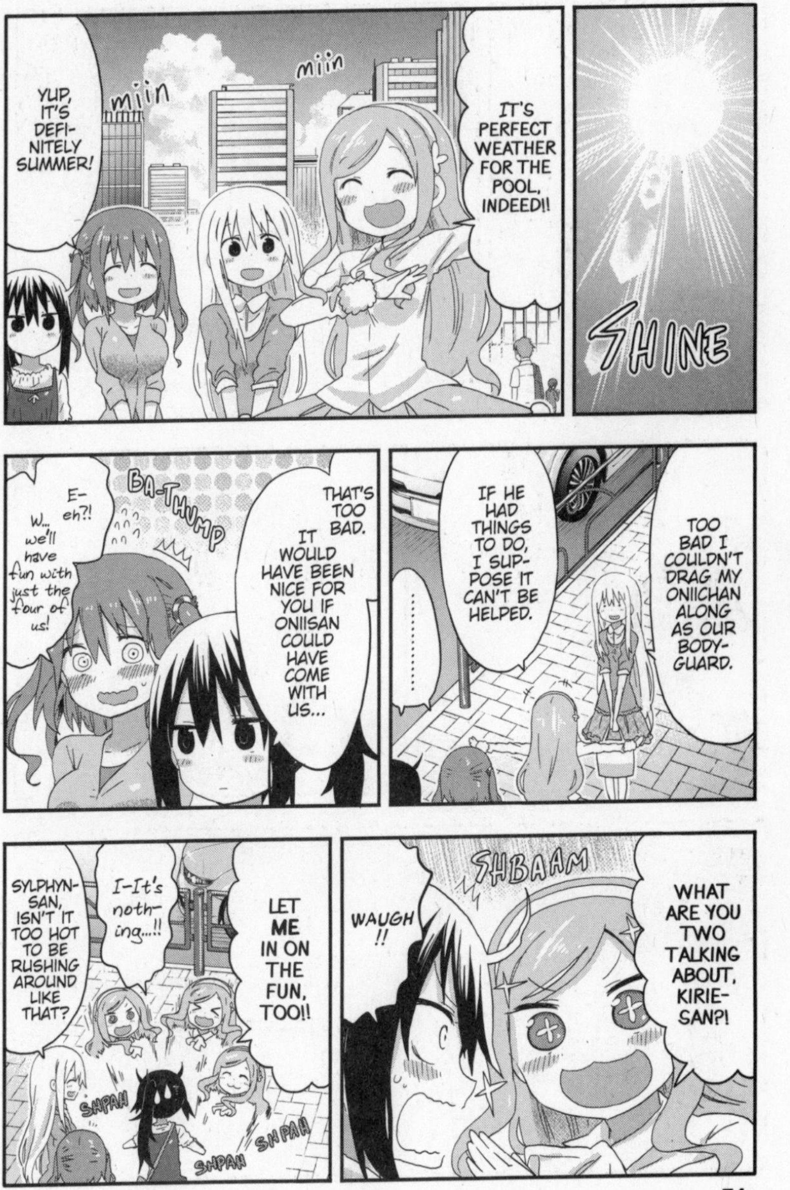
SHINE
IT'S PERFECT WEATHER FOR THE POOL, INDEED!!
miin
miin
YUP, IT'S DEFINITELY SUMMER!
TOO BAD I COULDN'T DRAG MY ONIICHAN ALONG AS OUR BODYGUARD.
IF HE HAD THINGS TO DO, I SUPPOSE IT CAN'T BE HELPED.
......
THAT'S TOO BAD.
IT WOULD HAVE BEEN NICE FOR YOU IF ONIISAN COULD HAVE COME WITH US...
BA-THUMP
E-eh?!
W... we'll have fun with just the four of us!
SHBAAM
WHAT ARE YOU TWO TALKING ABOUT, KIRIE-SAN?!
WAUGH!!
LET ME IN ON THE FUN, TOO!!
I-It's nothing....!!
SYLPHYN-SAN, ISN'T IT TOO HOT TO BE RUSHING AROUND LIKE THAT?
SHPAH
SHPAH
SHPAH

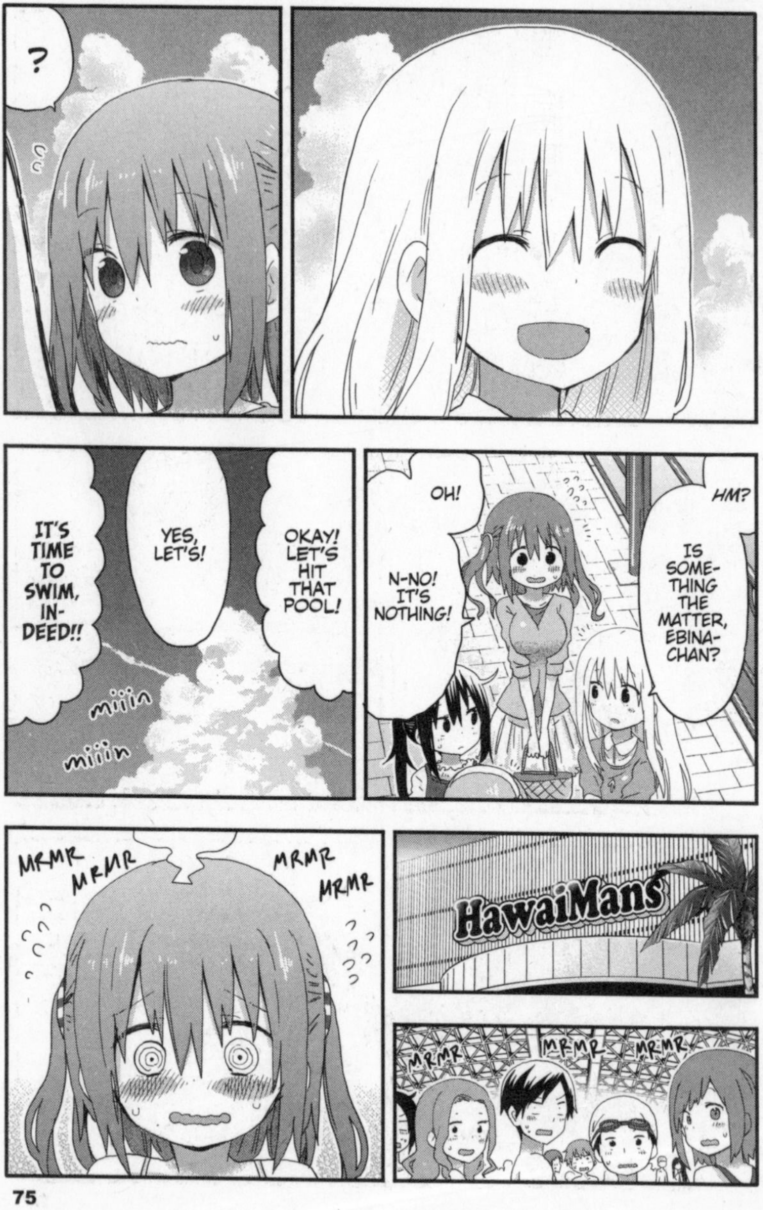
?
HM?
IS SOME-THING THE MATTER, EBINA-CHAN?
OH!
N-NO! IT'S NOTHING!
OKAY! LET'S HIT THAT POOL!
YES, LET'S!
IT'S TIME TO SWIM, IN-DEED!!
miiin
miiin
HawaiMans
MRMR
MRMR
MRMR
MRMR
MRMR
MRMR
MRMR

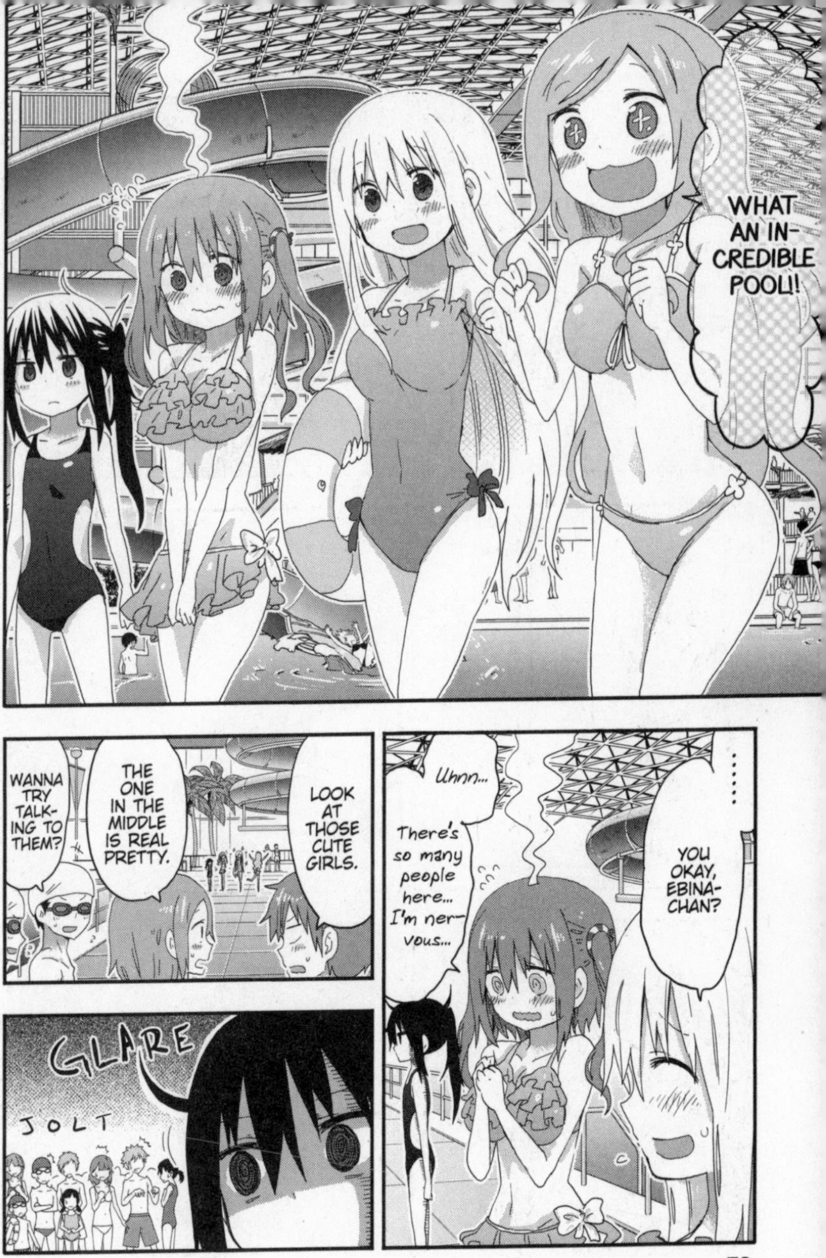
WHAT AN IN-CREDIBLE POOL!!
......
YOU OKAY, EBINA-CHAN?
Uhnn...
There's so many people here... I'm ner-vous...
LOOK AT THOSE CUTE GIRLS.
THE ONE IN THE MIDDLE IS REAL PRETTY.
WANNA TRY TALKING TO THEM?
GLARE
JOLT

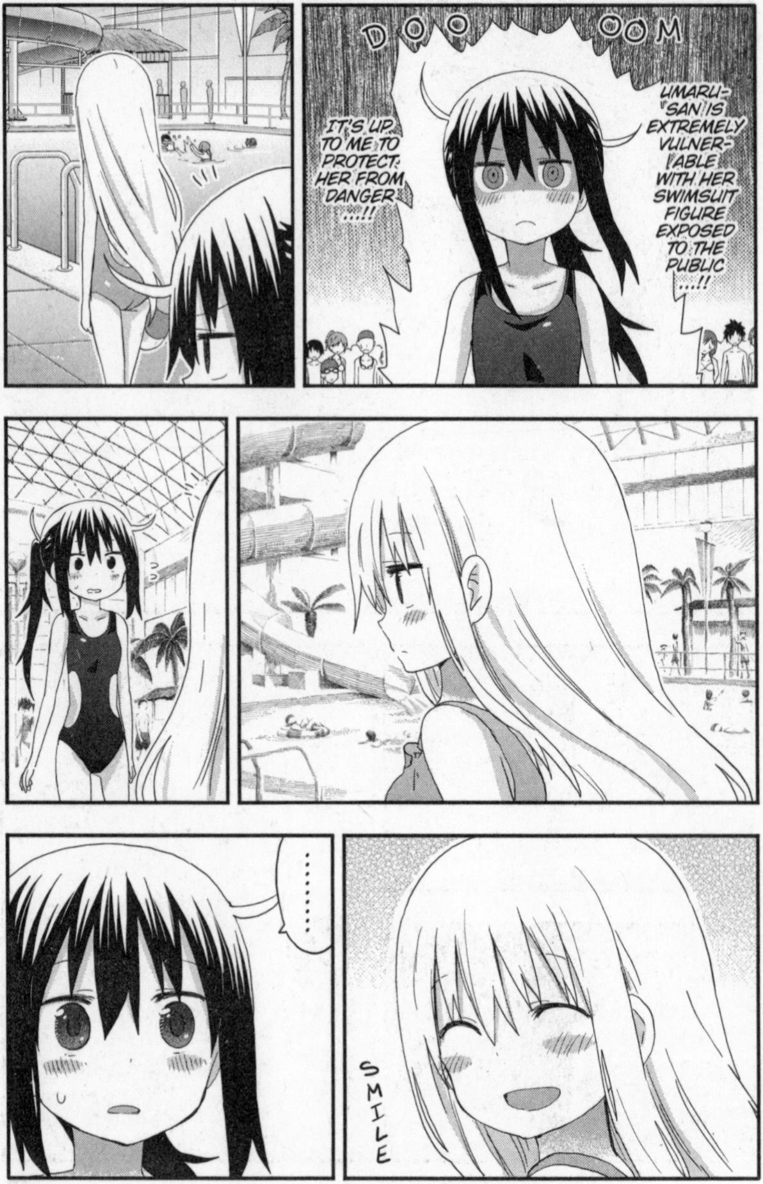
DOO OOM
UMARU-SAN IS EXTREMELY VULNERABLE WITH HER SWIMSUIT FIGURE EXPOSED TO THE PUBLIC ...!!
IT'S UP TO ME TO PROTECT HER FROM DANGER ...!!
SMILE
......

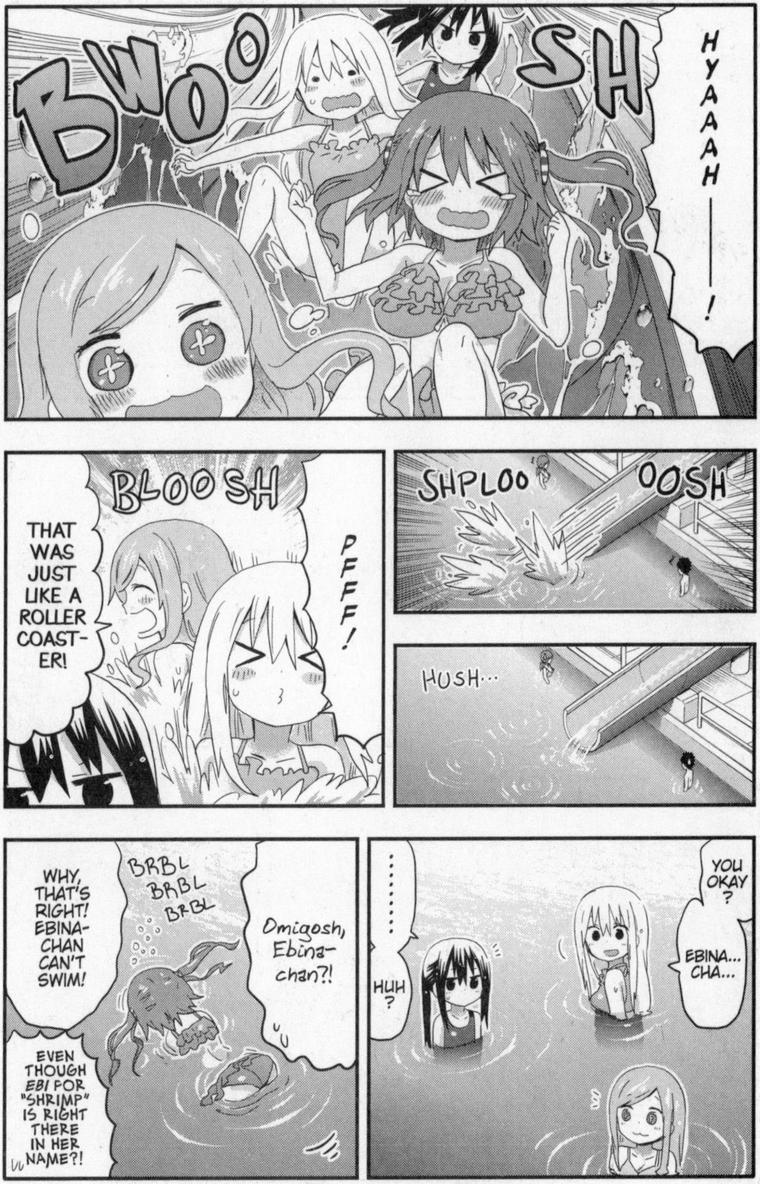
BWOOSH
HYAAAAH——!
SHPLOO OOSH
HUSH...
BLOOSH
THAT WAS JUST LIKE A ROLLER COASTER!
PFFF!
YOU OKAY?
....
HUH?
EBINA... CHA...
BRBL BRBL BRBL
Omigosh, Ebina-chan?!
WHY, THAT'S RIGHT! EBINA-CHAN CAN'T SWIM!
EVEN THOUGH *EBI* FOR "SHRIMP" IS RIGHT THERE IN HER NAME?!

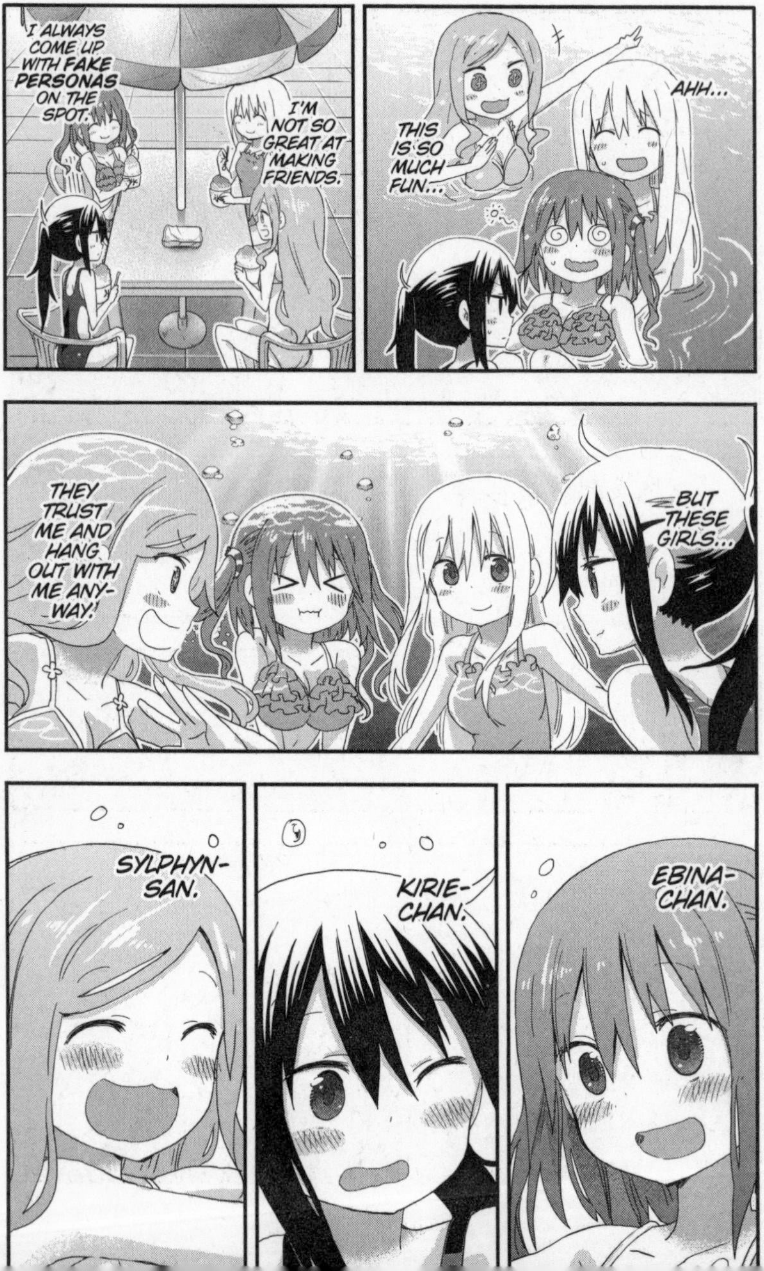
AHH...
THIS IS SO MUCH FUN...
I'M NOT SO GREAT AT MAKING FRIENDS.
I ALWAYS COME UP WITH FAKE PERSONAS ON THE SPOT.
BUT THESE GIRLS...
THEY TRUST ME AND HANG OUT WITH ME ANY-WAY!
EBINA-CHAN.
KIRIE-CHAN.
SYLPHYN-SAN.

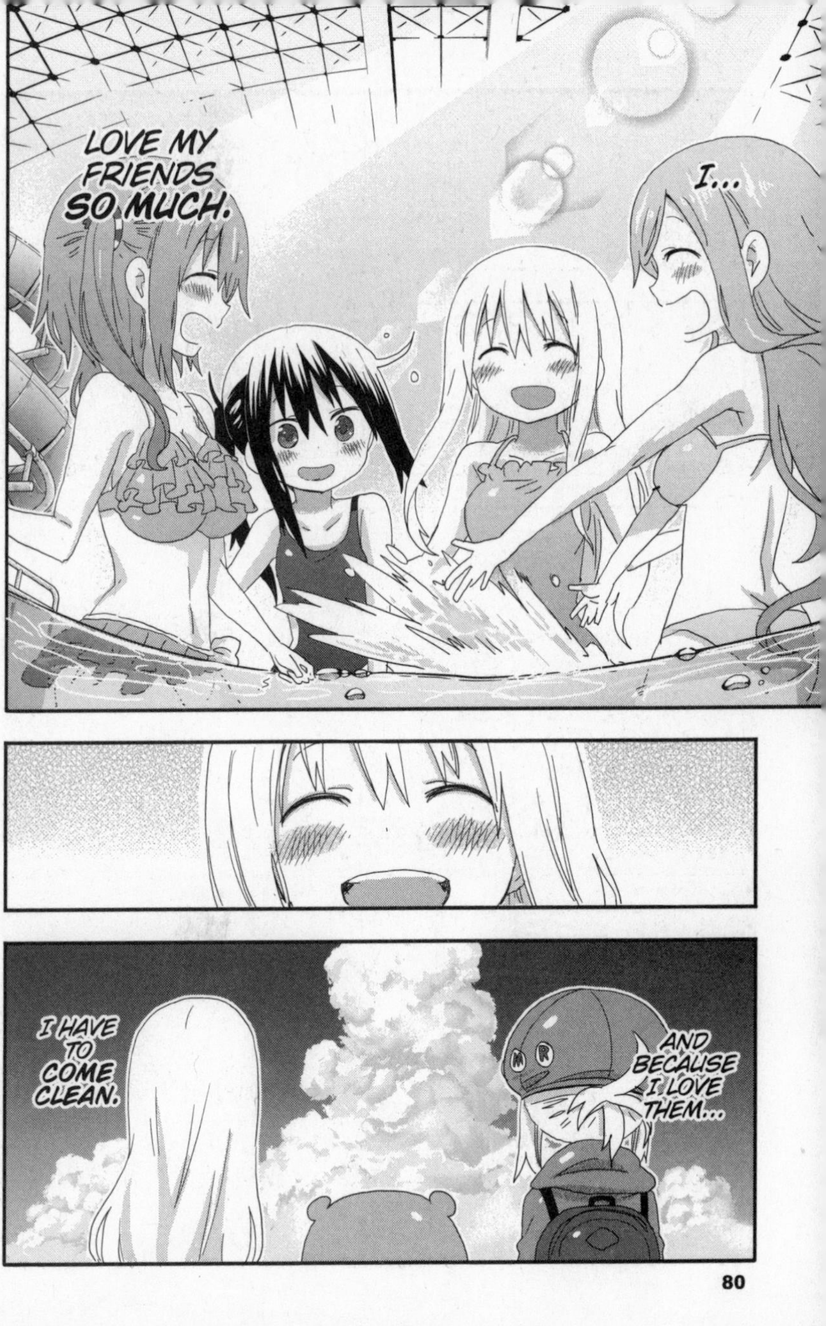
I...
LOVE MY FRIENDS SO MUCH.
AND BECAUSE I LOVE THEM...
I HAVE TO COME CLEAN.

No. 117 Umaru & the Pool: Part 2

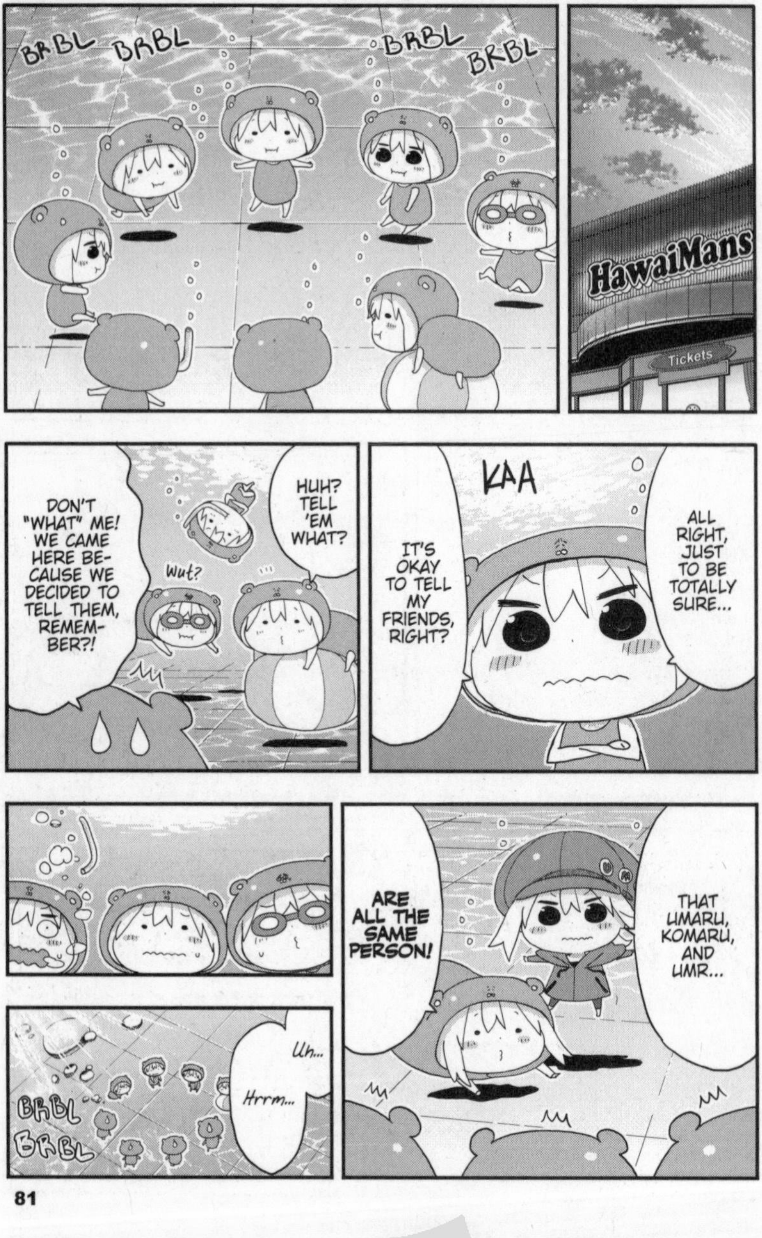
HawaiMans
Tickets
BRBL
BRBL
BRBL
BRBL
KAA
ALL RIGHT, JUST TO BE TOTALLY SURE...
IT'S OKAY TO TELL MY FRIENDS, RIGHT?
HUH? TELL 'EM WHAT?
Wut?
DON'T "WHAT" ME! WE CAME HERE BE-CAUSE WE DECIDED TO TELL THEM, REMEMBER?!
THAT UMARU, KOMARU, AND UMR...
ARE ALL THE SAME PERSON!
Un...
Hrrm...
BRBL
BRBL

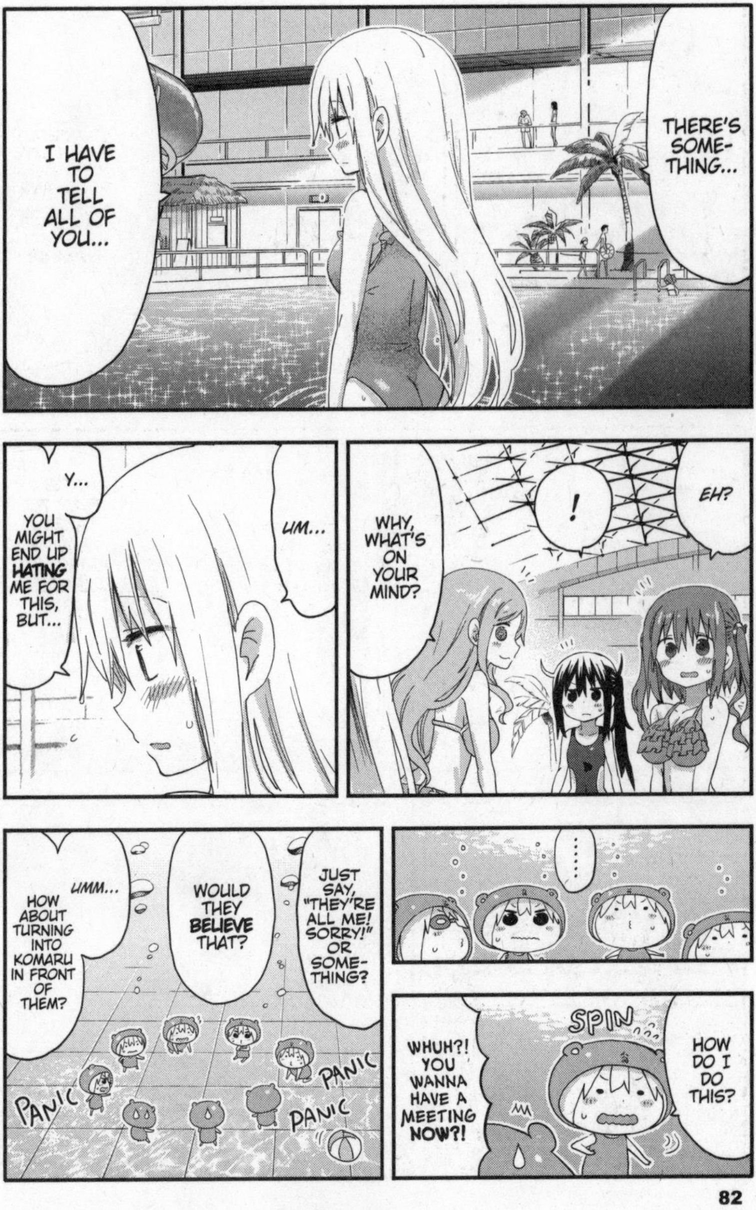
THERE'S SOMETHING...
I HAVE TO TELL ALL OF YOU...
EH?
!
WHY, WHAT'S ON YOUR MIND?
UM...
Y... YOU MIGHT END UP HATING ME FOR THIS, BUT...
......
HOW DO I DO THIS?
SPIN
WHUH?! YOU WANNA HAVE A MEETING NOW?!
JUST SAY, "THEY'RE ALL ME! SORRY!" OR SOMETHING?
WOULD THEY BELIEVE THAT?
UMM... HOW ABOUT TURNING INTO KOMARU IN FRONT OF THEM?
PANIC
PANIC
PANIC

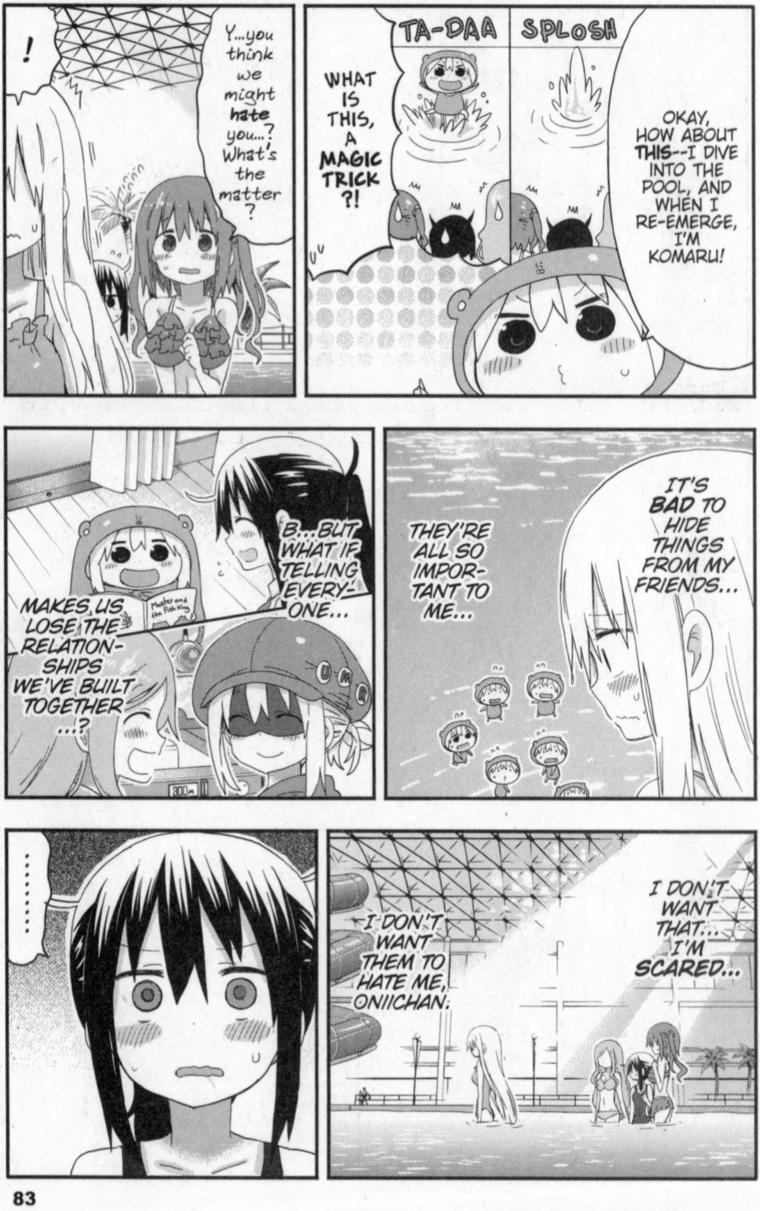
OKAY, HOW ABOUT THIS--I DIVE INTO THE POOL, AND WHEN I RE-EMERGE, I'M KOMARU!
SPLOSH
TA-DAA
WHAT IS THIS, A MAGIC TRICK?!
Y...you think we might hate you...? What's the matter?
!
IT'S BAD TO HIDE THINGS FROM MY FRIENDS...
THEY'RE ALL SO IMPORTANT TO ME...
B...BUT WHAT IF TELLING EVERYONE...
MAKES US LOSE THE RELATIONSHIPS WE'VE BUILT TOGETHER...?
I DON'T WANT THAT... I'M SCARED...
I DON'T WANT THEM TO HATE ME, ONIICHAN.
....

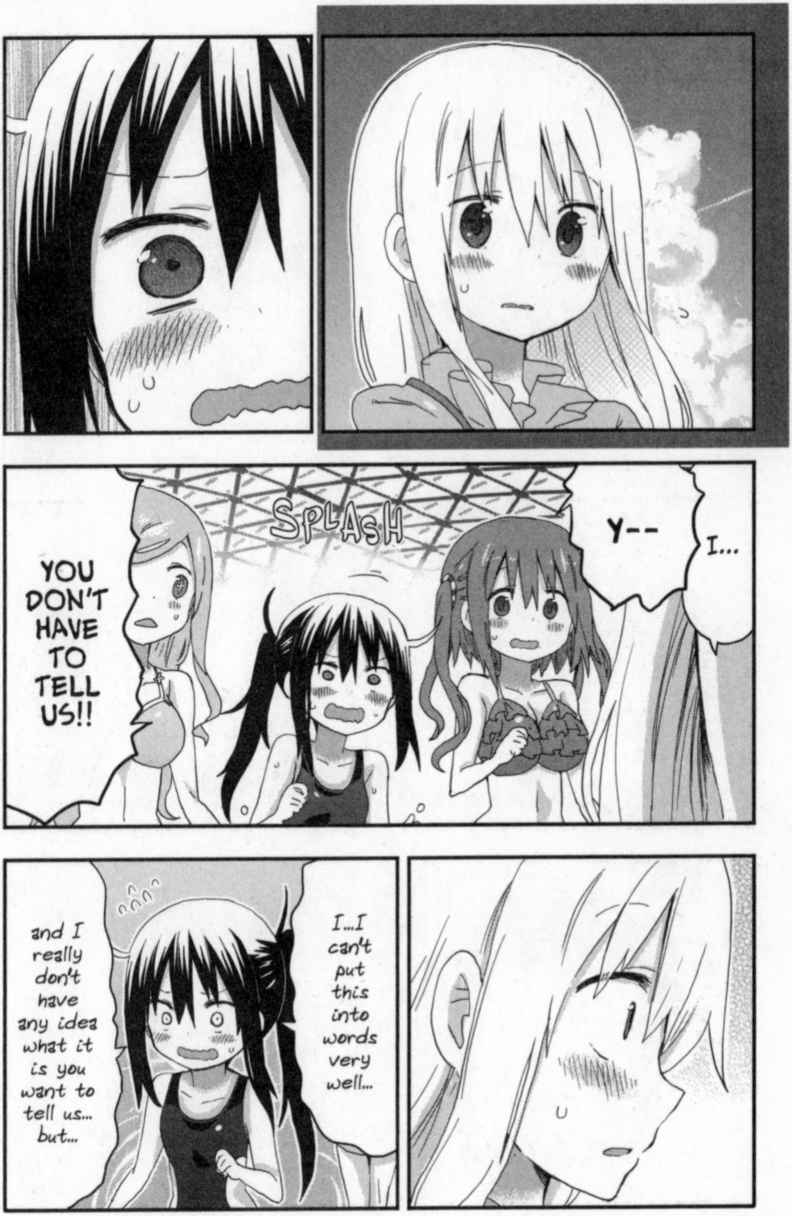
I...
Y--
SPLASH
YOU DON'T HAVE TO TELL US!!
I...I can't put this into words very well...
and I really don't have any idea what it is you want to tell us... but...

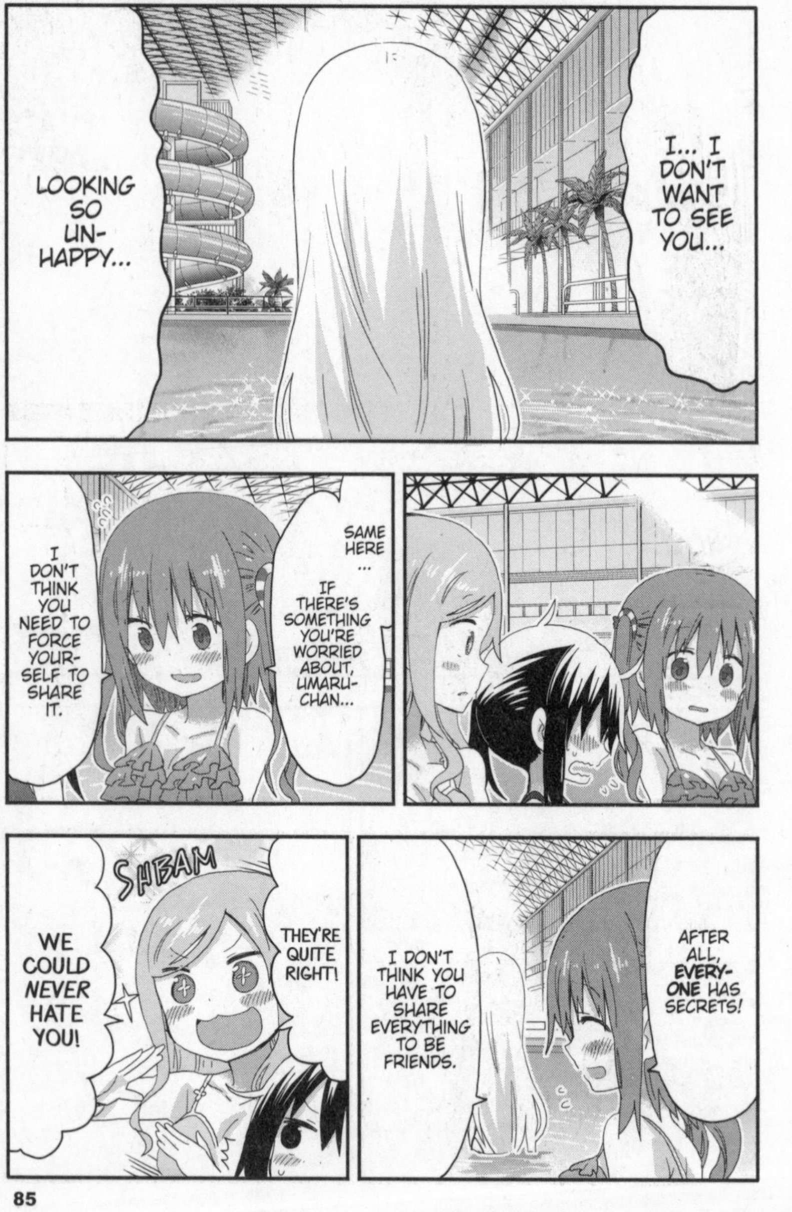
I... I DON'T WANT TO SEE YOU...
LOOKING SO UN-HAPPY...
SAME HERE ... IF THERE'S SOMETHING YOU'RE WORRIED ABOUT, UMARU-CHAN...
I DON'T THINK YOU NEED TO FORCE YOUR-SELF TO SHARE IT.
AFTER ALL, **EVERY-ONE** HAS SECRETS!
I DON'T THINK YOU HAVE TO SHARE EVERYTHING TO BE FRIENDS.
SHBAM
THEY'RE QUITE RIGHT!
WE COULD *NEVER* HATE YOU!

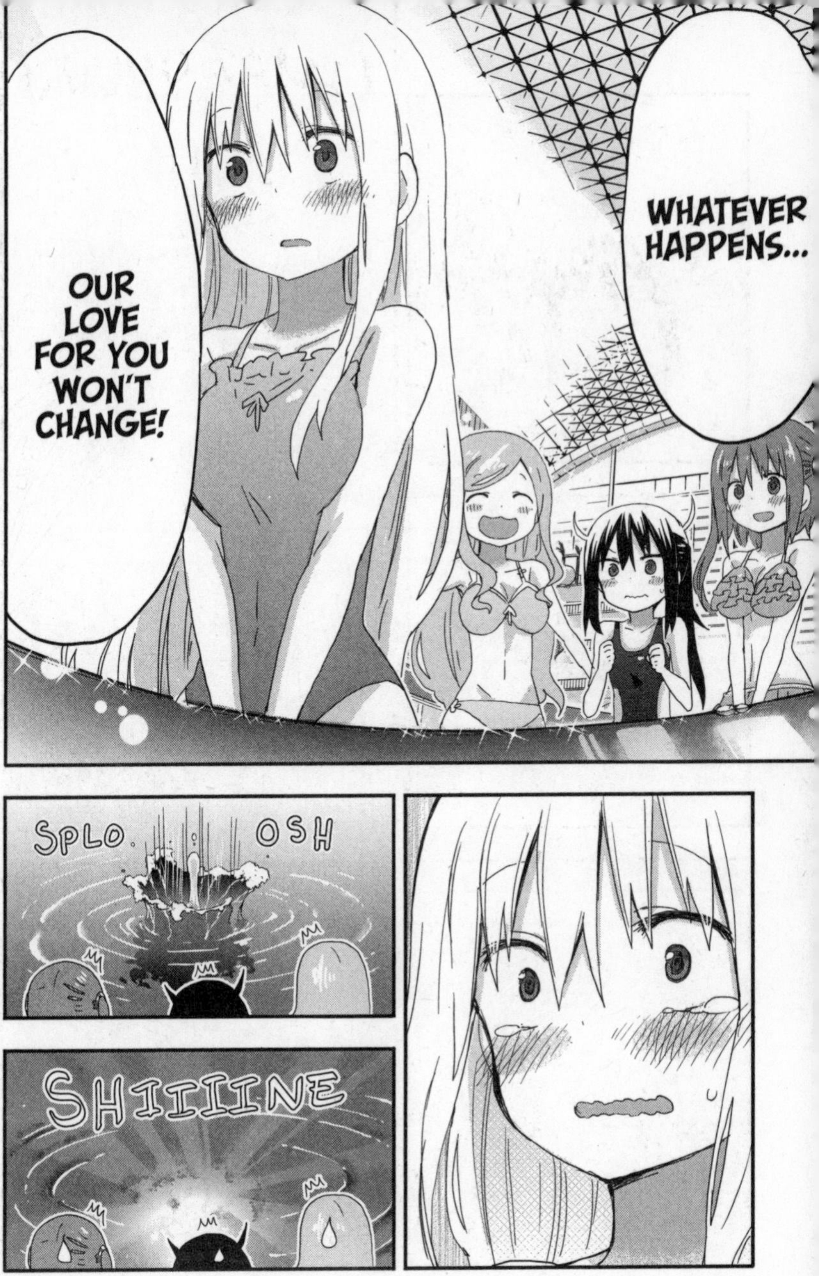
WHATEVER HAPPENS...
OUR LOVE FOR YOU WON'T CHANGE!
SPLO OSH
SHIIIINE

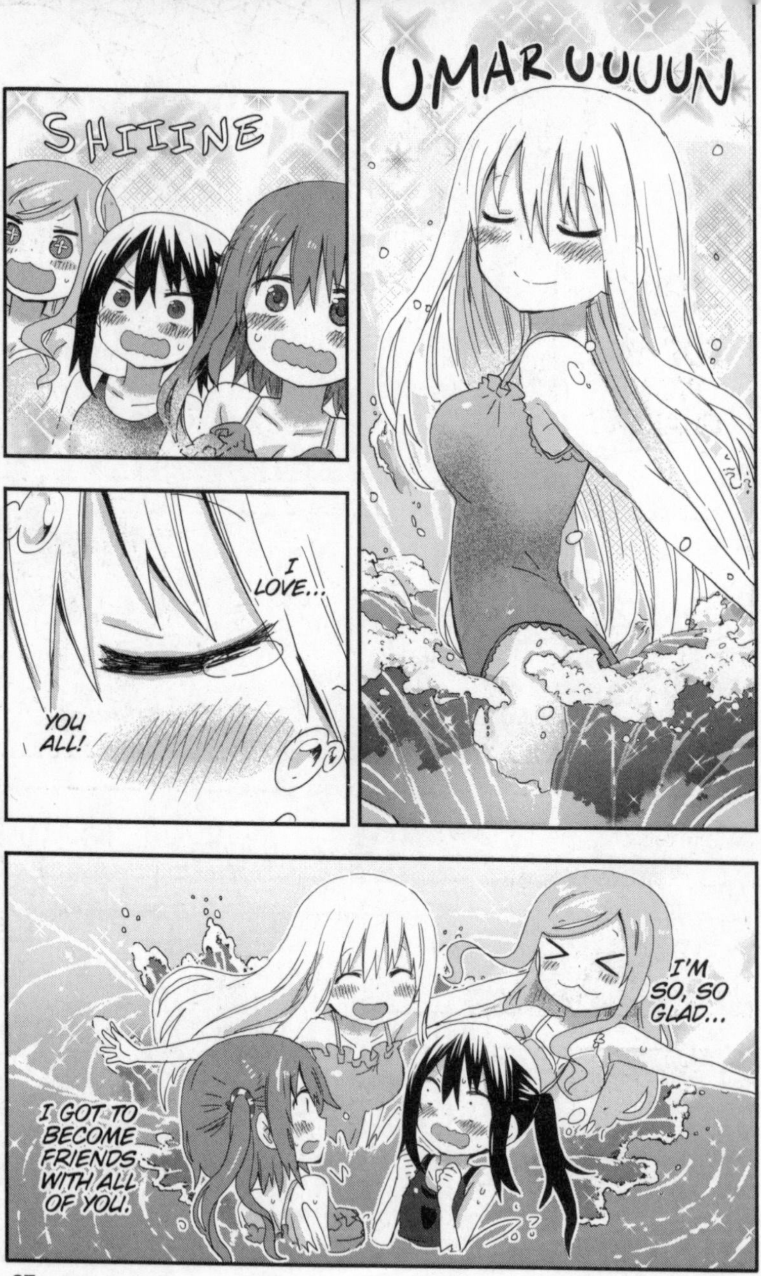
UMARUUUUN
SHIIINE
I LOVE...
YOU ALL!
I'M SO, SO GLAD...
I GOT TO BECOME FRIENDS WITH ALL OF YOU.

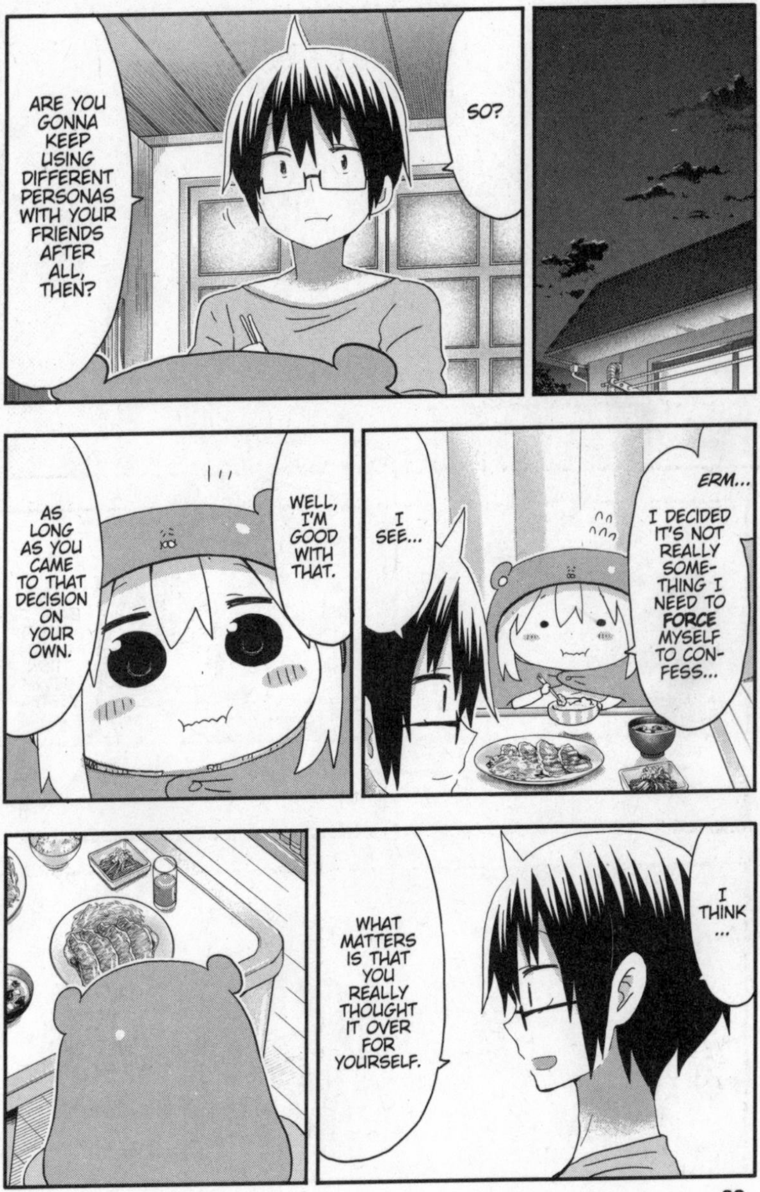
SO?
ARE YOU GONNA KEEP USING DIFFERENT PERSONAS WITH YOUR FRIENDS AFTER ALL, THEN?
ERM...
I DECIDED IT'S NOT REALLY SOME-THING I NEED TO FORCE MYSELF TO CON-FESS...
I SEE...
WELL, I'M GOOD WITH THAT.
AS LONG AS YOU CAME TO THAT DECISION ON YOUR OWN.
I THINK...
WHAT MATTERS IS THAT YOU REALLY THOUGHT IT OVER FOR YOURSELF.

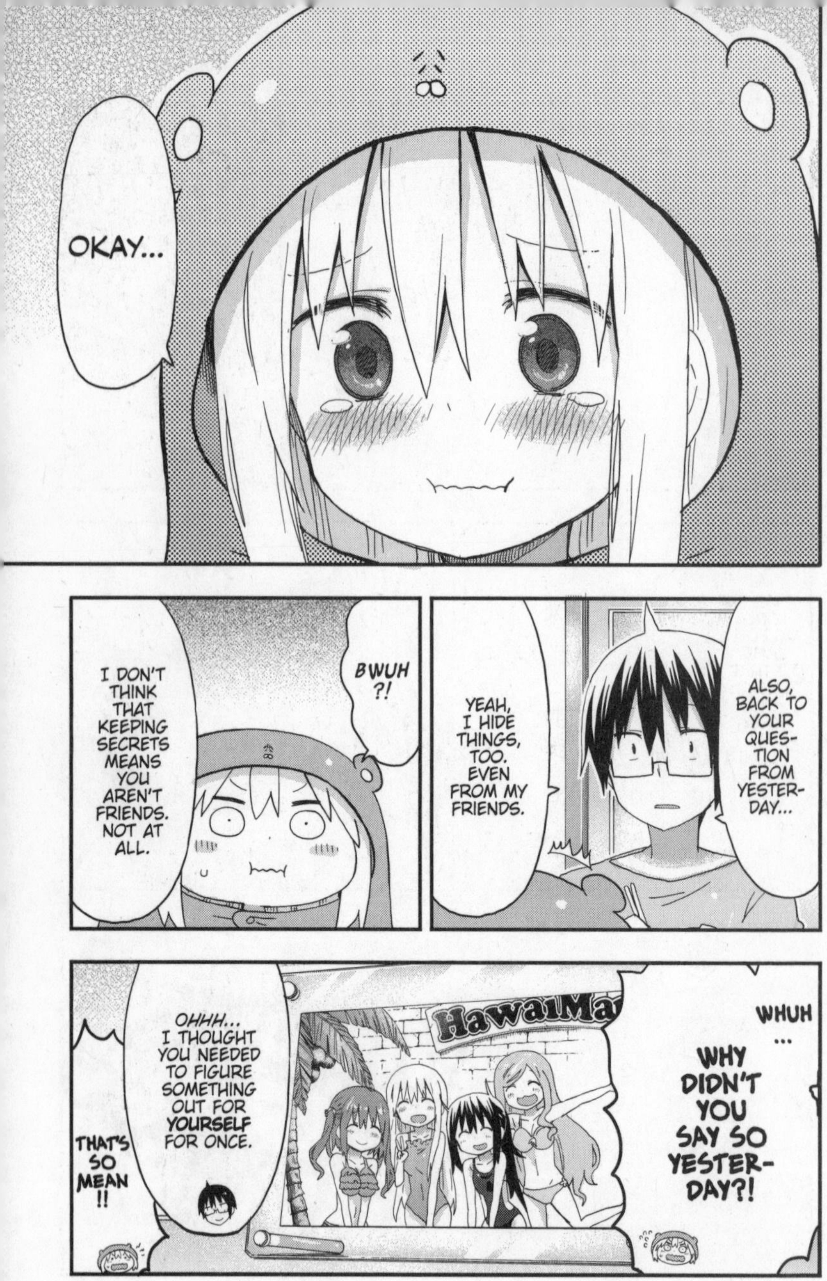
OKAY...
ALSO, BACK TO YOUR QUESTION FROM YESTERDAY...
YEAH, I HIDE THINGS, TOO. EVEN FROM MY FRIENDS.
BWUH?!
I DON'T THINK THAT KEEPING SECRETS MEANS YOU AREN'T FRIENDS. NOT AT ALL.
WHUH...
WHY DIDN'T YOU SAY SO YESTERDAY?!
OHHH... I THOUGHT YOU NEEDED TO FIGURE SOMETHING OUT FOR **YOURSELF** FOR ONCE.
THAT'S SO MEAN!!

HIMOUTO! UMARU-CHAN

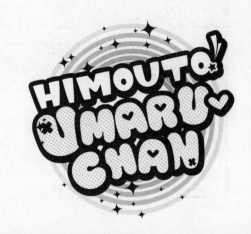

No. 118 **Umaru & the Remote**

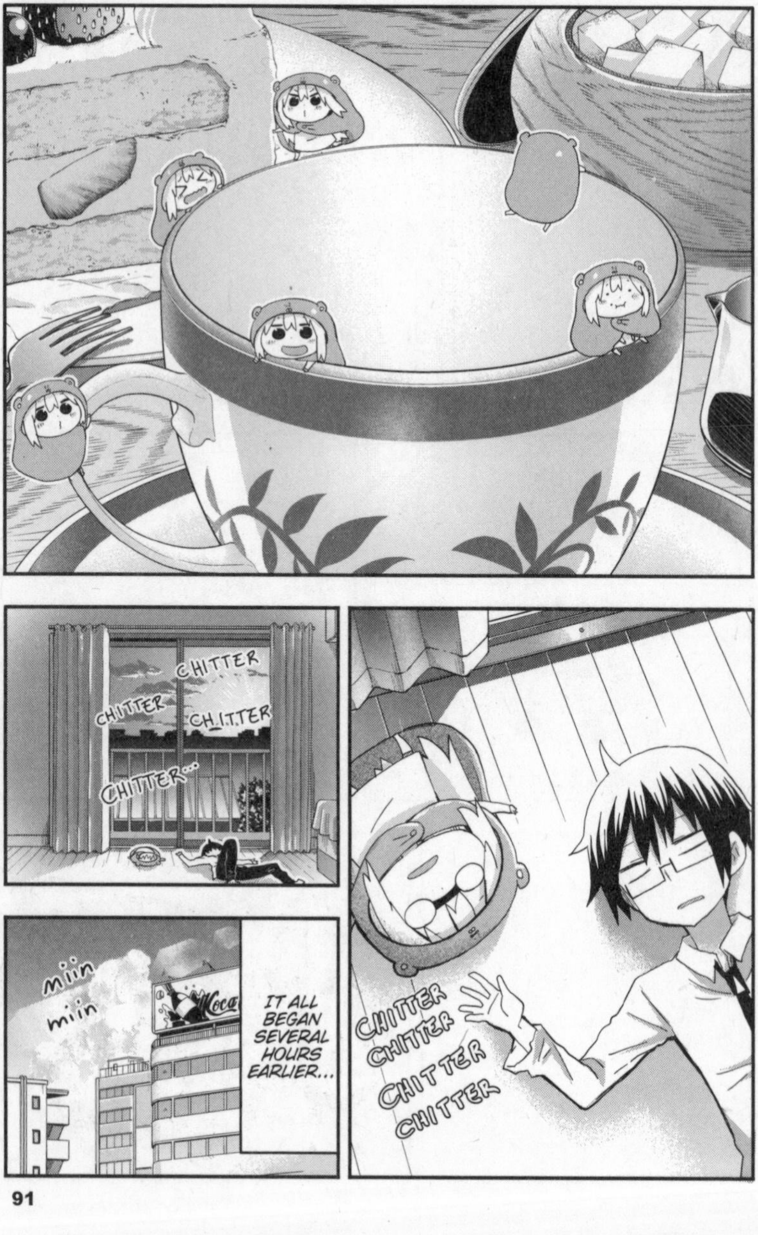

CHITTER
CHITTER
CHITTER
CHITTER
CHITTER
CHITTER
CHITTER
CHITTER...
IT ALL BEGAN SEVERAL HOURS EARLIER...
miin
miin

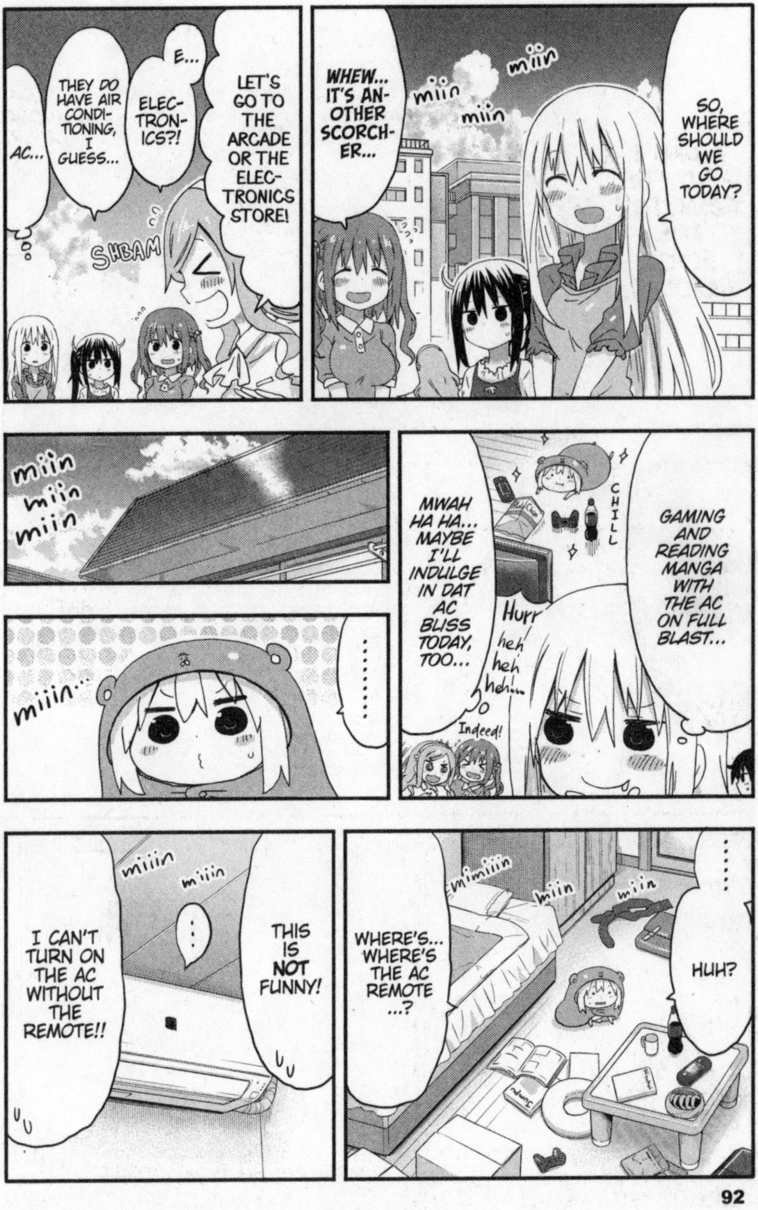
SO, WHERE SHOULD WE GO TODAY?
miin
miin
miin
WHEW... IT'S ANOTHER SCORCHER...
LET'S GO TO THE ARCADE OR THE ELECTRONICS STORE!
E... ELECTRONICS?!
THEY DO HAVE AIR CONDITIONING, I GUESS...
AC...
SHBAM
GAMING AND READING MANGA WITH THE AC ON FULL BLAST...
CHILL
MWAH HA HA... MAYBE I'LL INDULGE IN DAT AC BLISS TODAY, TOO...
Hurr heh heh heh...
Indeed!
miin
miin
miin
......
miiin...
......
HUH?
miin
miin
mimiiin
WHERE'S... WHERE'S THE AC REMOTE ...?
THIS IS NOT FUNNY!
miiin
miiin
...
I CAN'T TURN ON THE AC WITHOUT THE REMOTE!!

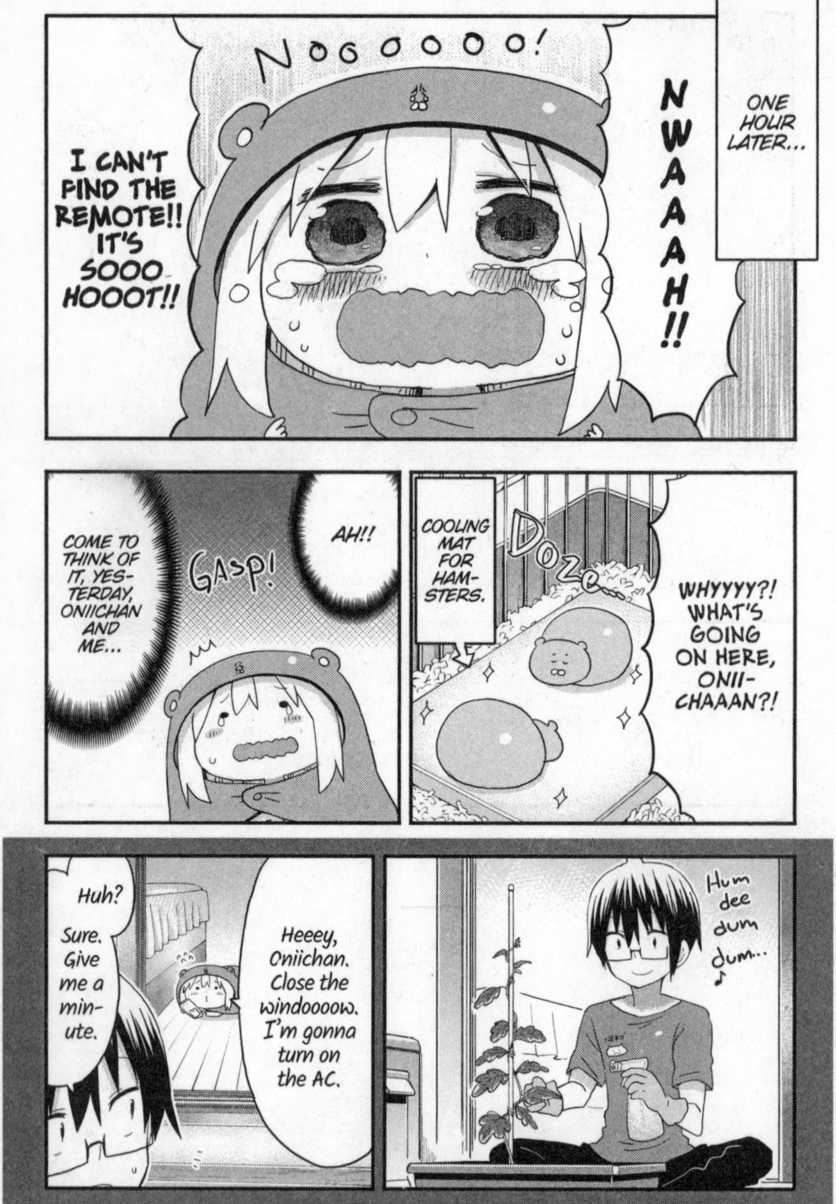
ONE HOUR LATER...
NWAAAAH!!
NOOOOOO!
I CAN'T FIND THE REMOTE!! IT'S SOOO HOOOT!!
WHYYYY?! WHAT'S GOING ON HERE, ONII-CHAAAN?!
COOLING MAT FOR HAMSTERS.
Doze...
AH!!
GASP!
COME TO THINK OF IT, YESTERDAY, ONIICHAN AND ME...
Hum dee dum dum...
Heeey, Oniichan. Close the windooow. I'm gonna turn on the AC.
Huh?
Sure. Give me a minute.

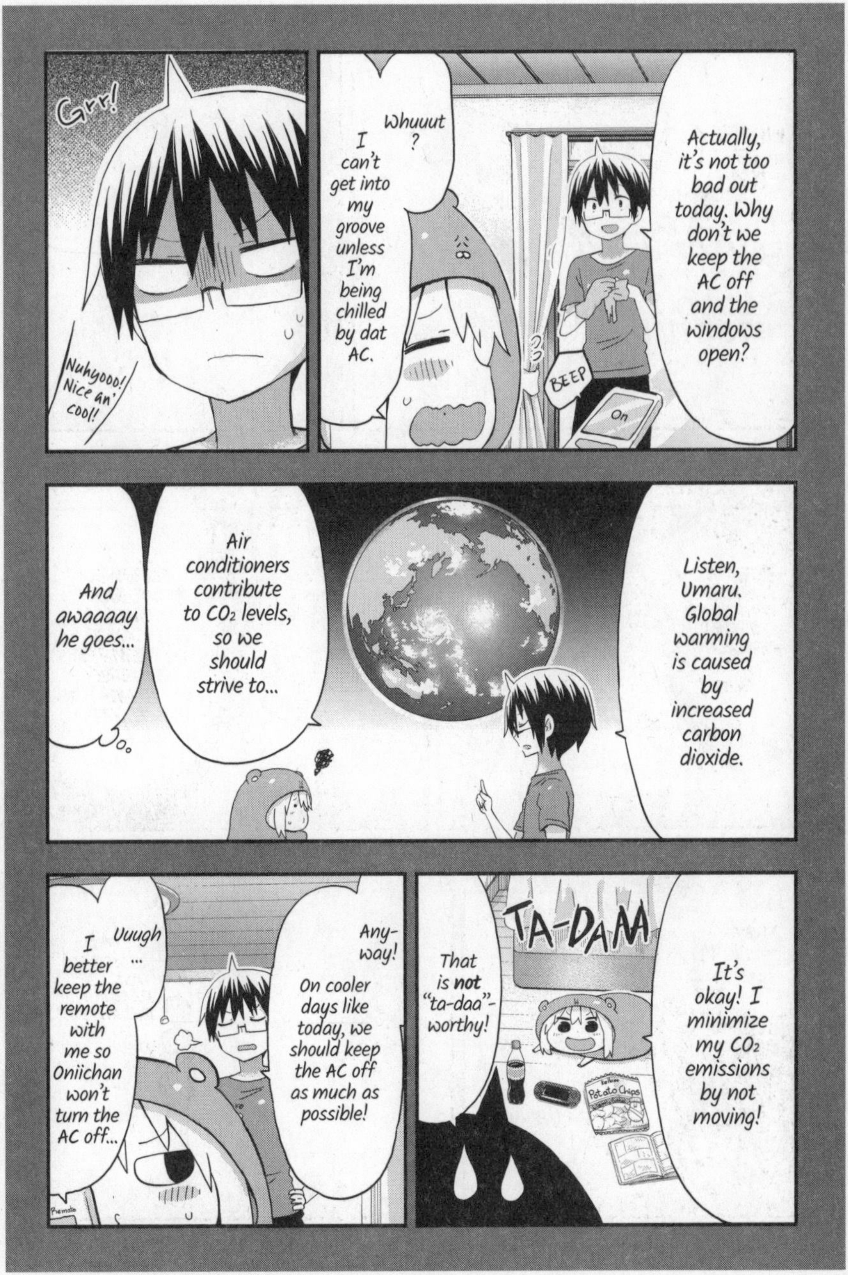
Actually, it's not too bad out today. Why don't we keep the AC off and the windows open?
Whuuut?
I can't get into my groove unless I'm being chilled by dat AC.
BEEP
On
Grr!
Nuhyooo! Nice an' cool!
Listen, Umaru. Global warming is caused by increased carbon dioxide.
Air conditioners contribute to CO_2 levels, so we should strive to...
And awaaaay he goes...
TA-DAA
It's okay! I minimize my CO_2 emissions by not moving!
That is **not** "ta-daa"-worthy!
Potato Chips
Any-way!
On cooler days like today, we should keep the AC off as much as possible!
Uuugh...
I better keep the remote with me so Oniichan won't turn the AC off...

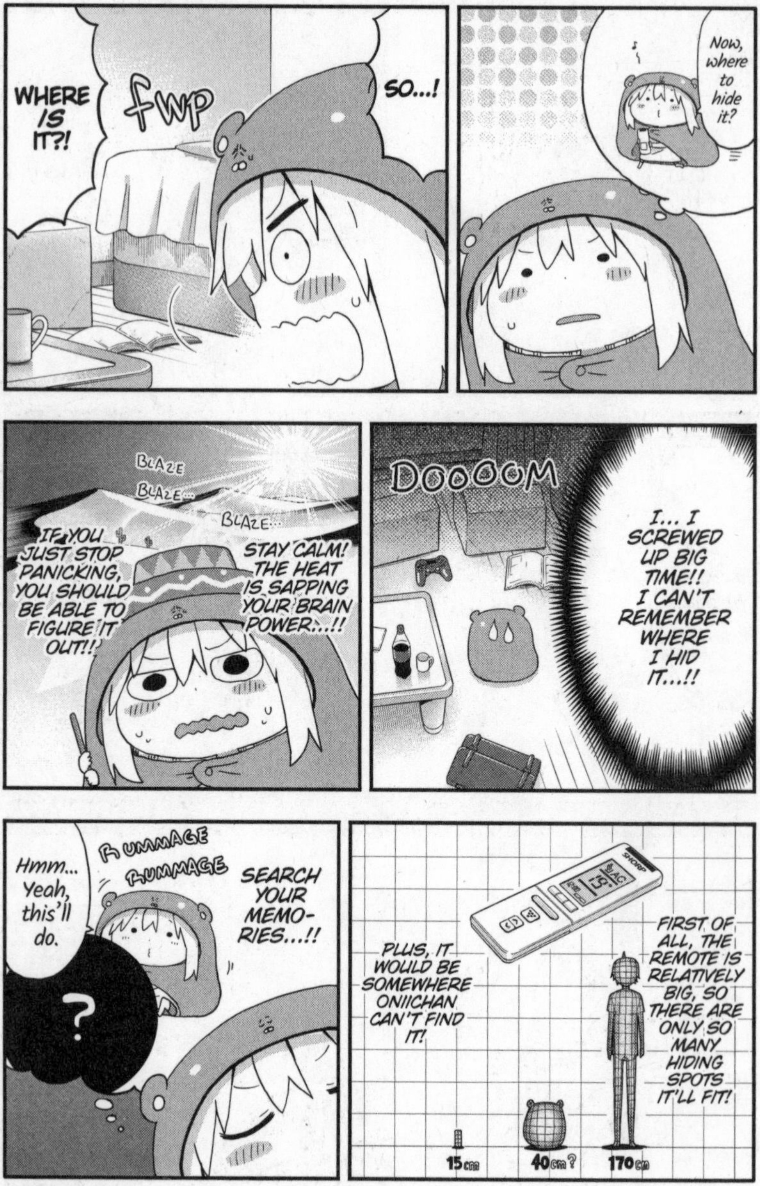
Now, where to hide it?
SO...!
fwp
WHERE IS IT?!
DOOOOM
I... I SCREWED UP BIG TIME!! I CAN'T REMEMBER WHERE I HID IT...!!
BLAZE
BLAZE...
BLAZE...
STAY CALM! THE HEAT IS SAPPING YOUR BRAIN POWER...!!
IF YOU JUST STOP PANICKING, YOU SHOULD BE ABLE TO FIGURE IT OUT!!
SHORP
AC
FIRST OF ALL, THE REMOTE IS RELATIVELY BIG, SO THERE ARE ONLY SO MANY HIDING SPOTS IT'LL FIT!
PLUS, IT WOULD BE SOMEWHERE ONIICHAN CAN'T FIND IT!
15cm
40cm?
170cm
SEARCH YOUR MEMO-RIES...!!
RUMMAGE
RUMMAGE
Hmm... Yeah, this'll do.
?

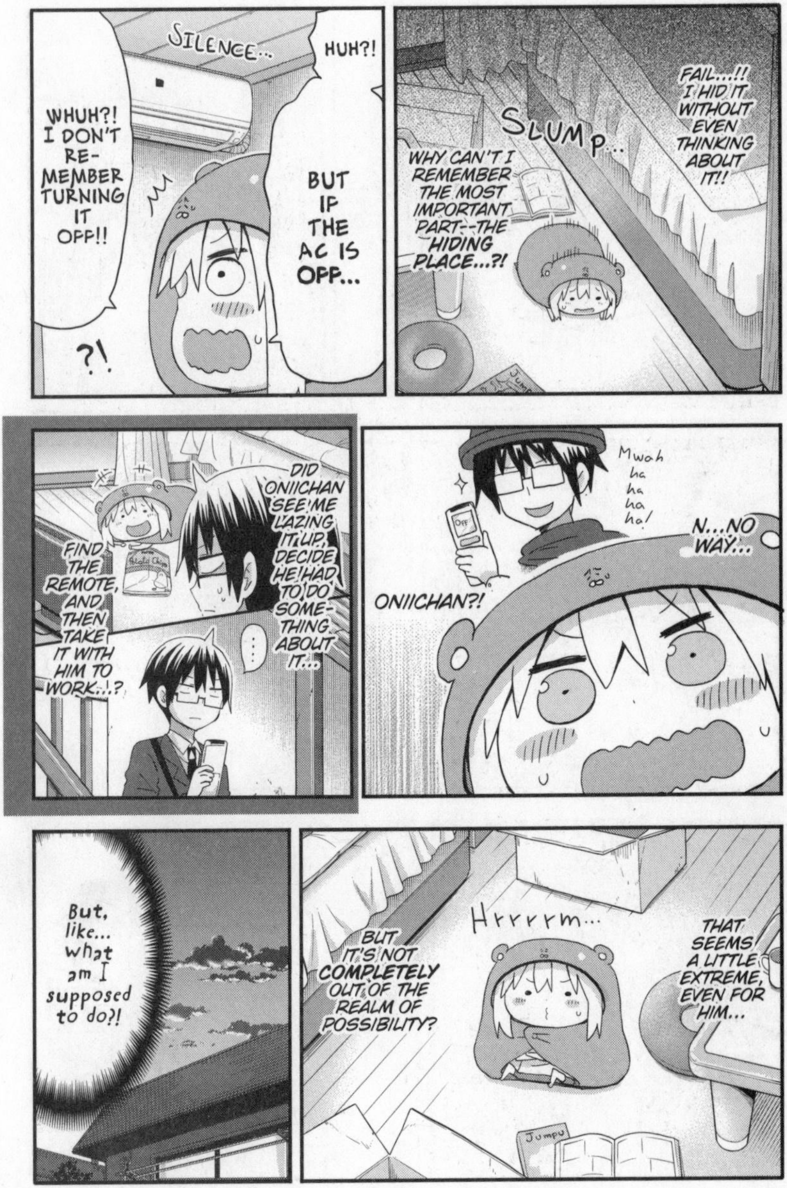
FAIL...!! I HID IT WITHOUT EVEN THINKING ABOUT IT!!
SLUMP...
WHY CAN'T I REMEMBER THE MOST IMPORTANT PART--THE HIDING PLACE...?!
SILENCE...
HUH?!
BUT IF THE AC IS OFF...
WHUH?! I DON'T RE-MEMBER TURNING IT OFF!!
?!
Mwah ha ha ha ha!
OFF
N...NO WAY...
ONIICHAN?!
DID ONIICHAN SEE ME LAZING IT UP, DECIDE HE HAD TO DO SOME-THING ABOUT IT...
FIND THE REMOTE, AND THEN TAKE IT WITH HIM TO WORK...?
.....
Hrrrrm...
THAT SEEMS A LITTLE EXTREME, EVEN FOR HIM...
BUT IT'S NOT COMPLETELY OUT OF THE REALM OF POSSIBILITY?
Jumpu
But, like... what am I supposed to do?!

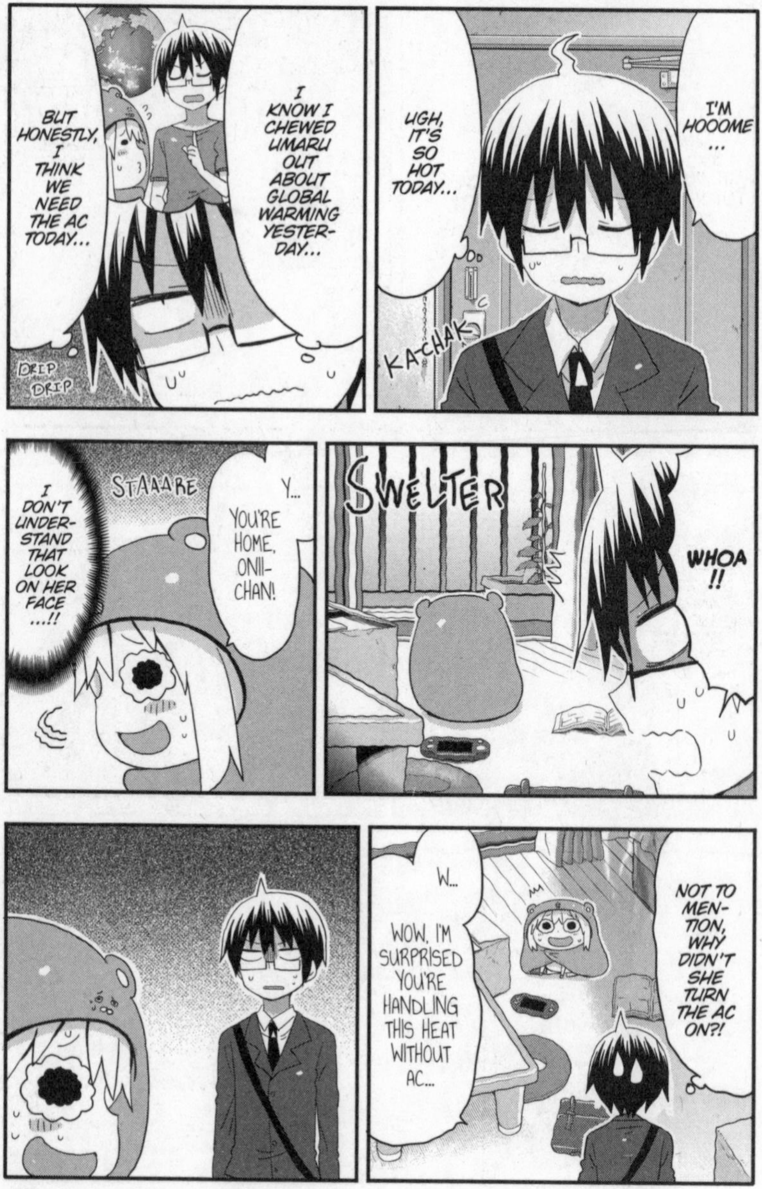
I'M HOOOME ...
UGH, IT'S SO HOT TODAY...
KA-CHAK
I KNOW I CHEWED UMARU OUT ABOUT GLOBAL WARMING YESTERDAY...
BUT HONESTLY, I THINK WE NEED THE AC TODAY...
DRIP DRIP
SWELTER
WHOA !!
Y...
YOU'RE HOME, ONII-CHAN!
STAAARE
I DON'T UNDERSTAND THAT LOOK ON HER FACE ...!!
NOT TO MENTION, WHY DIDN'T SHE TURN THE AC ON?!
W...
WOW, I'M SURPRISED YOU'RE HANDLING THIS HEAT WITHOUT AC...

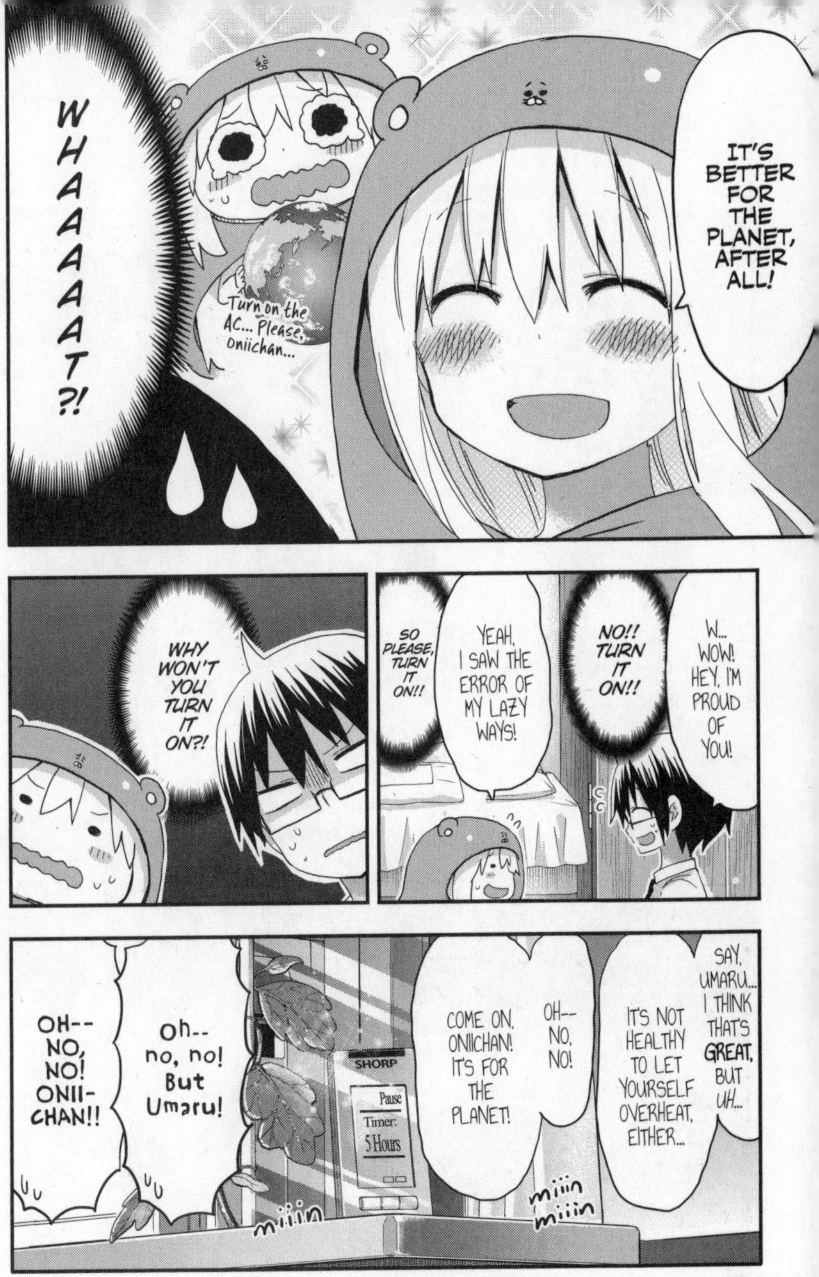
IT'S BETTER FOR THE PLANET, AFTER ALL!
Turn on the AC... Please, oniichan...
WHAAAAAAAT?!
W... WOW! HEY, I'M PROUD OF YOU!
NO!! TURN IT ON!!
YEAH, I SAW THE ERROR OF MY LAZY WAYS!
SO PLEASE, TURN IT ON!!
WHY WON'T YOU TURN IT ON?!
SAY, UMARU... I THINK THAT'S **GREAT,** BUT UH...
IT'S NOT HEALTHY TO LET YOURSELF OVERHEAT, EITHER...
OH-- NO, NO!
COME ON, ONIICHAN! IT'S FOR THE PLANET!
miiin miiin
SHORP
Pause
Timer:
5 Hours
Oh-- no, no! But Umaru!
OH-- NO, NO! ONII-CHAN!!
miiin

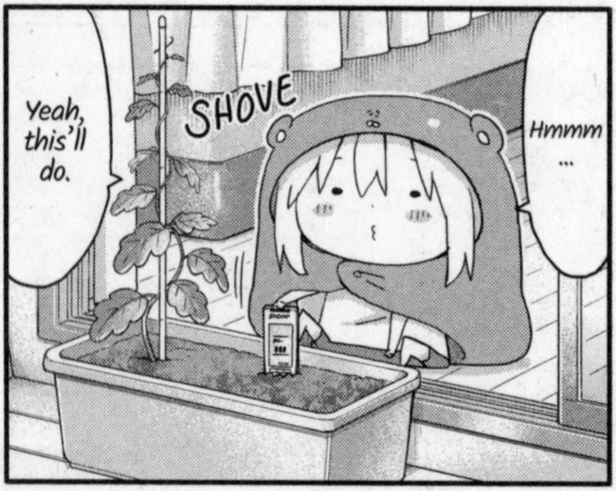
Hmmm ...
SHOVE
Yeah, this'll do.

Guest Chapter in *Jump Square*

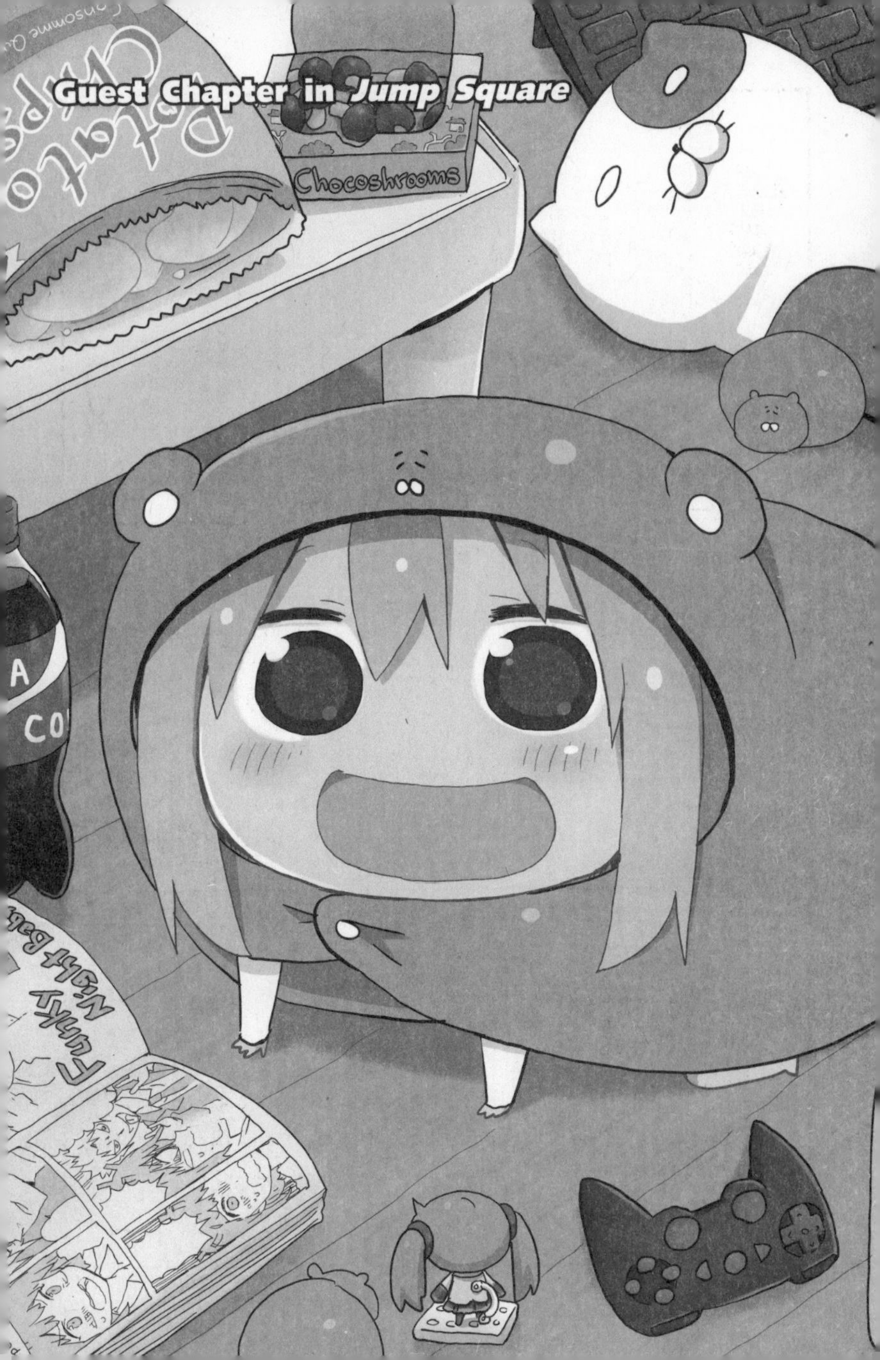
Chocoshrooms

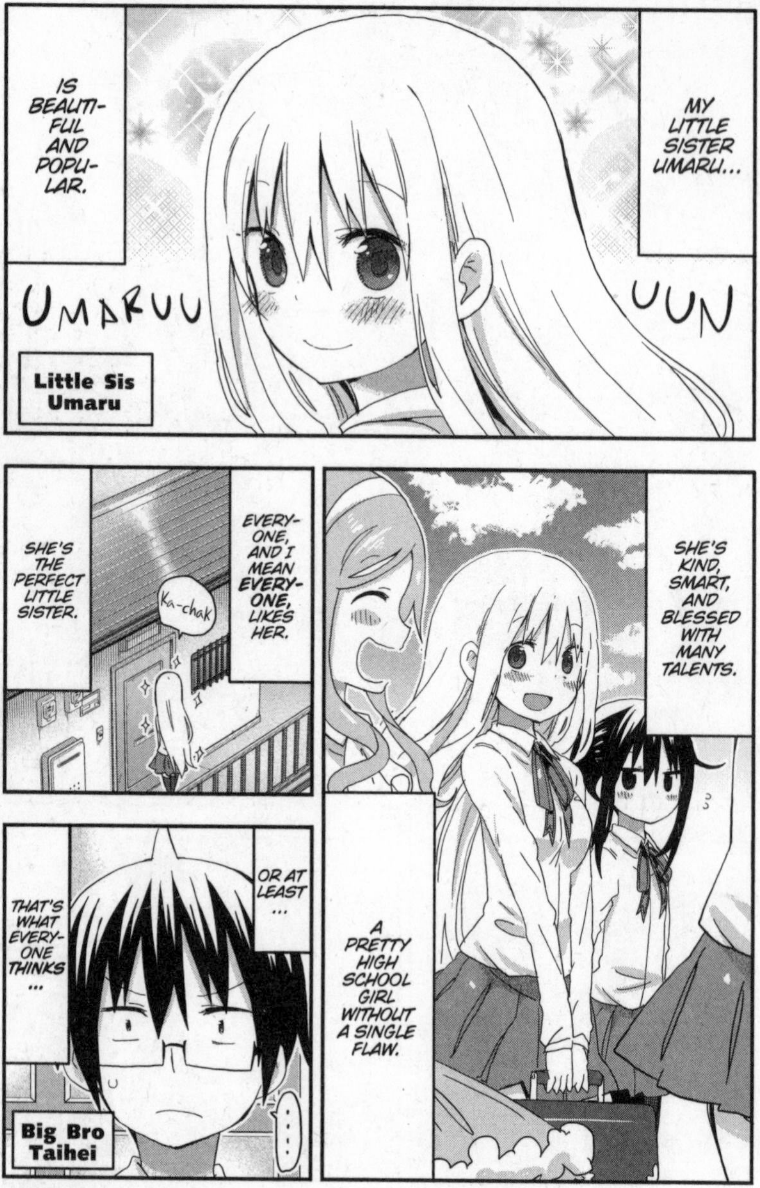

MY LITTLE SISTER UMARU...
IS BEAUTIFUL AND POPULAR.
UMARUU
UUN
Little Sis Umaru
SHE'S KIND, SMART, AND BLESSED WITH MANY TALENTS.
A PRETTY HIGH SCHOOL GIRL WITHOUT A SINGLE FLAW.
EVERYONE, AND I MEAN EVERYONE, LIKES HER.
Ka-chak
SHE'S THE PERFECT LITTLE SISTER.
OR AT LEAST ...
THAT'S WHAT EVERYONE THINKS ...
....
Big Bro Taihei

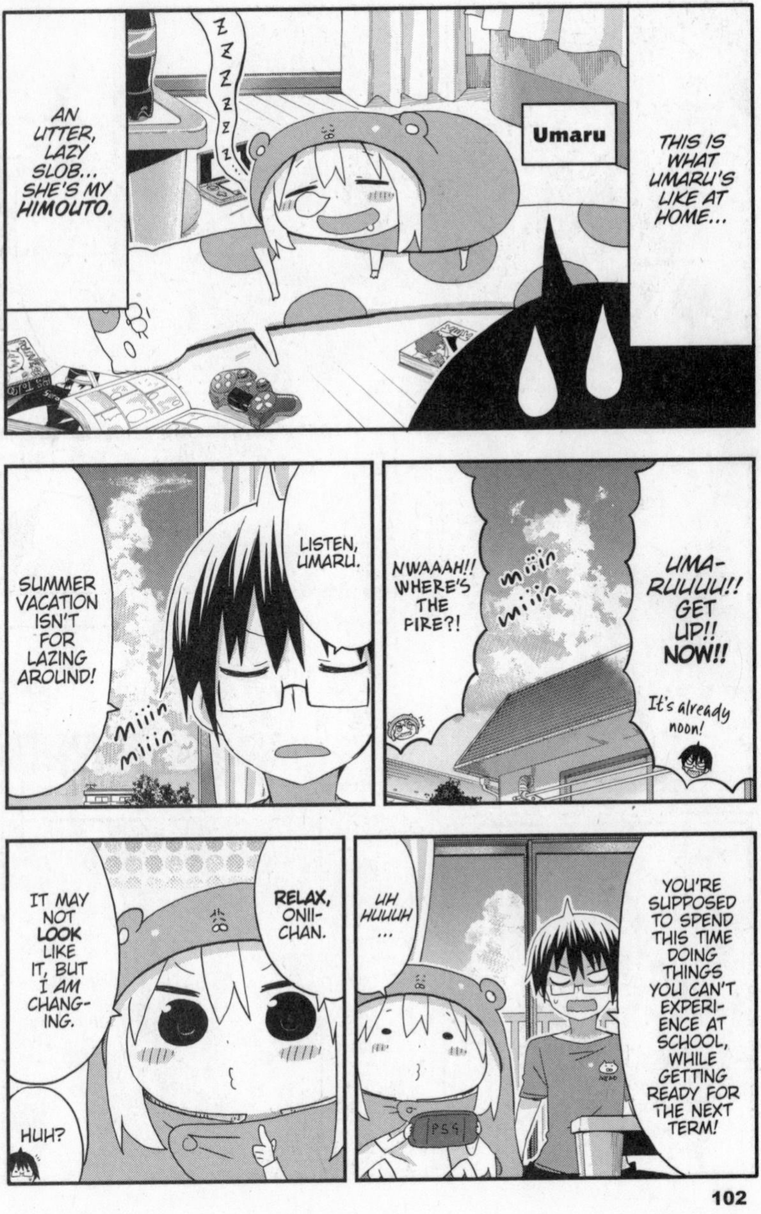
THIS IS WHAT UMARU'S LIKE AT HOME...
Umaru
ZZZZZZ...
AN UTTER, LAZY SLOB... SHE'S MY HIMOUTO.
UMA-RUUUU!! GET UP!! NOW!!
It's already noon!
miiin miiin
NWAAAH!! WHERE'S THE FIRE?!
LISTEN, UMARU.
SUMMER VACATION ISN'T FOR LAZING AROUND!
miiin miiin
YOU'RE SUPPOSED TO SPEND THIS TIME DOING THINGS YOU CAN'T EXPERIENCE AT SCHOOL, WHILE GETTING READY FOR THE NEXT TERM!
UH HUUUH...
RELAX, ONII-CHAN.
IT MAY NOT LOOK LIKE IT, BUT I AM CHANGING.
HUH?

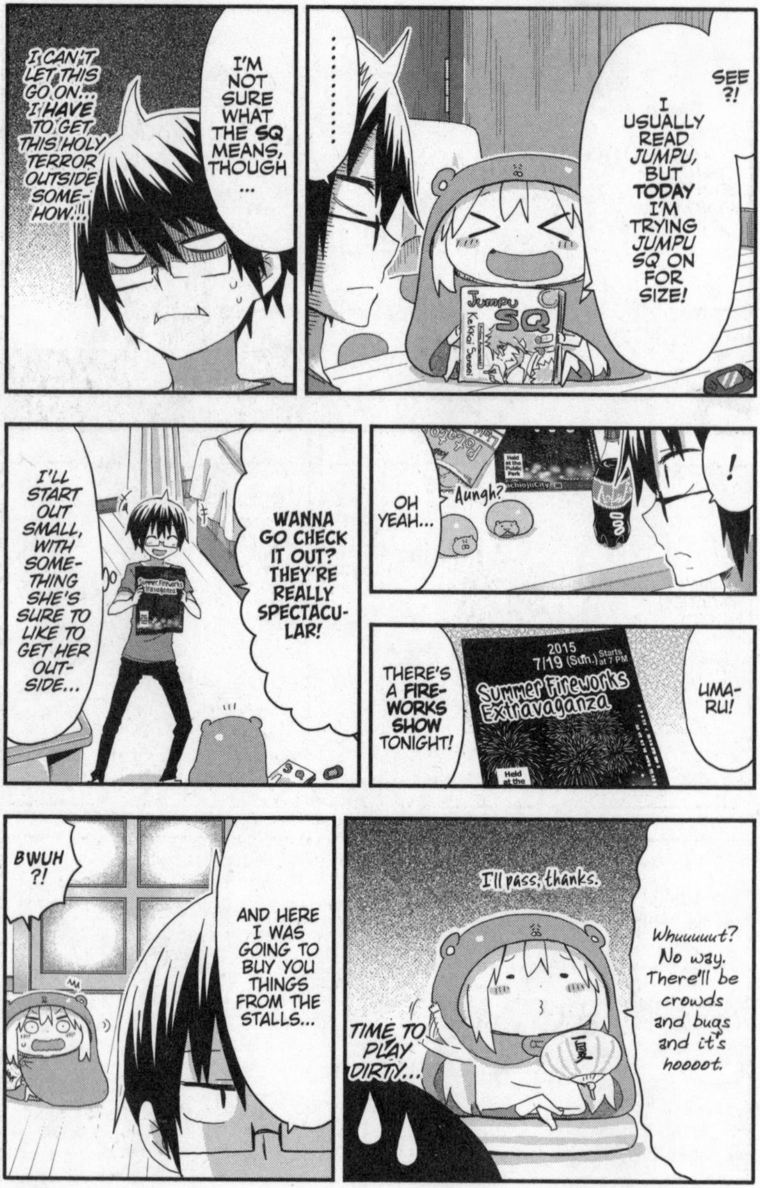
SEE?! I USUALLY READ JUMPU, BUT TODAY I'M TRYING JUMPU SQ ON FOR SIZE!
Jumpu SQ
Kekkai Sensei
......
I'M NOT SURE WHAT THE SQ MEANS, THOUGH...
I CAN'T LET THIS GO ON... I HAVE TO GET THIS HOLY TERROR OUTSIDE SOMEHOW...!!
!
OH YEAH...
Aungh?
UMA-RU!
THERE'S A FIREWORKS SHOW TONIGHT!
2015 7/19 (Sun.) Starts at 7 PM
Summer Fireworks Extravaganza
WANNA GO CHECK IT OUT? THEY'RE REALLY SPECTACULAR!
I'LL START OUT SMALL, WITH SOMETHING SHE'S SURE TO LIKE TO GET HER OUTSIDE...
Whuuuuut? No way. There'll be crowds and bugs and it's hoooot.
I'll pass, thanks.
TIME TO PLAY DIRTY...
AND HERE I WAS GOING TO BUY YOU THINGS FROM THE STALLS...
BWUH?!

Fan: Summer.

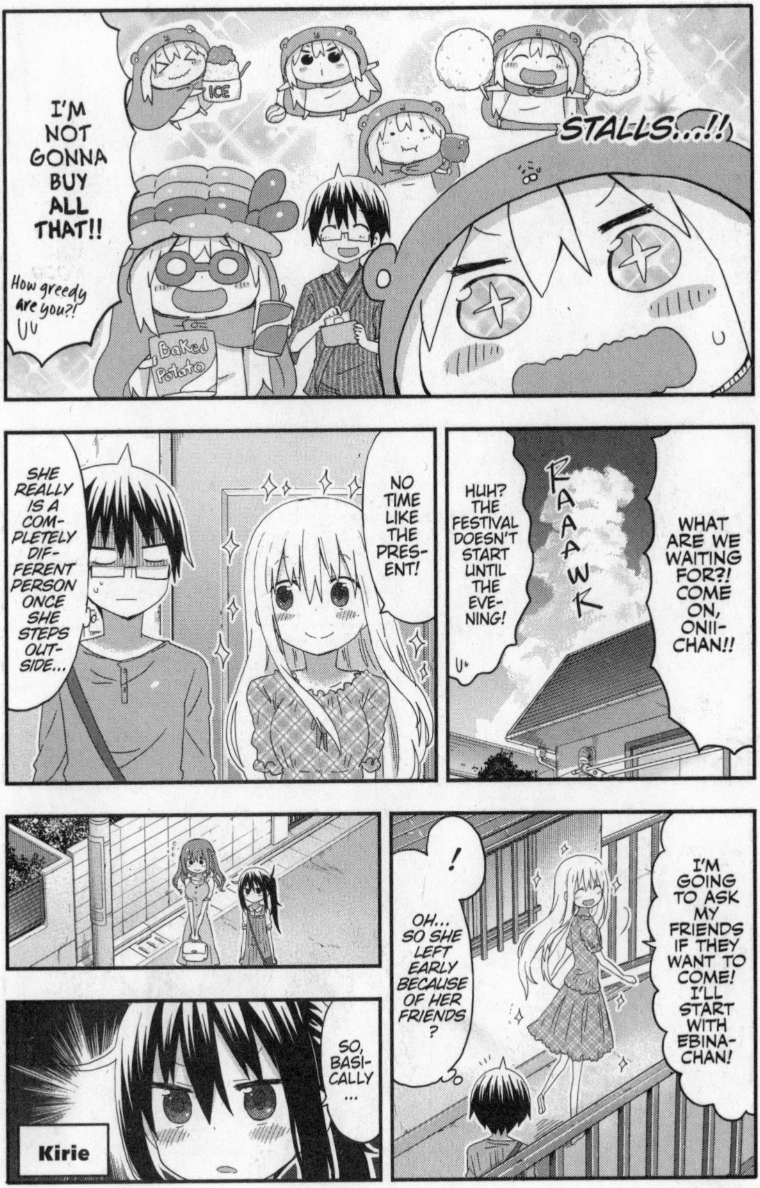

STALLS...!!
ICE
I'M NOT GONNA BUY ALL THAT!!
How greedy are you?!
Baked Potato
WHAT ARE WE WAITING FOR?! COME ON, ONII-CHAN!!
RAAAWK
HUH? THE FESTIVAL DOESN'T START UNTIL THE EVENING!
NO TIME LIKE THE PRESENT!
SHE REALLY IS A COMPLETELY DIFFERENT PERSON ONCE SHE STEPS OUTSIDE...
I'M GOING TO ASK MY FRIENDS IF THEY WANT TO COME! I'LL START WITH EBINA-CHAN!
!
OH... SO SHE LEFT EARLY BECAUSE OF HER FRIENDS?
SO, BASICALLY...
Kirie

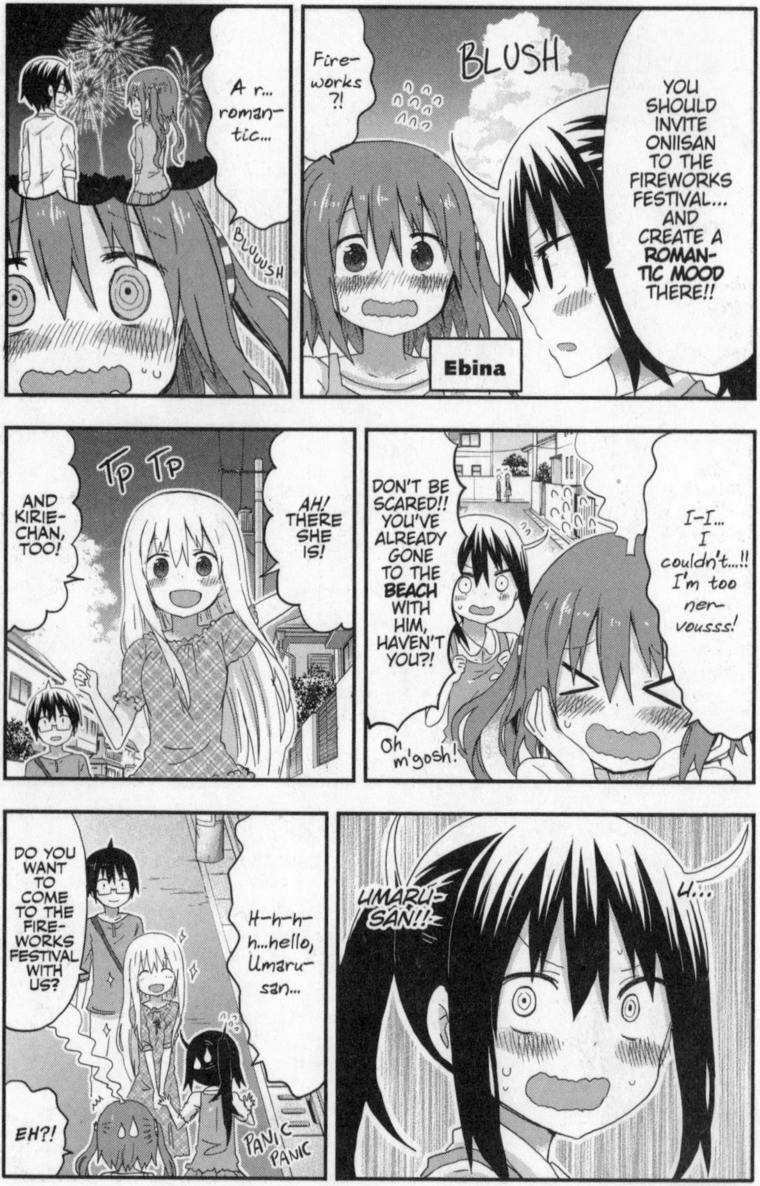
YOU SHOULD INVITE ONIISAN TO THE FIREWORKS FESTIVAL... AND CREATE A ROMANTIC MOOD THERE!!
BLUSH
Fireworks?!
Ebina
A r... romantic...
BLUUUSH
I-I... I couldn't...!! I'm too nervousss!
DON'T BE SCARED!! YOU'VE ALREADY GONE TO THE BEACH WITH HIM, HAVEN'T YOU?!
Oh m'gosh!
AH! THERE SHE IS!
Tp Tp
AND KIRIE-CHAN, TOO!
U...
UMARU-SAN!!
H-h-h-h...hello, Umaru-san...
DO YOU WANT TO COME TO THE FIREWORKS FESTIVAL WITH US?
PANIC PANIC
EH?!

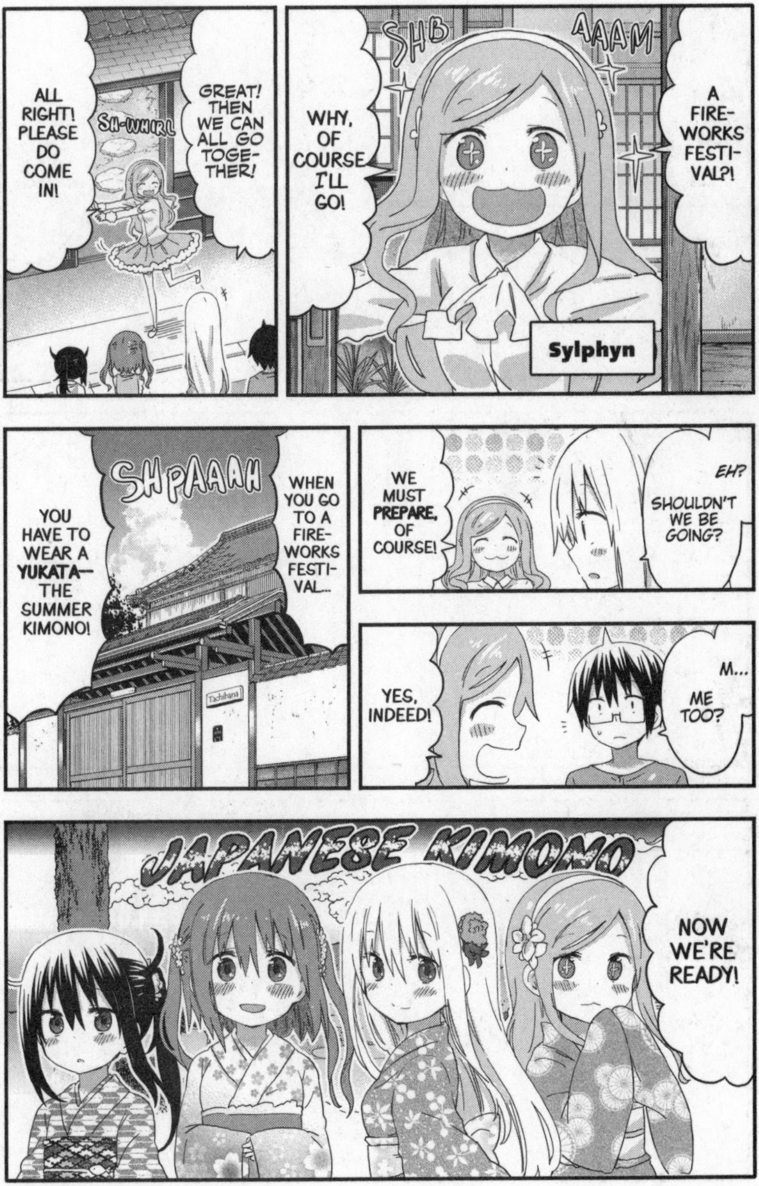
AAAM
SHB
A FIREWORKS FESTIVAL?!
WHY, OF COURSE I'LL GO!
Sylphyn
GREAT! THEN WE CAN ALL GO TOGETHER!
SH-WHIRL
ALL RIGHT! PLEASE DO COME IN!
EH?
SHOULDN'T WE BE GOING?
WE MUST PREPARE, OF COURSE!
M...
ME TOO?
YES, INDEED!
WHEN YOU GO TO A FIREWORKS FESTIVAL...
SHPAAAH
YOU HAVE TO WEAR A YUKATA—THE SUMMER KIMONO!
Tachibana
NOW WE'RE READY!
JAPANESE KIMONO

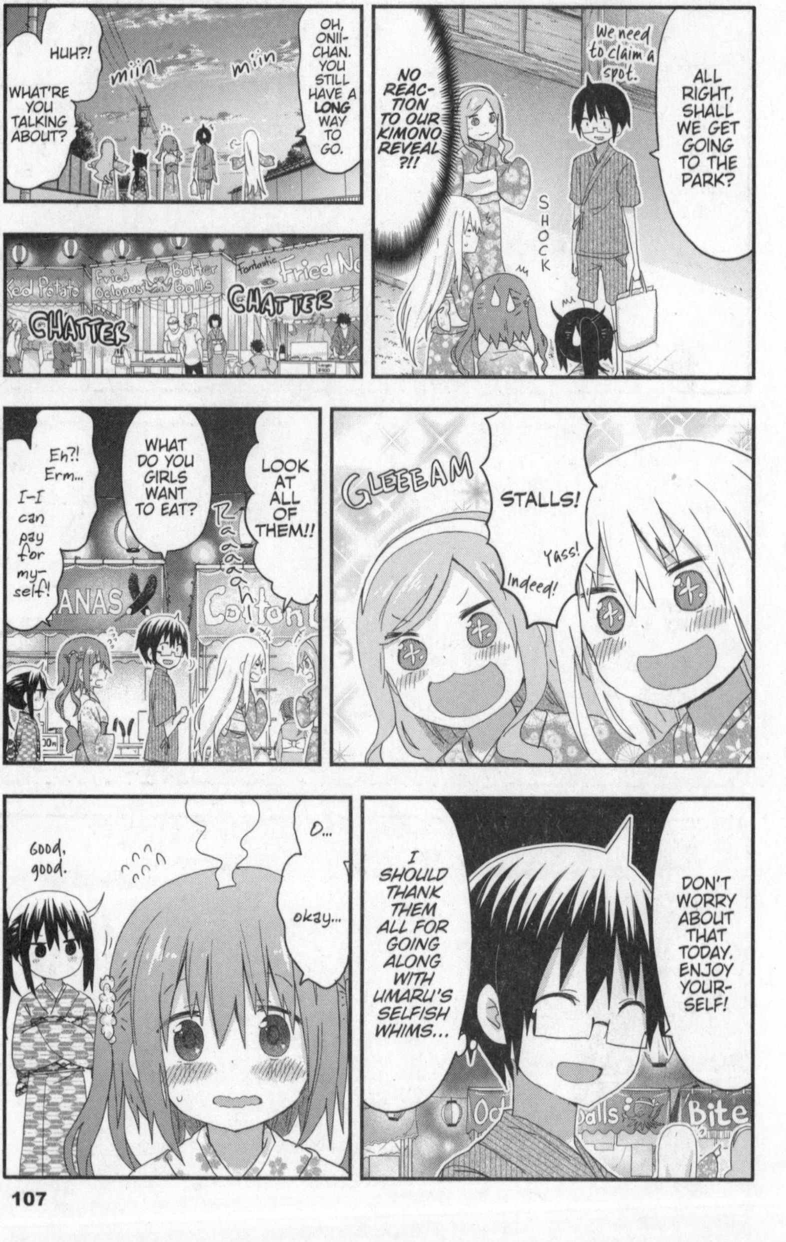
ALL RIGHT, SHALL WE GET GOING TO THE PARK?
We need to claim a spot.
NO REACTION TO OUR KIMONO REVEAL?!!
SHOCK
OH, ONII-CHAN. YOU STILL HAVE A LONG WAY TO GO.
miin
miin
HUH?! WHAT'RE YOU TALKING ABOUT?
Fantastic Fried No
Fried Octopus Batter Balls
ked Potato
CHATTER
CHATTER
GLEEEAM
STALLS!
Yass!
Indeed!
LOOK AT ALL OF THEM!!
Raaaaah
WHAT DO YOU GIRLS WANT TO EAT?
Eh?! Erm... I-I can pay for myself!
ANAS
Cotton
DON'T WORRY ABOUT THAT TODAY. ENJOY YOURSELF!
I SHOULD THANK THEM ALL FOR GOING ALONG WITH UMARU'S SELFISH WHIMS...
Oc
Balls
Bite
O...
okay...
Good, good.

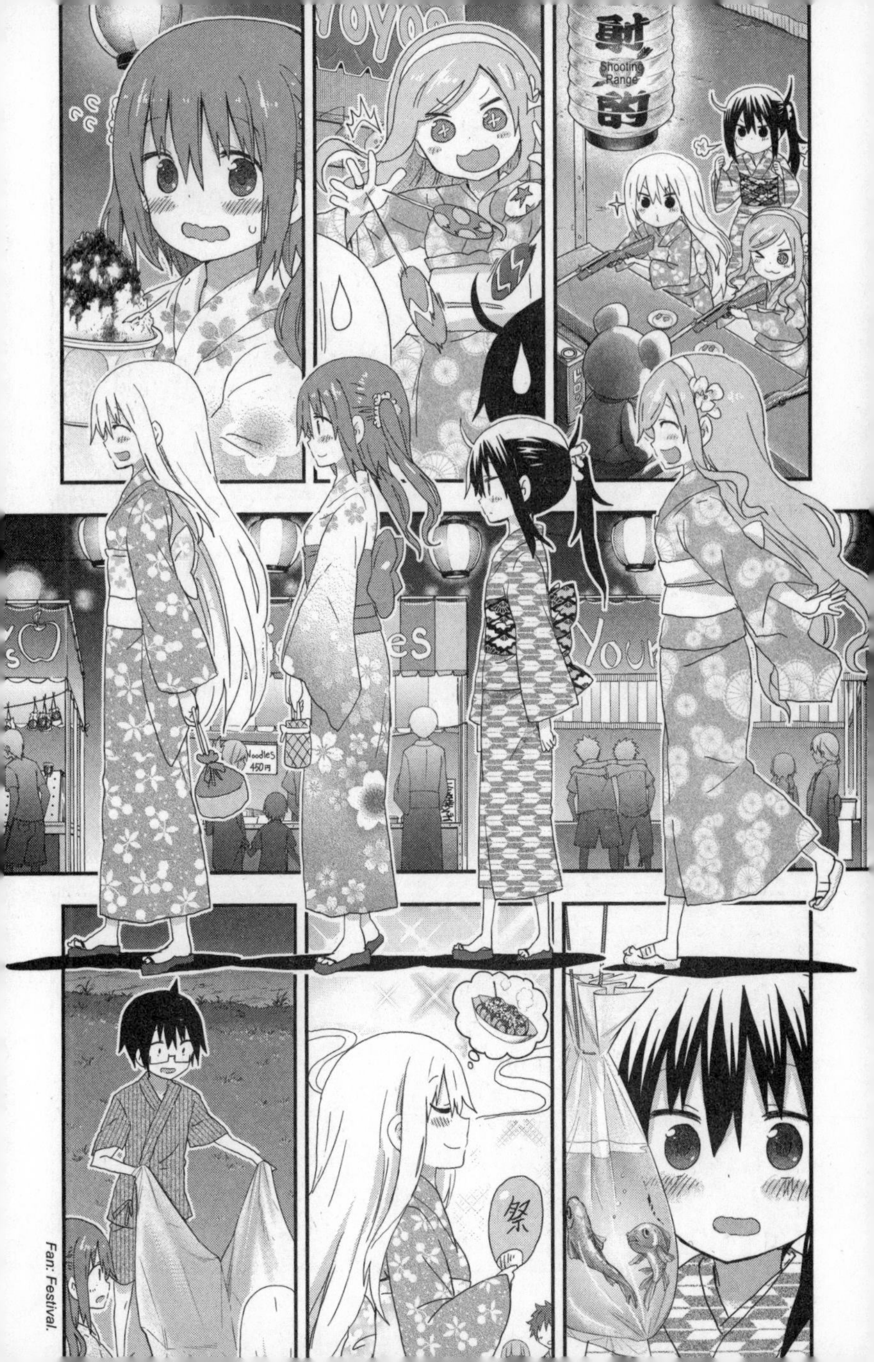
射的
Shooting Range
Yoyos
Your
es
Noodles 450円
祭

Fan: Festival.

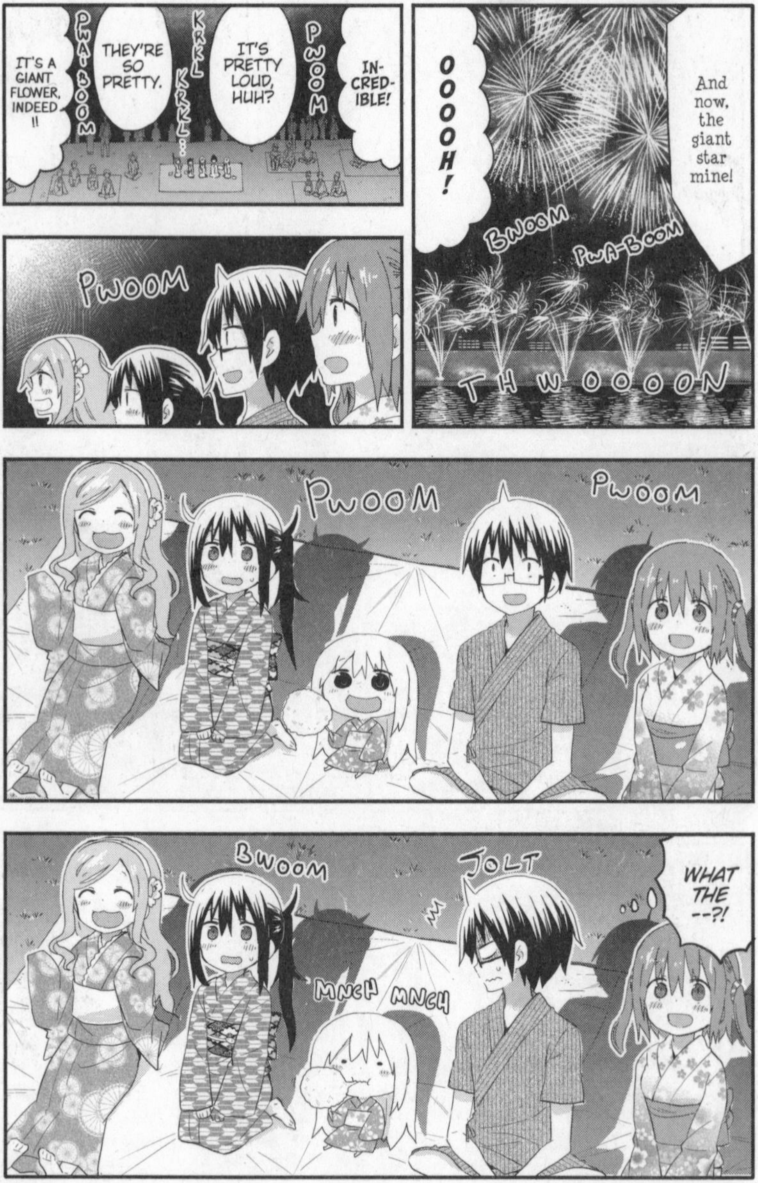
And now, the giant star mine!
OOOOOH!
BWOOM
PWA-BOOM
THWOOOON
INCREDIBLE!
PWOOM
IT'S PRETTY LOUD, HUH?
KRKL KRKL...
THEY'RE SO PRETTY.
PWA-BOOM
IT'S A GIANT FLOWER, INDEED!!
PWOOM
PWOOM
PWOOM
WHAT THE--?!
JOLT
BWOOM
MNCH MNCH

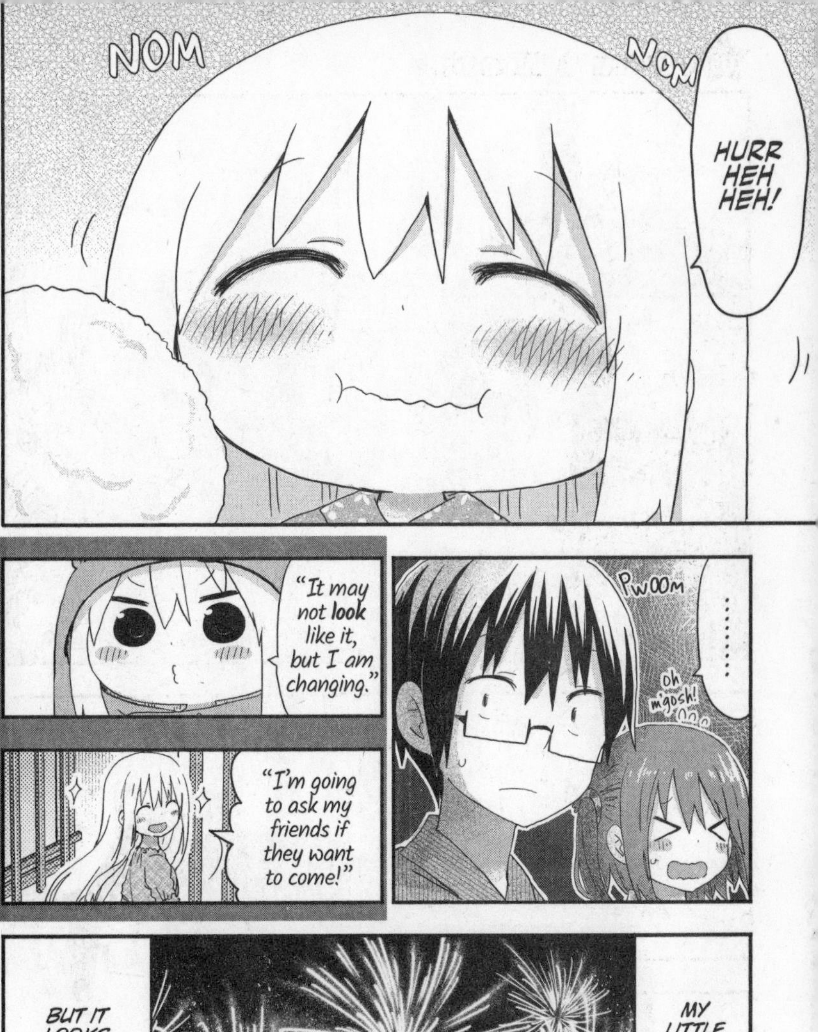
NOM
HURR HEH HEH!
NOM
PWOOM
......
oh m'gosh!
"It may not **look** like it, but I am changing."
"I'm going to ask my friends if they want to come!"
MY LITTLE SISTER IS A HIMOU-TO...
BUT IT LOOKS LIKE SHE REALLY IS CHANGING-- LITTLE BY LITTLE, AT LEAST.

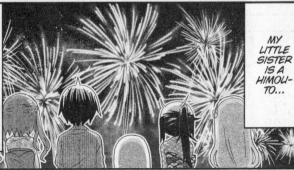

No. 119 Umaru & Weeding

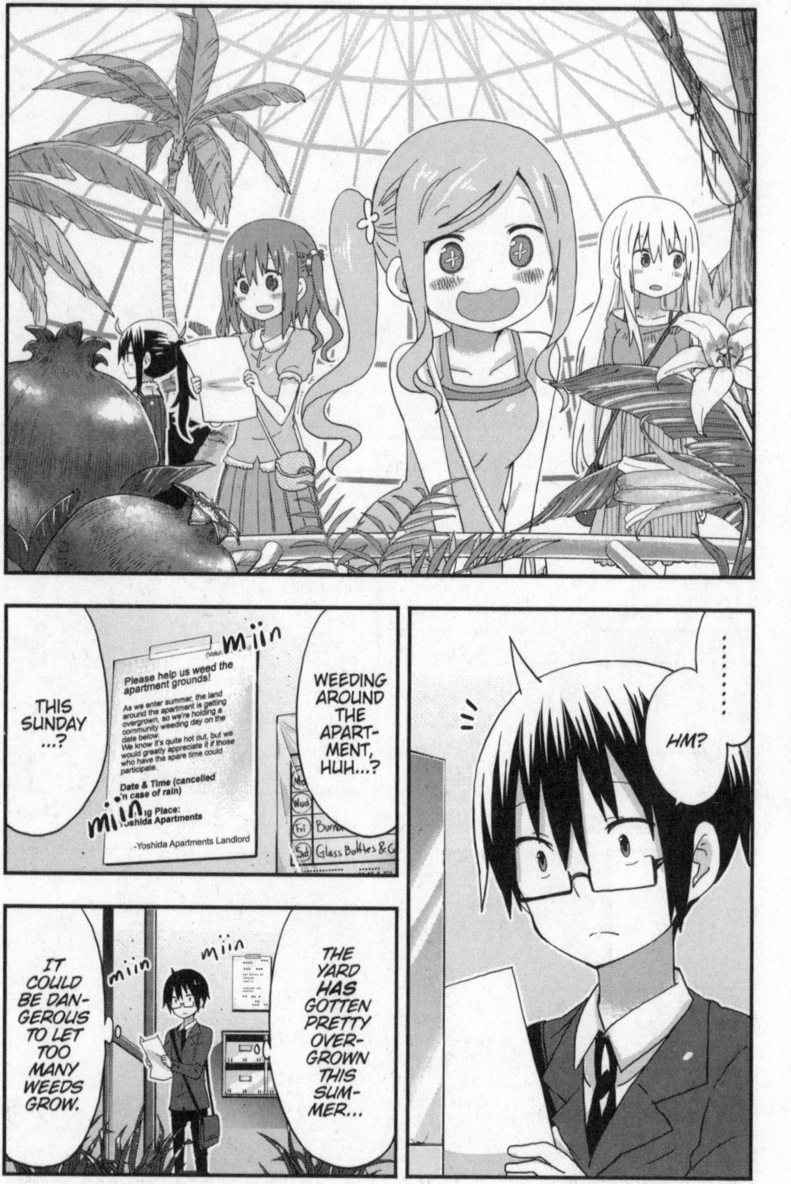
......
HM?
WEEDING AROUND THE APARTMENT, HUH...?
miin
Please help us weed the apartment grounds!
As we enter summer, the land around the apartment is getting overgrown, so we're holding a community weeding day on the date below.
We know it's quite hot out, but we would greatly appreciate it if those who have the spare time could participate.
Date & Time (cancelled
n case of rain)
Place:
-Yoshida Apartments Landlord
Wed
Fri
Sat
Glass Bottles &
miin
THIS SUNDAY...?
THE YARD HAS GOTTEN PRETTY OVERGROWN THIS SUMMER...
miin
miin
IT COULD BE DANGEROUS TO LET TOO MANY WEEDS GROW.

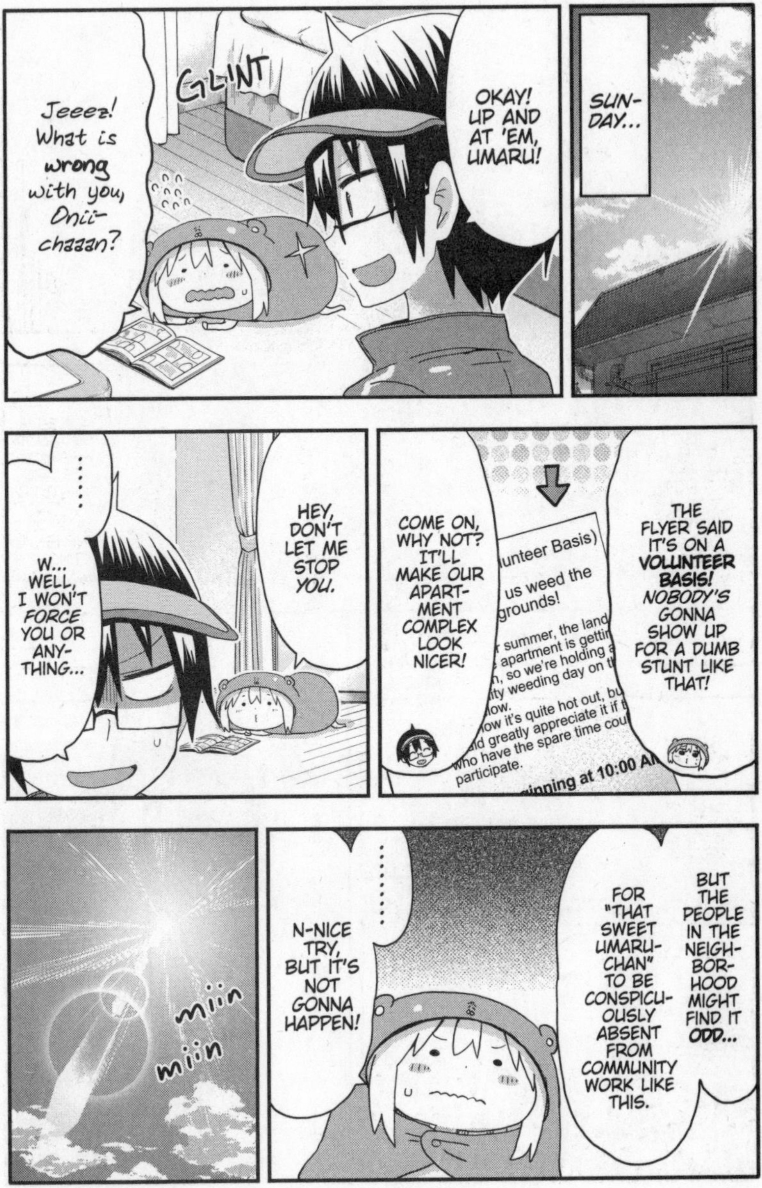
SUN-DAY...
OKAY! UP AND AT 'EM, UMARU!
GLINT
Jeeez! What is wrong with you, Onii-chaaan?
THE FLYER SAID IT'S ON A VOLUNTEER BASIS! NOBODY'S GONNA SHOW UP FOR A DUMB STUNT LIKE THAT!
lunteer Basis)
us weed the
grounds!
r summer, the land
e apartment is gettin
h, so we're holding a
ity weeding day on th
ow.
now it's quite hot out, bu
uld greatly appreciate it if t
who have the spare time cou
participate.
ginning at 10:00 A
COME ON, WHY NOT? IT'LL MAKE OUR APARTMENT COMPLEX LOOK NICER!
HEY, DON'T LET ME STOP YOU.
......
W... WELL, I WON'T FORCE YOU OR ANYTHING...
BUT THE PEOPLE IN THE NEIGHBORHOOD MIGHT FIND IT ODD...
FOR "THAT SWEET UMARU-CHAN" TO BE CONSPICUOUSLY ABSENT FROM COMMUNITY WORK LIKE THIS.
......
N-NICE TRY, BUT IT'S NOT GONNA HAPPEN!
miin
miin

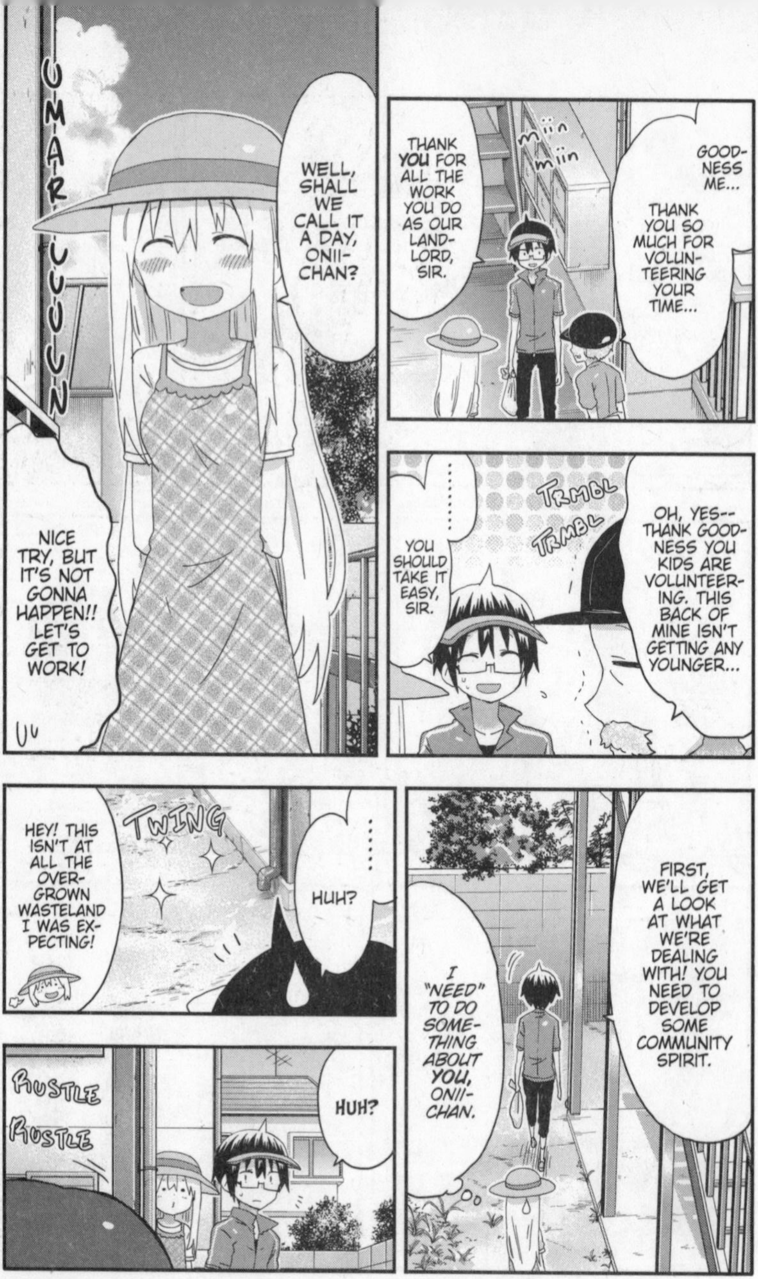
GOODNESS ME... THANK YOU SO MUCH FOR VOLUNTEERING YOUR TIME...
miin miin
THANK YOU FOR ALL THE WORK YOU DO AS OUR LANDLORD, SIR.
OH, YES-- THANK GOODNESS YOU KIDS ARE VOLUNTEERING. THIS BACK OF MINE ISN'T GETTING ANY YOUNGER...
TRMBL TRMBL
......
YOU SHOULD TAKE IT EASY, SIR.
WELL, SHALL WE CALL IT A DAY, ONII-CHAN?
UMARUUUUUN
NICE TRY, BUT IT'S NOT GONNA HAPPEN!! LET'S GET TO WORK!
UU
FIRST, WE'LL GET A LOOK AT WHAT WE'RE DEALING WITH! YOU NEED TO DEVELOP SOME COMMUNITY SPIRIT.
I "NEED" TO DO SOMETHING ABOUT YOU, ONII-CHAN.
......
HUH?
TWING
HEY! THIS ISN'T AT ALL THE OVERGROWN WASTELAND I WAS EXPECTING!
HUH?
RUSTLE RUSTLE

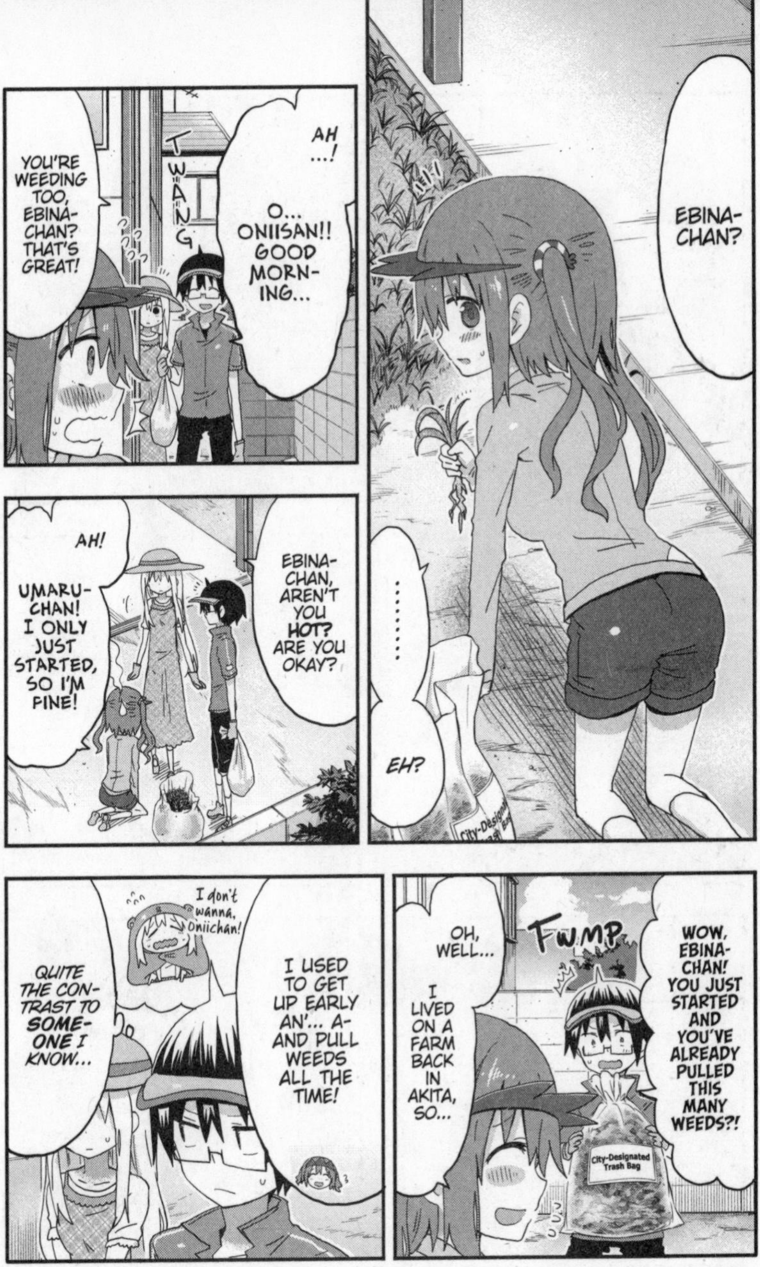
EBINA-CHAN?
......
EH?
City-Designated Trash Bag
AH ...!
O... ONIISAN!! GOOD MORNING...
TWANG
YOU'RE WEEDING TOO, EBINA-CHAN? THAT'S GREAT!
EBINA-CHAN, AREN'T YOU HOT? ARE YOU OKAY?
AH!
UMARU-CHAN! I ONLY JUST STARTED, SO I'M FINE!
WOW, EBINA-CHAN! YOU JUST STARTED AND YOU'VE ALREADY PULLED THIS MANY WEEDS?!
FWMP
OH, WELL...
I LIVED ON A FARM BACK IN AKITA, SO...
City-Designated Trash Bag
I USED TO GET UP EARLY AN'... A-AND PULL WEEDS ALL THE TIME!
I don't wanna, Oniichan!
QUITE THE CONTRAST TO SOMEONE I KNOW...

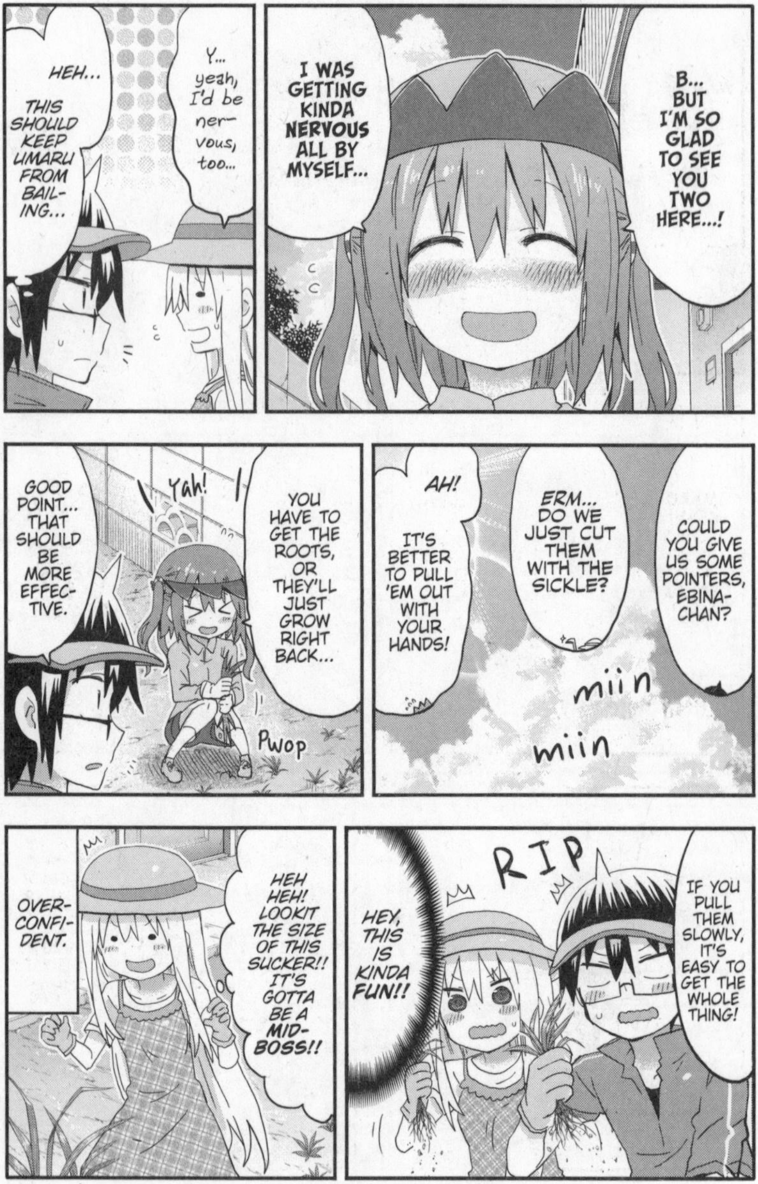
B... BUT I'M SO GLAD TO SEE YOU TWO HERE...!
I WAS GETTING KINDA NERVOUS ALL BY MYSELF...
Y... yeah, I'd be ner-vous, too...
HEH... THIS SHOULD KEEP UMARU FROM BAILING...
COULD YOU GIVE US SOME POINTERS, EBINA-CHAN?
ERM... DO WE JUST CUT THEM WITH THE SICKLE?
AH! IT'S BETTER TO PULL 'EM OUT WITH YOUR HANDS!
miin
miin
YOU HAVE TO GET THE ROOTS, OR THEY'LL JUST GROW RIGHT BACK...
Yah!
Pwop
GOOD POINT... THAT SHOULD BE MORE EFFEC-TIVE.
IF YOU PULL THEM SLOWLY, IT'S EASY TO GET THE WHOLE THING!
RIP
HEY, THIS IS KINDA FUN!!
HEH HEH! LOOKIT THE SIZE OF THIS SUCKER!! IT'S GOTTA BE A MID-BOSS!!
OVER-CONFI-DENT.

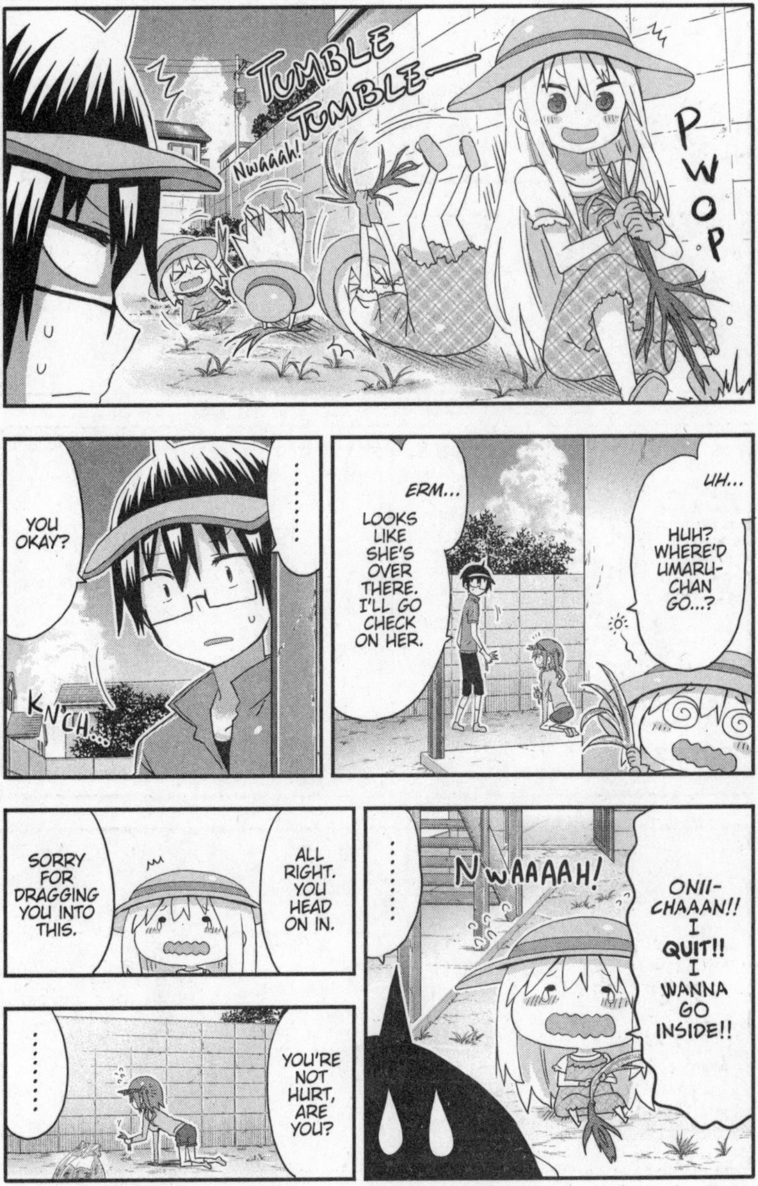
PWOP
TUMBLE TUMBLE—
Nwaaah!
UH...
HUH? WHERE'D UMARU-CHAN GO...?
ERM...
LOOKS LIKE SHE'S OVER THERE. I'LL GO CHECK ON HER.
......
YOU OKAY?
KNCH...
......
NWAAAAH!
ONII-CHAAAN!! I QUIT!! I WANNA GO INSIDE!!
ALL RIGHT. YOU HEAD ON IN.
SORRY FOR DRAGGING YOU INTO THIS.
YOU'RE NOT HURT, ARE YOU?
......

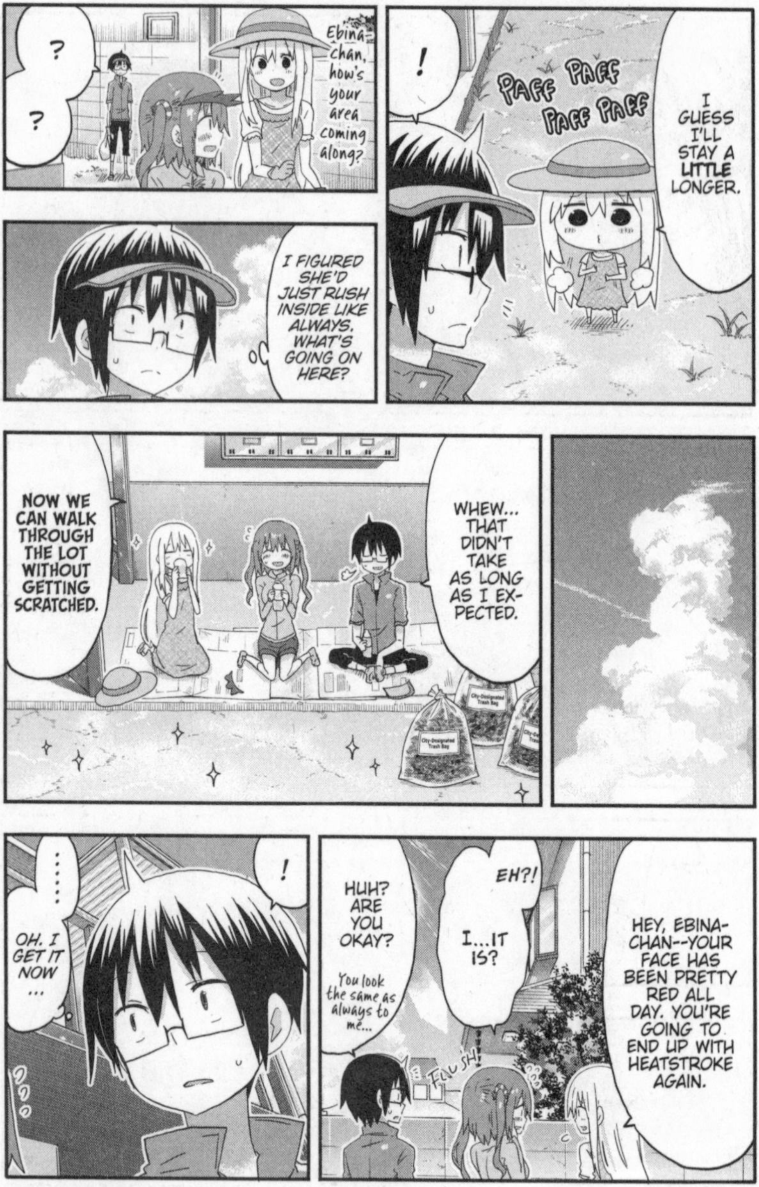
!
PAFF PAFF PAFF PAFF
I GUESS I'LL STAY A LITTLE LONGER.
Ebina-chan, how's your area coming along?
?
?
I FIGURED SHE'D JUST RUSH INSIDE LIKE ALWAYS. WHAT'S GOING ON HERE?
WHEW... THAT DIDN'T TAKE AS LONG AS I EXPECTED.
NOW WE CAN WALK THROUGH THE LOT WITHOUT GETTING SCRATCHED.
City-Designated Trash Bag
HEY, EBINA-CHAN--YOUR FACE HAS BEEN PRETTY RED ALL DAY. YOU'RE GOING TO END UP WITH HEATSTROKE AGAIN.
EH?!
I...IT IS?
HUH? ARE YOU OKAY?
You look the same as always to me...
FLUSH!
!
......
OH. I GET IT NOW ...

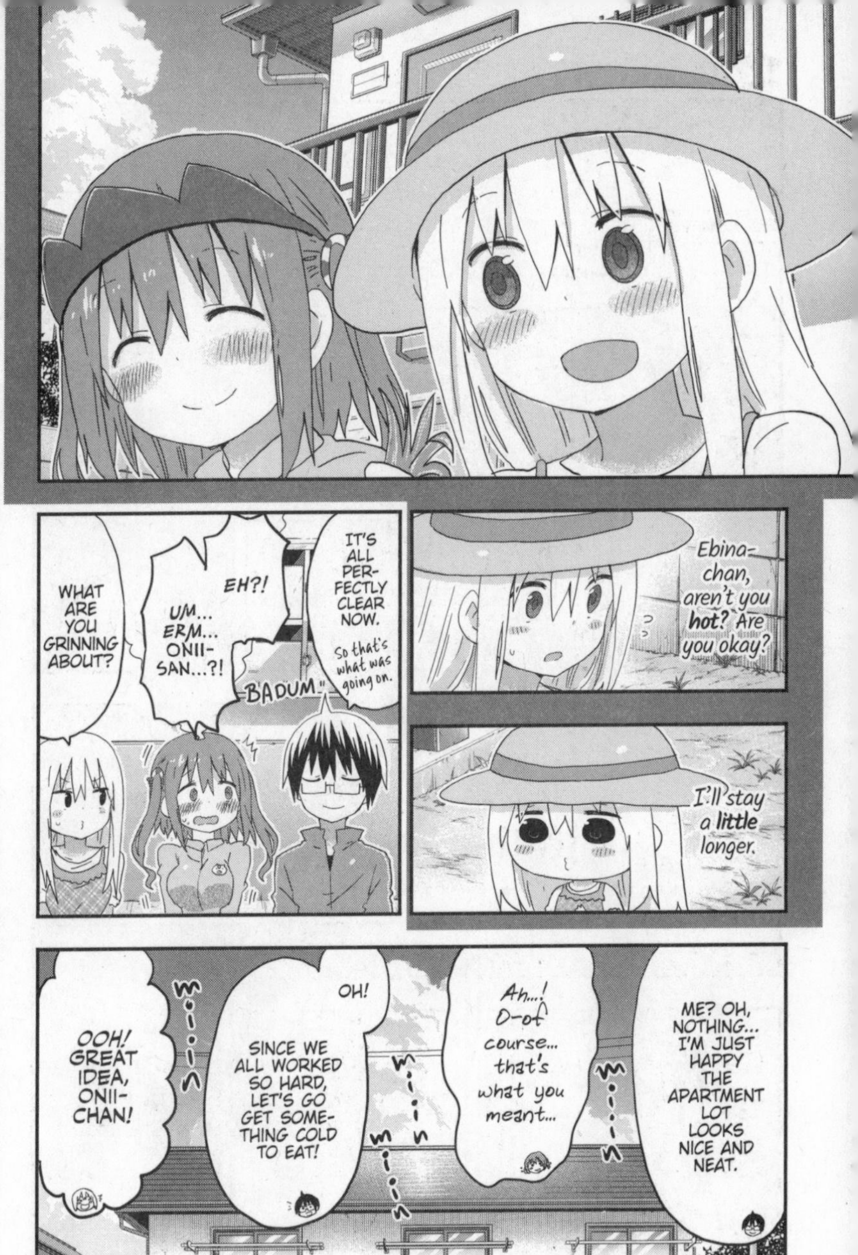
Ebina-chan, aren't you hot? Are you okay?
I'll stay a little longer.
IT'S ALL PERFECTLY CLEAR NOW.
So that's what was going on.
EH?!
UM... ERM... ONII-SAN...?!
BADUM
WHAT ARE YOU GRINNING ABOUT?
ME? OH, NOTHING... I'M JUST HAPPY THE APARTMENT LOT LOOKS NICE AND NEAT.
mi-i-n
Ah...! O-of course... that's what you meant...
mi-i-n
OH!
SINCE WE ALL WORKED SO HARD, LET'S GO GET SOMETHING COLD TO EAT!
mi-i-n
OOH! GREAT IDEA, ONII-CHAN!

No. 120 Umaru & the Siblings

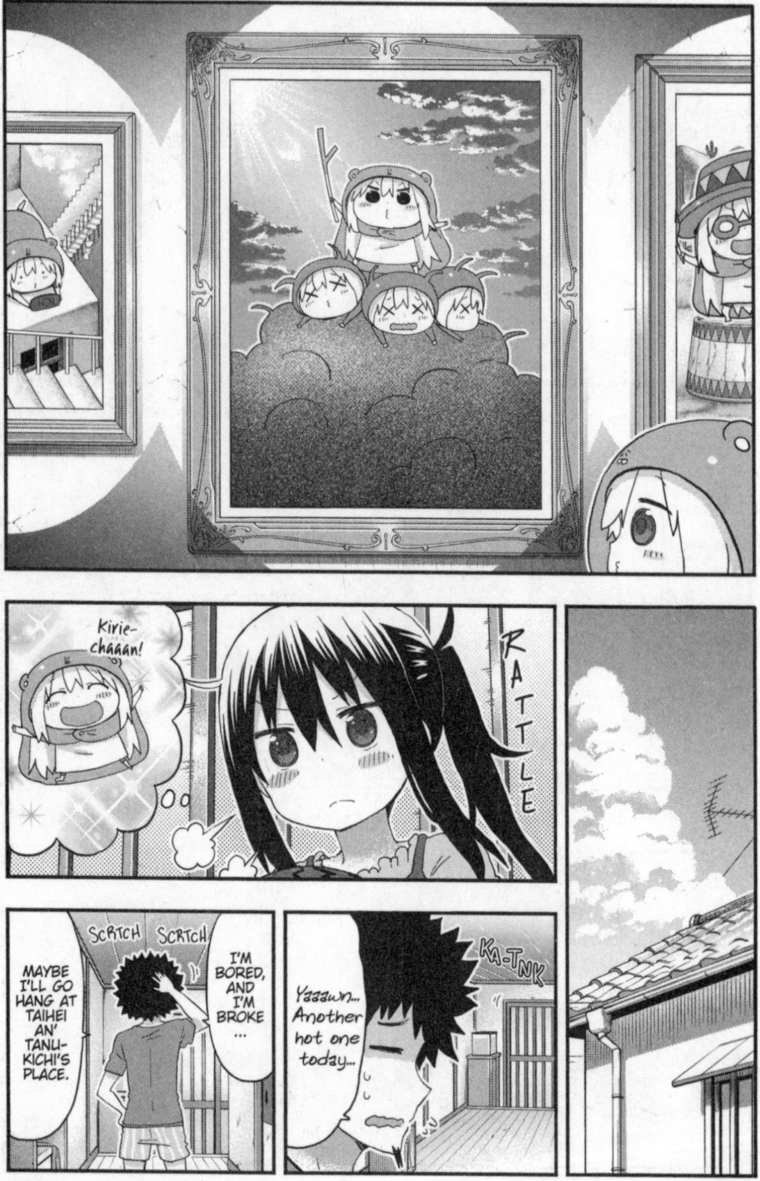
RATTLE
Kirie-chaaan!
KA-TNK
Yaaawn... Another hot one today...
SCRTCH SCRTCH
I'M BORED, AND I'M BROKE...
MAYBE I'LL GO HANG AT TAIHEI AN' TANUKICHI'S PLACE.

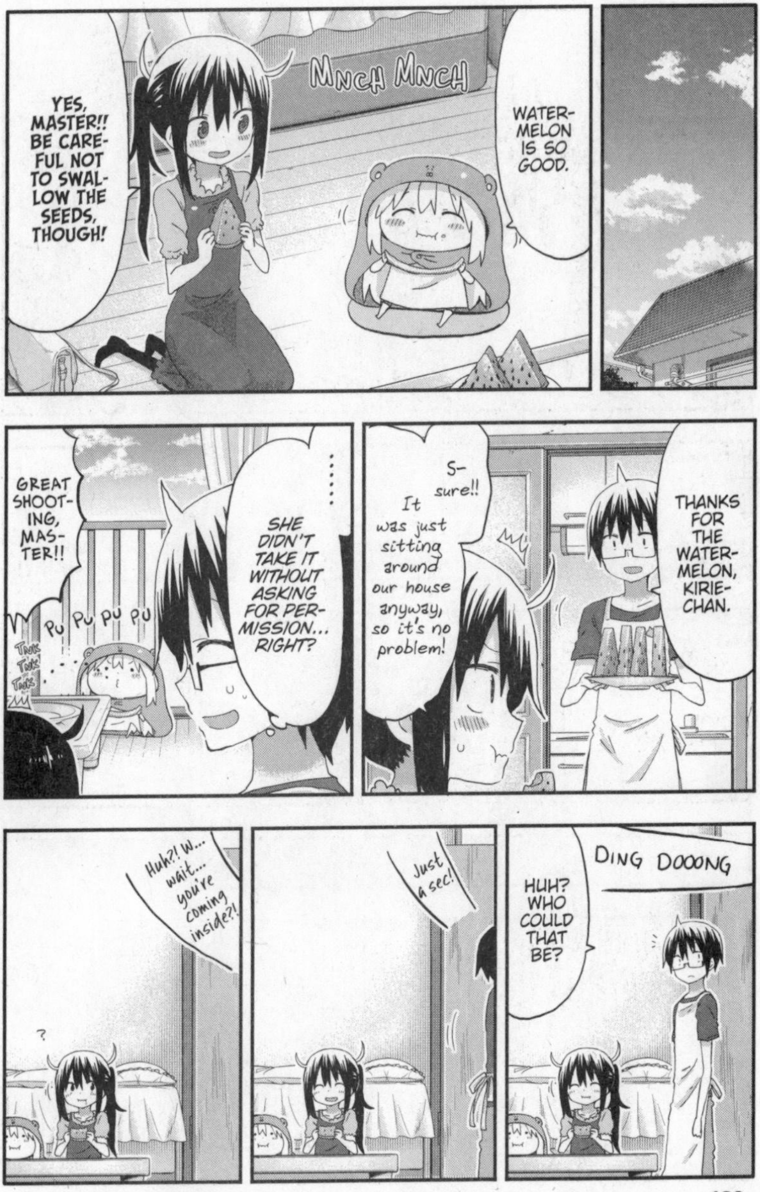
WATER-MELON IS SO GOOD.
MNCH MNCH
YES, MASTER!! BE CARE-FUL NOT TO SWAL-LOW THE SEEDS, THOUGH!
THANKS FOR THE WATER-MELON, KIRIE-CHAN.
S-sure!!
It was just sitting around our house anyway, so it's no problem!
......
SHE DIDN'T TAKE IT WITHOUT ASKING FOR PER-MISSION... RIGHT?
GREAT SHOOT-ING, MAS-TER!!
PU PU PU PU
TNK TNK TNK
DING DOOONG
HUH? WHO COULD THAT BE?
Just a sec!
Huh?! W... wait... you're coming inside?!
?

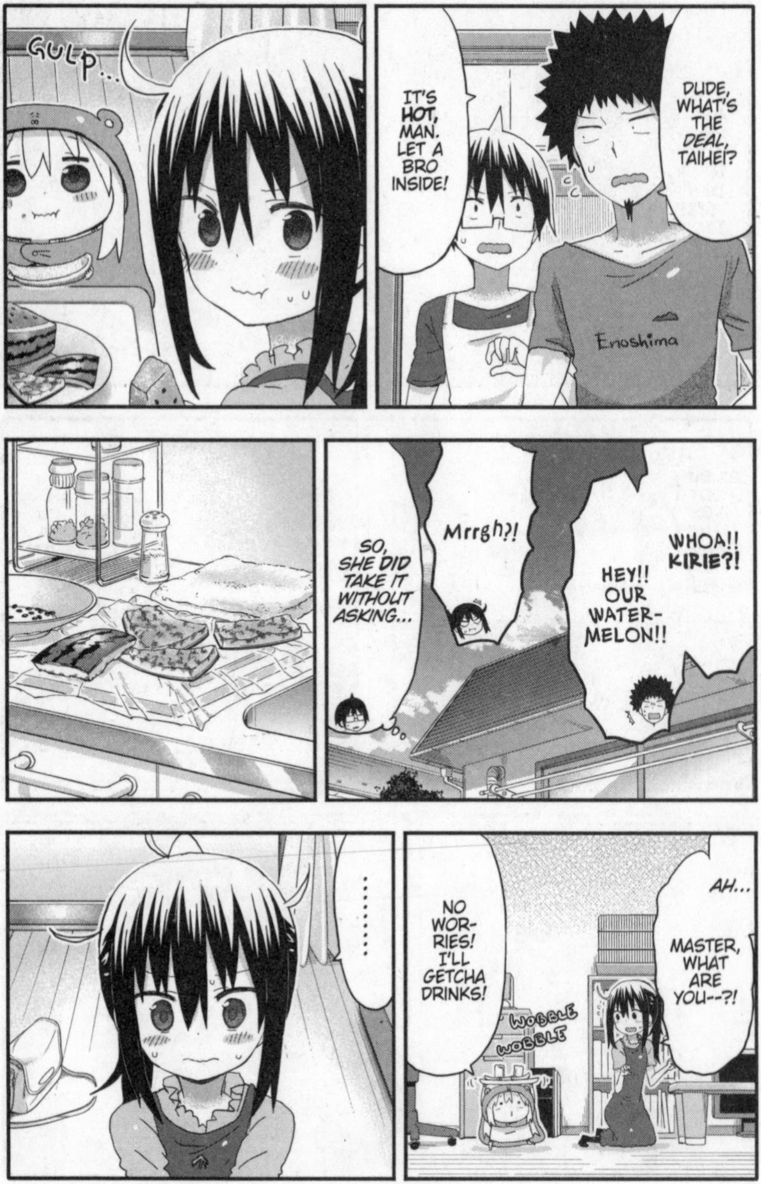
DUDE, WHAT'S THE DEAL, TAIHEI?
IT'S HOT, MAN. LET A BRO INSIDE!
Enoshima
GULP...
WHOA!! KIRIE?!
HEY!! OUR WATER-MELON!!
Mrrgh?!
SO, SHE DID TAKE IT WITHOUT ASKING...
AH...
MASTER, WHAT ARE YOU--?!
WOBBLE WOBBLE
NO WOR-RIES! I'LL GETCHA DRINKS!
......

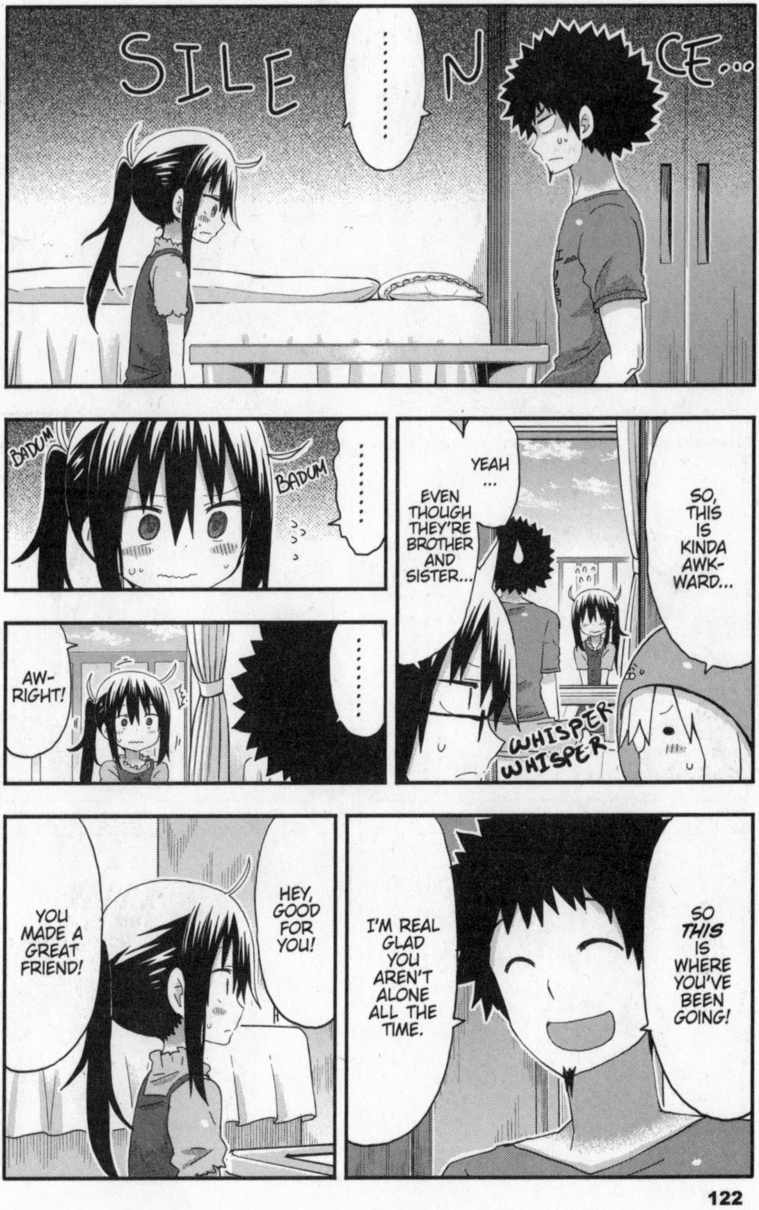
SILENCE...
......
SO, THIS IS KINDA AWK-WARD...
YEAH ... EVEN THOUGH THEY'RE BROTHER AND SISTER...
WHISPER WHISPER
BADUM BADUM
......
......
AW-RIGHT!
SO THIS IS WHERE YOU'VE BEEN GOING!
I'M REAL GLAD YOU AREN'T ALONE ALL THE TIME.
HEY, GOOD FOR YOU!
YOU MADE A GREAT FRIEND!

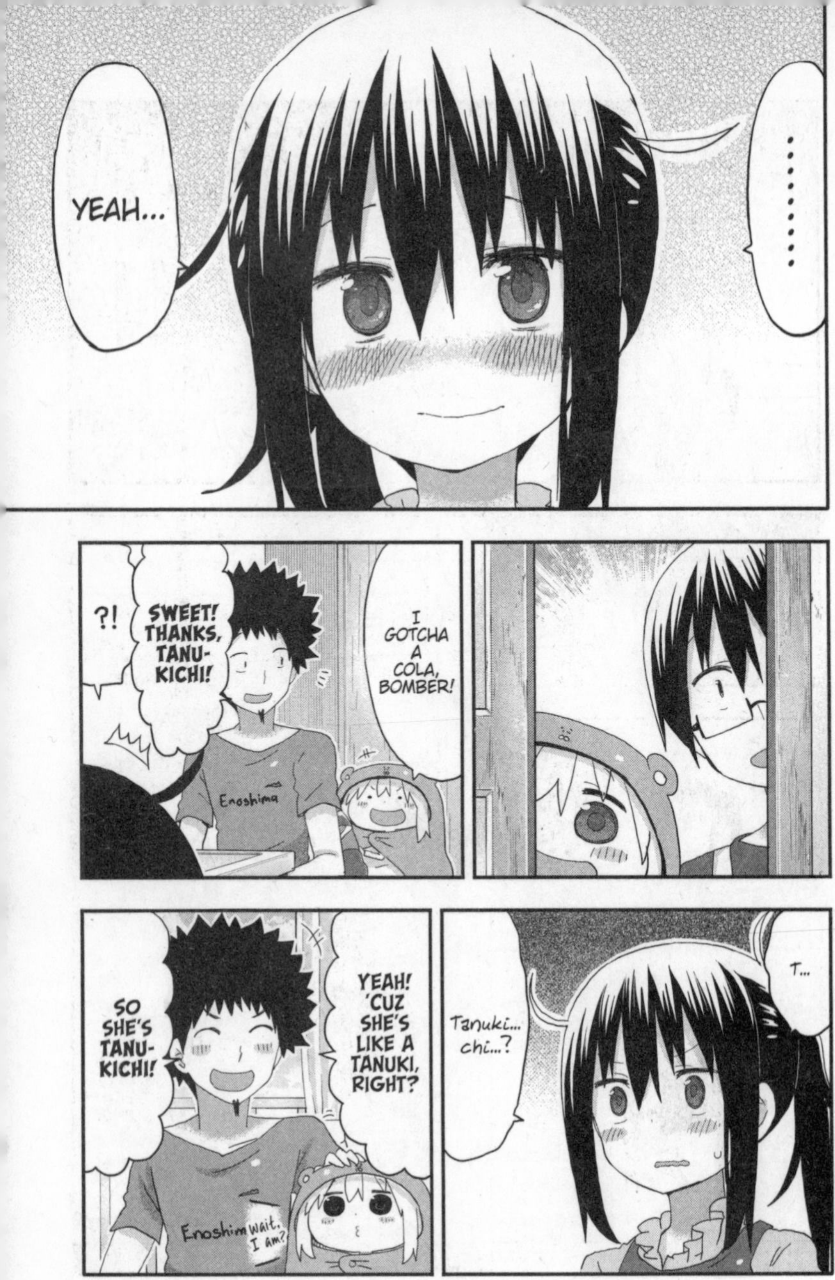
......
YEAH...
I GOTCHA A COLA, BOMBER!
SWEET! THANKS, TANU-KICHI!
?!
Enoshima
T...
Tanuki... chi...?
YEAH! 'CUZ SHE'S LIKE A TANUKI, RIGHT?
SO SHE'S TANU-KICHI!
Enoshim
Wait, I am?

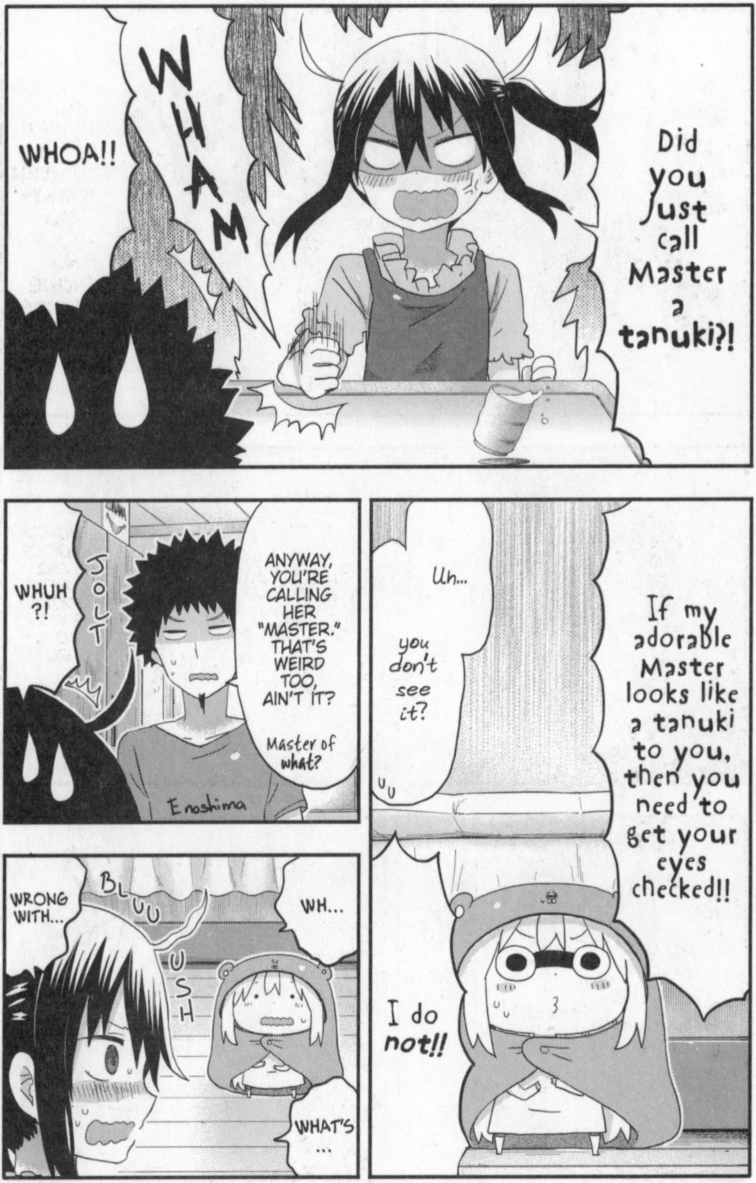
Did you just call Master a tanuki?!
WHAM
WHOA!!
If my adorable Master looks like a tanuki to you, then you need to get your eyes checked!!
Uh...
you don't see it?
I do not!!
ANYWAY, YOU'RE CALLING HER "MASTER." THAT'S WEIRD TOO, AIN'T IT?
Master of what?
JOLT
WHUH ?!
Enoshima
WH...
BLUUUSH
WRONG WITH...
WHAT'S ...

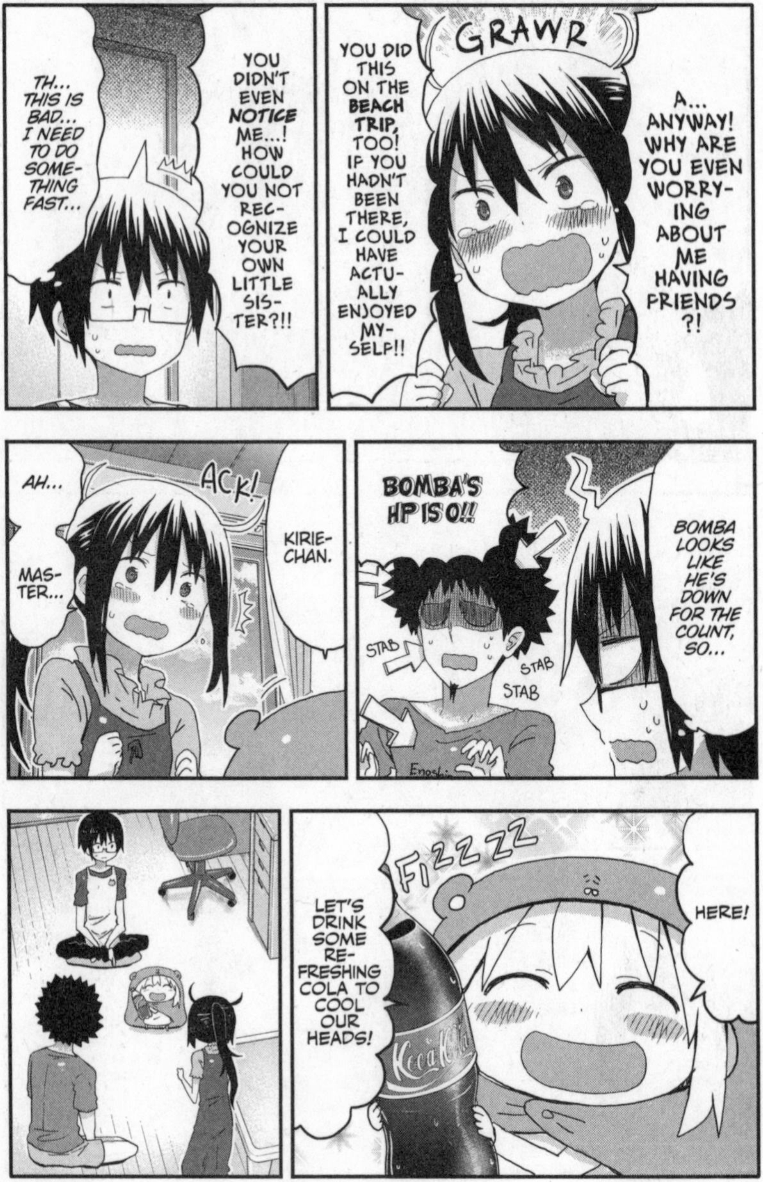
GRAWR
A... ANYWAY! WHY ARE YOU EVEN WORRYING ABOUT ME HAVING FRIENDS?!
YOU DID THIS ON THE BEACH TRIP, TOO! IF YOU HADN'T BEEN THERE, I COULD HAVE ACTUALLY ENJOYED MYSELF!!
YOU DIDN'T EVEN NOTICE ME...! HOW COULD YOU NOT RECOGNIZE YOUR OWN LITTLE SISTER?!!
TH... THIS IS BAD... I NEED TO DO SOMETHING FAST...
BOMBA LOOKS LIKE HE'S DOWN FOR THE COUNT, SO...
BOMBA'S HP IS 0!!
STAB
STAB
STAB
KIRIE-CHAN.
ACK!
AH...
MASTER...
HERE!
FIZZZZ
LET'S DRINK SOME REFRESHING COLA TO COOL OUR HEADS!

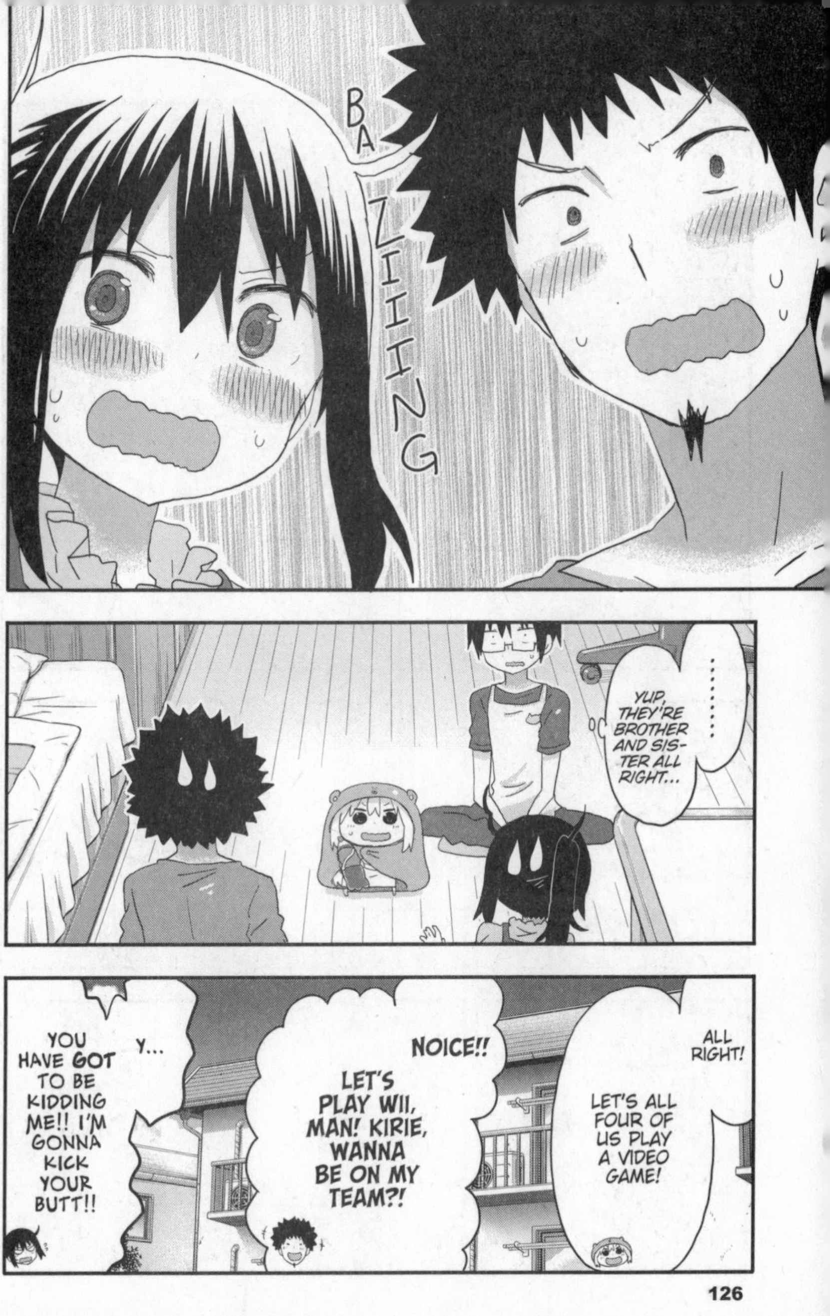
BA
ZIIING
......
YUP, THEY'RE BROTHER AND SISTER ALL RIGHT...
ALL RIGHT!
LET'S ALL FOUR OF US PLAY A VIDEO GAME!
NOICE!!
LET'S PLAY WII, MAN! KIRIE, WANNA BE ON MY TEAM?!
Y...
YOU HAVE GOT TO BE KIDDING ME!! I'M GONNA KICK YOUR BUTT!!

No. 121 Umaru & a Friend's Room

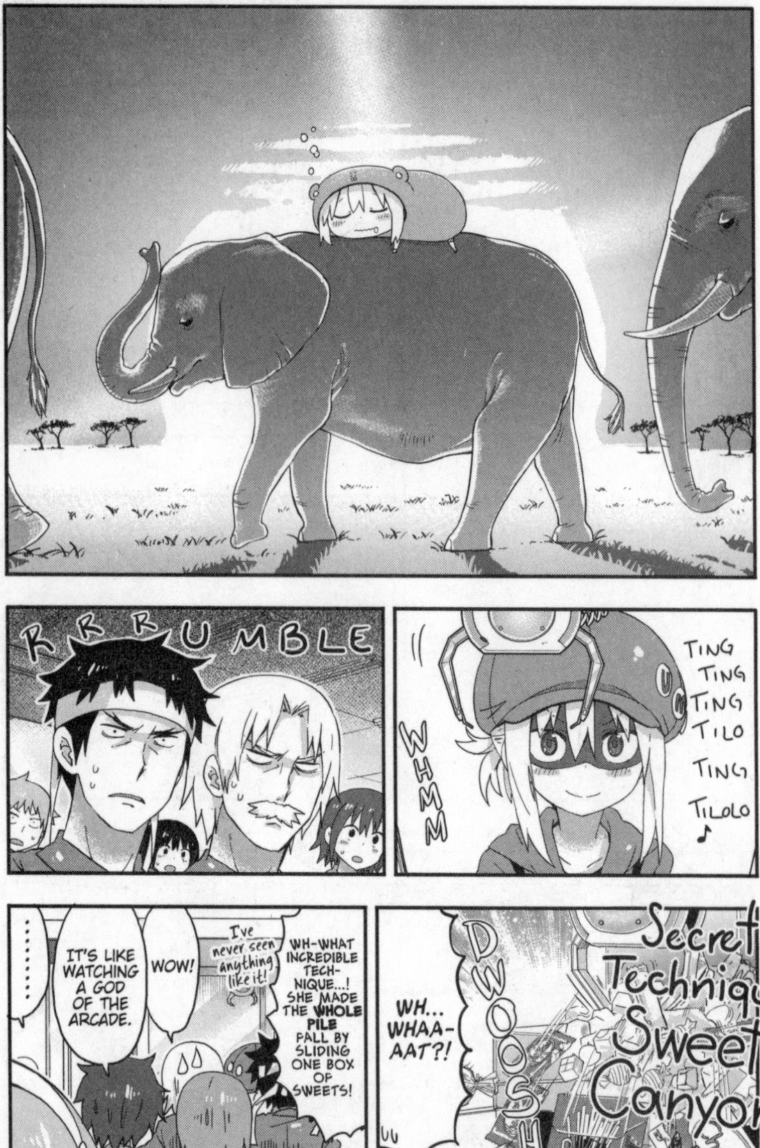
WHMM
TING TING TING TILO TING TILOLO ♪
RRRUMBLE
DWOOOSH
WH... WHAAA-AAT?!
Secret Technique Sweets Canyon
Poppy
Choco
WH-WHAT INCREDIBLE TECH-NIQUE...! SHE MADE THE WHOLE PILE FALL BY SLIDING ONE BOX OF SWEETS!
I've never seen anything like it!
WOW!
IT'S LIKE WATCHING A GOD OF THE ARCADE.
......

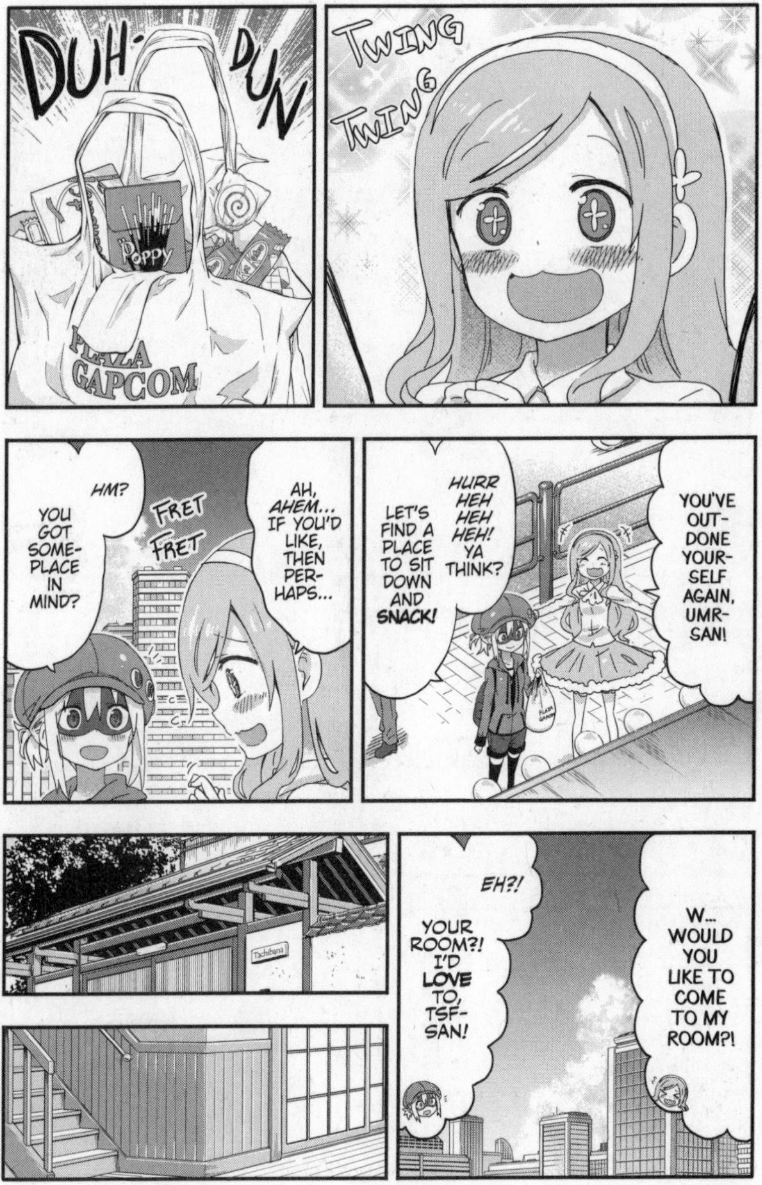
TWING TWING
DUH-DUN
Poppy
PLAZA GAPCOM
YOU'VE OUTDONE YOURSELF AGAIN, UMR-SAN!
HURR HEH HEH HEH! YA THINK?
LET'S FIND A PLACE TO SIT DOWN AND **SNACK!**
AH, *AHEM...* IF YOU'D LIKE, THEN PERHAPS...
FRET FRET
HM?
YOU GOT SOMEPLACE IN MIND?
W... WOULD YOU LIKE TO COME TO MY ROOM?!
EH?!
YOUR ROOM?! I'D **LOVE** TO, TSF-SAN!
Tachibana

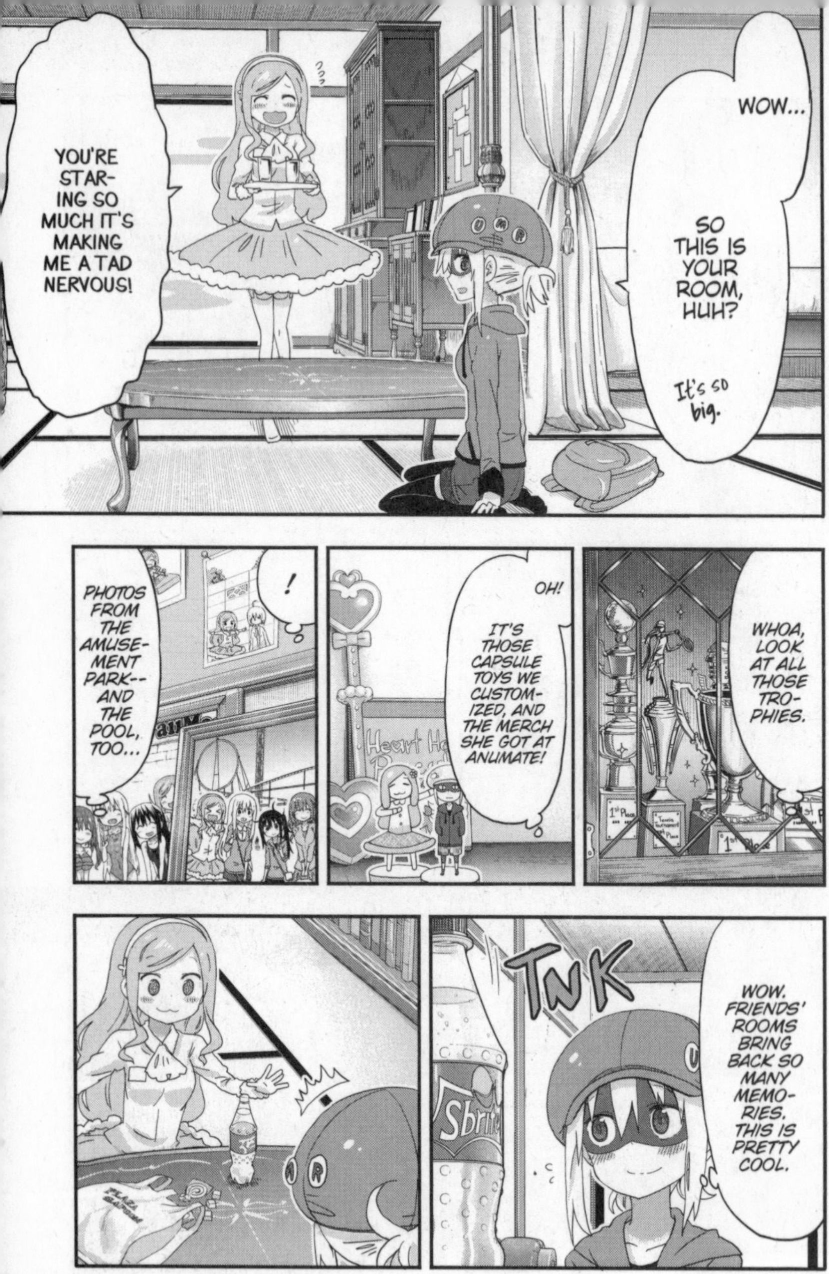
WOW...
SO THIS IS YOUR ROOM, HUH?
It's so big.
YOU'RE STARING SO MUCH IT'S MAKING ME A TAD NERVOUS!
WHOA, LOOK AT ALL THOSE TROPHIES.
OH!
IT'S THOSE CAPSULE TOYS WE CUSTOMIZED, AND THE MERCH SHE GOT AT ANUMATE!
!
PHOTOS FROM THE AMUSEMENT PARK--AND THE POOL, TOO...
TNK
WOW. FRIENDS' ROOMS BRING BACK SO MANY MEMORIES. THIS IS PRETTY COOL.

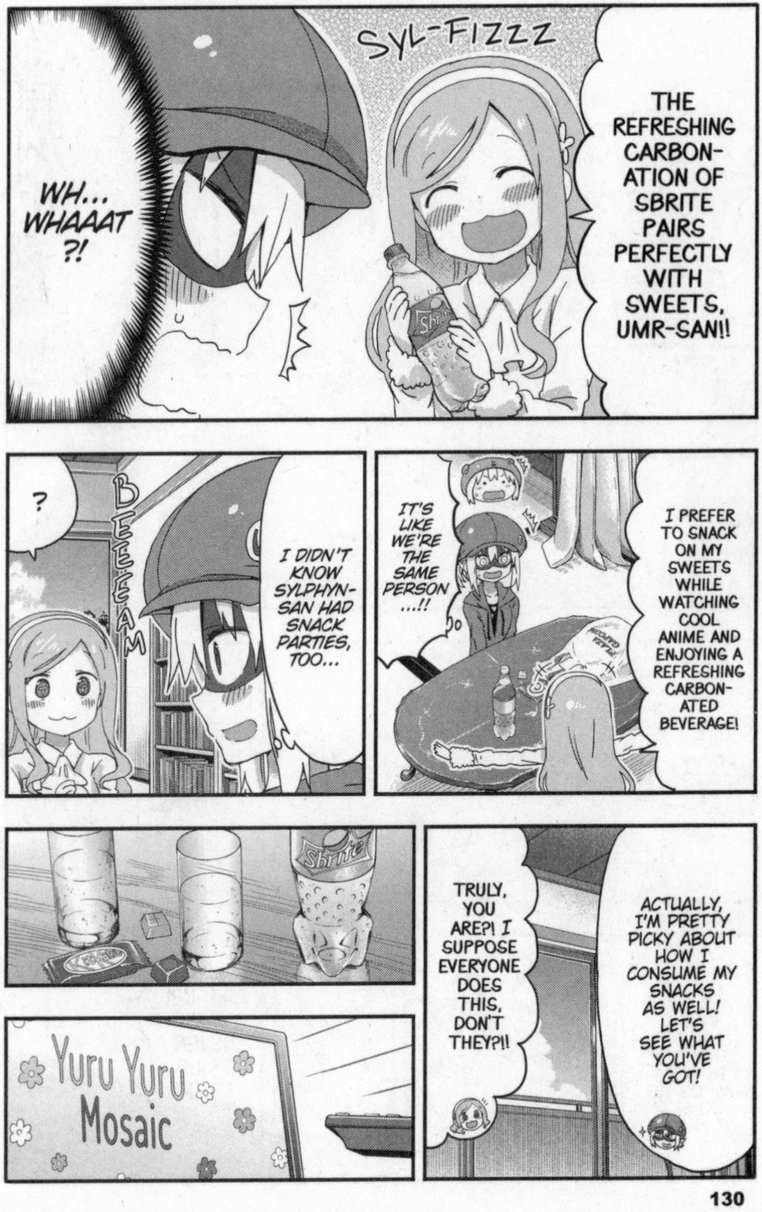
THE REFRESHING CARBON-ATION OF SBRITE PAIRS PERFECTLY WITH SWEETS, UMR-SAN!!
SYL-FIZZZ
WH... WHAAAT?!
I PREFER TO SNACK ON MY SWEETS WHILE WATCHING COOL ANIME AND ENJOYING A REFRESHING CARBON-ATED BEVERAGE!
IT'S LIKE WE'RE THE SAME PERSON ...!!
I DIDN'T KNOW SYLPHYN-SAN HAD SNACK PARTIES, TOO...
BEEEEAM
?
ACTUALLY, I'M PRETTY PICKY ABOUT HOW I CONSUME MY SNACKS AS WELL! LET'S SEE WHAT YOU'VE GOT!
TRULY, YOU ARE?! I SUPPOSE EVERYONE DOES THIS, DON'T THEY?!!
Sbrite
Yuru Yuru Mosaic

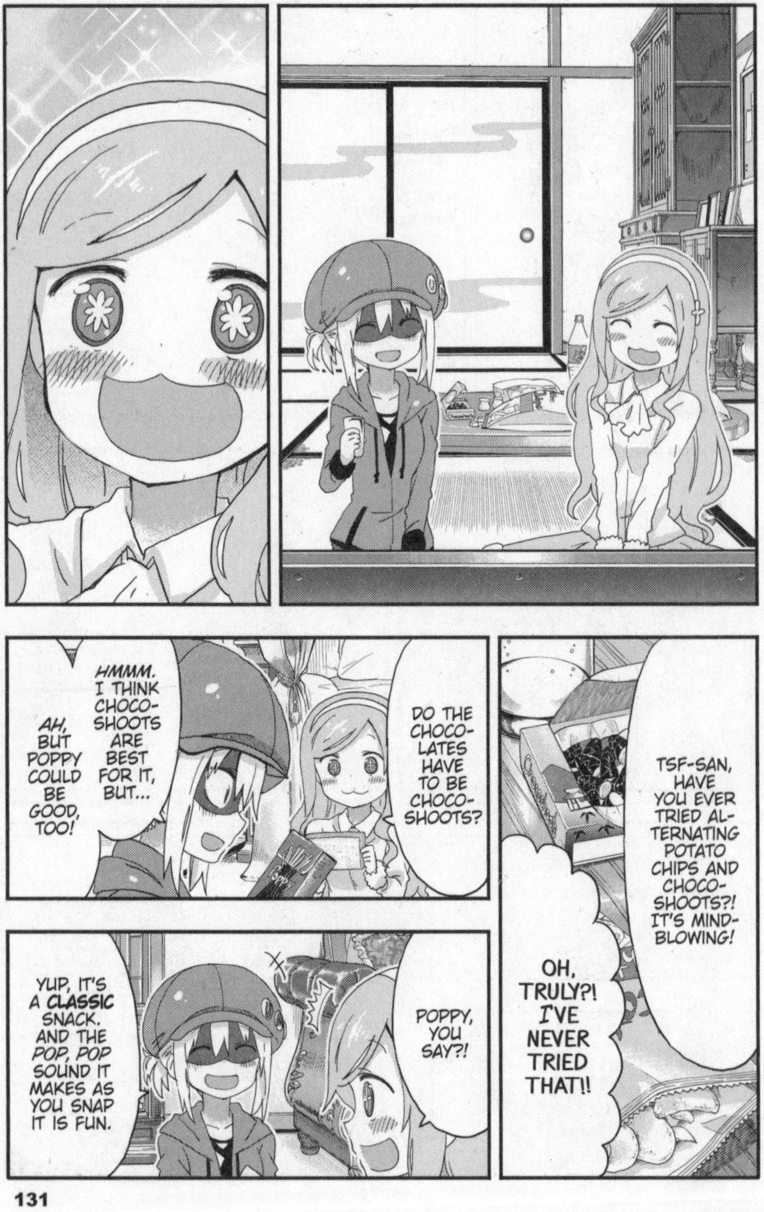
TSF-SAN, HAVE YOU EVER TRIED AL-TERNATING POTATO CHIPS AND CHOCO-SHOOTS?! IT'S MIND-BLOWING!
OH, TRULY?! I'VE NEVER TRIED THAT!!
DO THE CHOCO-LATES HAVE TO BE CHOCO-SHOOTS?
HMMM. I THINK CHOCO-SHOOTS ARE BEST FOR IT, BUT...
AH, BUT POPPY COULD BE GOOD, TOO!
POPPY, YOU SAY?!
YUP, IT'S A CLASSIC SNACK. AND THE POP, POP SOUND IT MAKES AS YOU SNAP IT IS FUN.

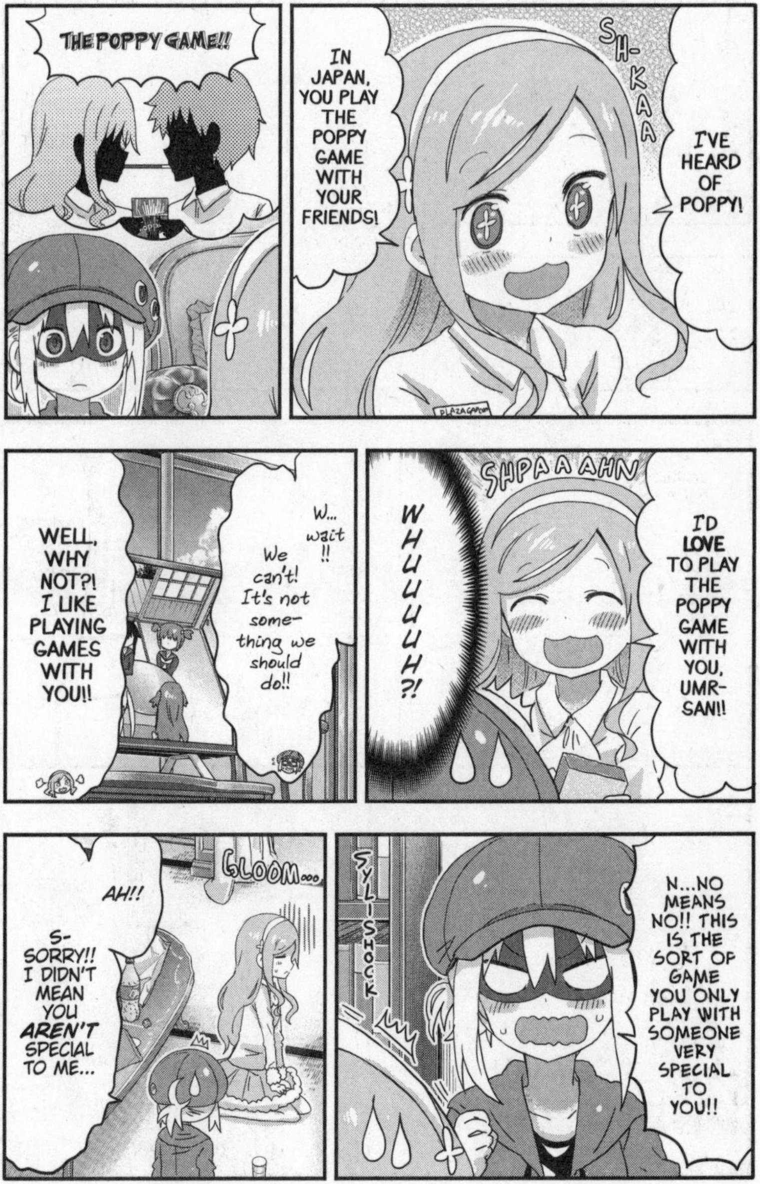
SH-KAA
I'VE HEARD OF POPPY!
IN JAPAN, YOU PLAY THE POPPY GAME WITH YOUR FRIENDS!
THE POPPY GAME!!
SHPAAAHN
I'D LOVE TO PLAY THE POPPY GAME WITH YOU, UMR-SAN!!
WHUUUUUH?!
W... wait!!
We can't! It's not some-thing we should do!!
WELL, WHY NOT?! I LIKE PLAYING GAMES WITH YOU!!
SYLISHOCK
N...NO MEANS NO!! THIS IS THE SORT OF GAME YOU ONLY PLAY WITH SOMEONE VERY SPECIAL TO YOU!!
GLOOM...
AH!!
S-SORRY!! I DIDN'T MEAN YOU AREN'T SPECIAL TO ME...

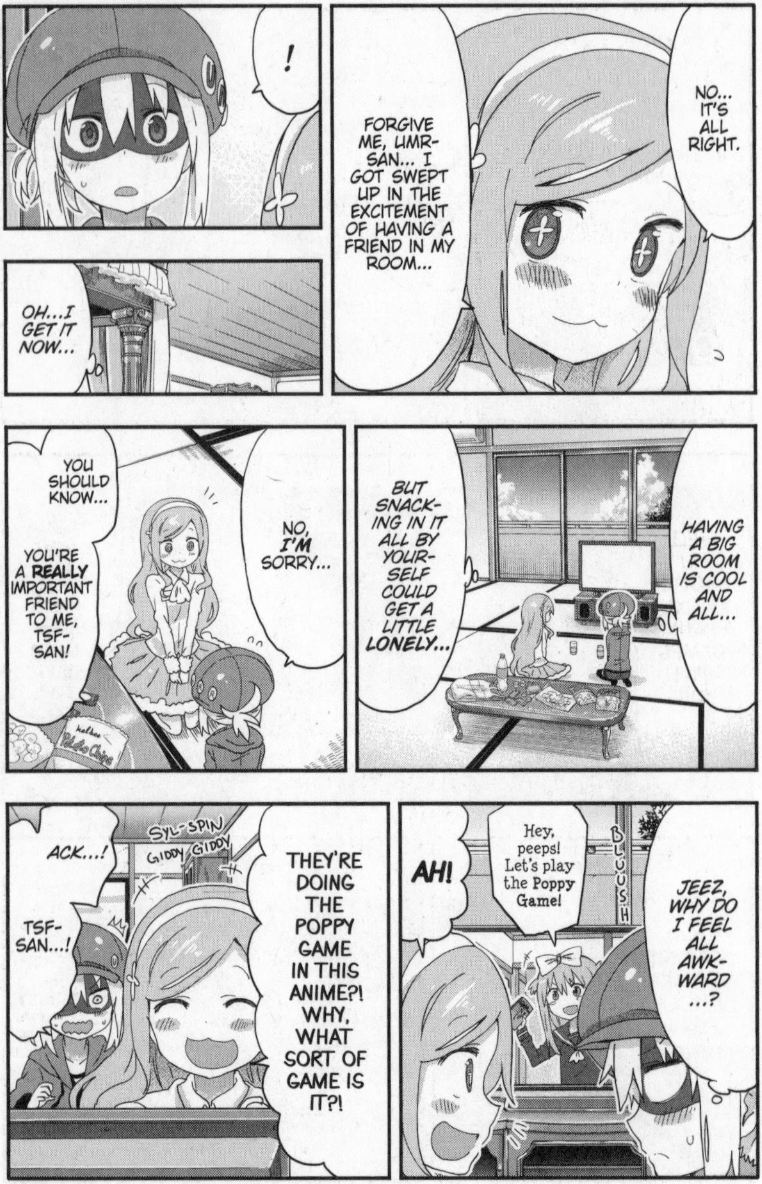
NO... IT'S ALL RIGHT.
FORGIVE ME, UMR-SAN... I GOT SWEPT UP IN THE EXCITEMENT OF HAVING A FRIEND IN MY ROOM...
!
OH...I GET IT NOW...
HAVING A BIG ROOM IS COOL AND ALL...
BUT SNACKING IN IT ALL BY YOURSELF COULD GET A LITTLE LONELY...
NO, I'M SORRY...
YOU SHOULD KNOW...
YOU'RE A REALLY IMPORTANT FRIEND TO ME, TSF-SAN!
JEEZ, WHY DO I FEEL ALL AWKWARD...?
BLUUSH
Hey, peeps! Let's play the Poppy Game!
AH!
THEY'RE DOING THE POPPY GAME IN THIS ANIME?! WHY, WHAT SORT OF GAME IS IT?!
SYL-SPIN
GIDDY GIDDY
ACK...!
TSF-SAN...!

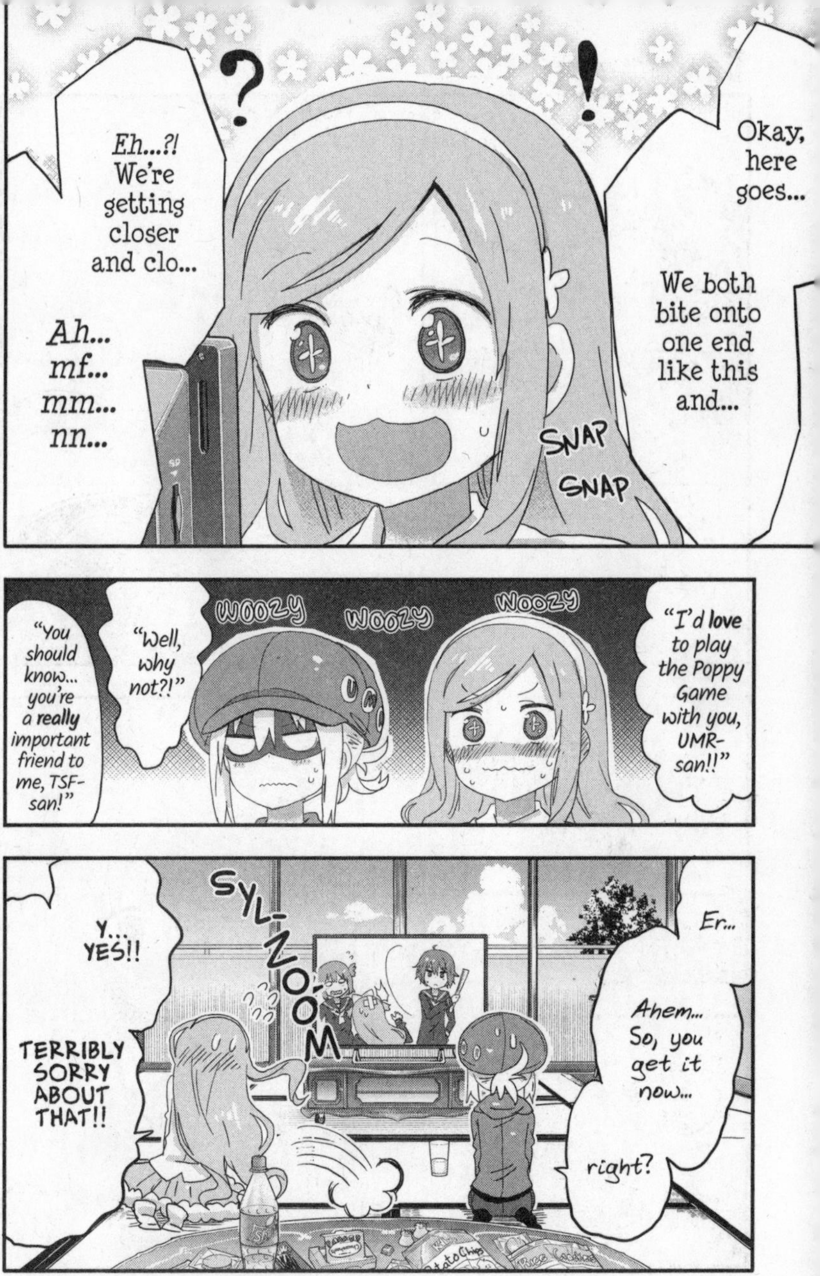
Okay, here goes...
We both bite onto one end like this and...
SNAP
SNAP
Eh...?! We're getting closer and clo...
Ah... mf... mm... nn...
"I'd **love** to play the Poppy Game with you, UMR-san!!"
WOOZY
WOOZY
WOOZY
"Well, why not?!"
"You should know... you're a **really** important friend to me, TSF-san!"
Er...
Ahem... So, you get it now...
right?
SYL-ZOOOM
Y... YES!!
TERRIBLY SORRY ABOUT THAT!!

No. 122 Umaru & Cooking

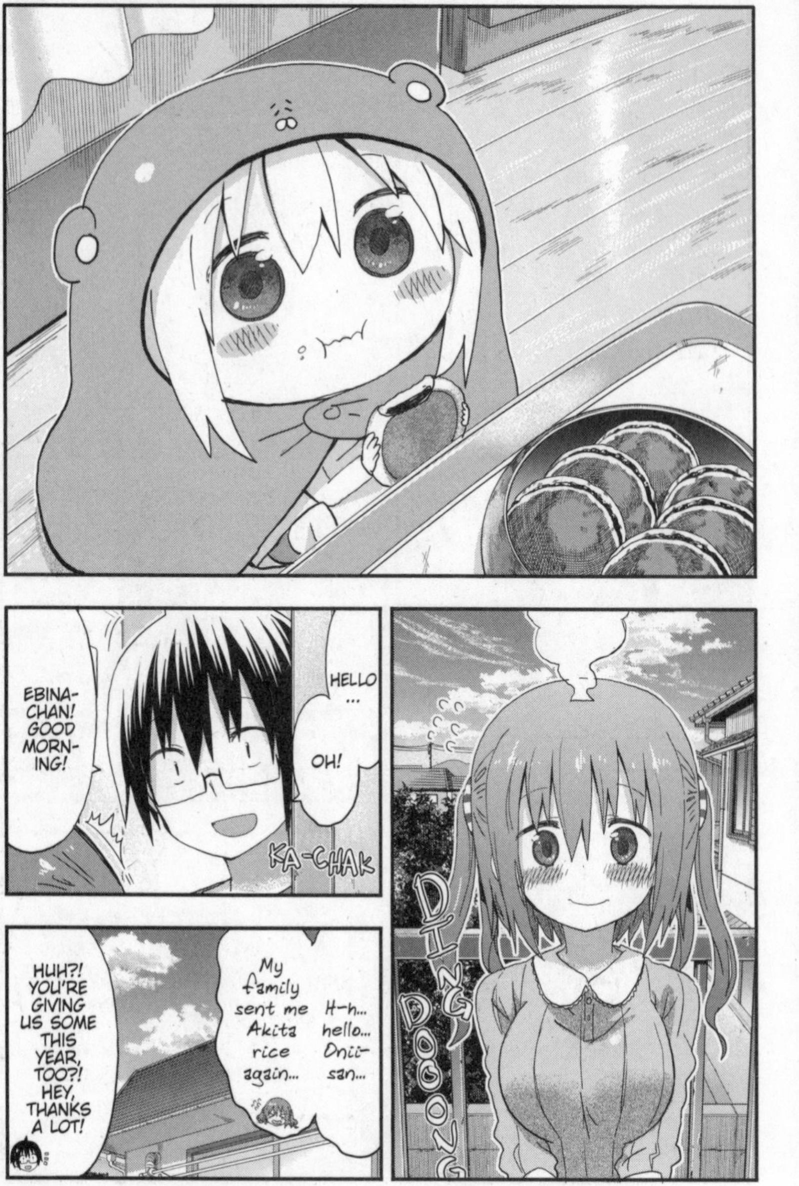
DING DONG
HELLO...
OH!
EBINA-CHAN! GOOD MORNING!
KA-CHAK
H-h... hello... Onii-san...
My family sent me Akita rice again...
HUH?! YOU'RE GIVING US SOME THIS YEAR, TOO?! HEY, THANKS A LOT!

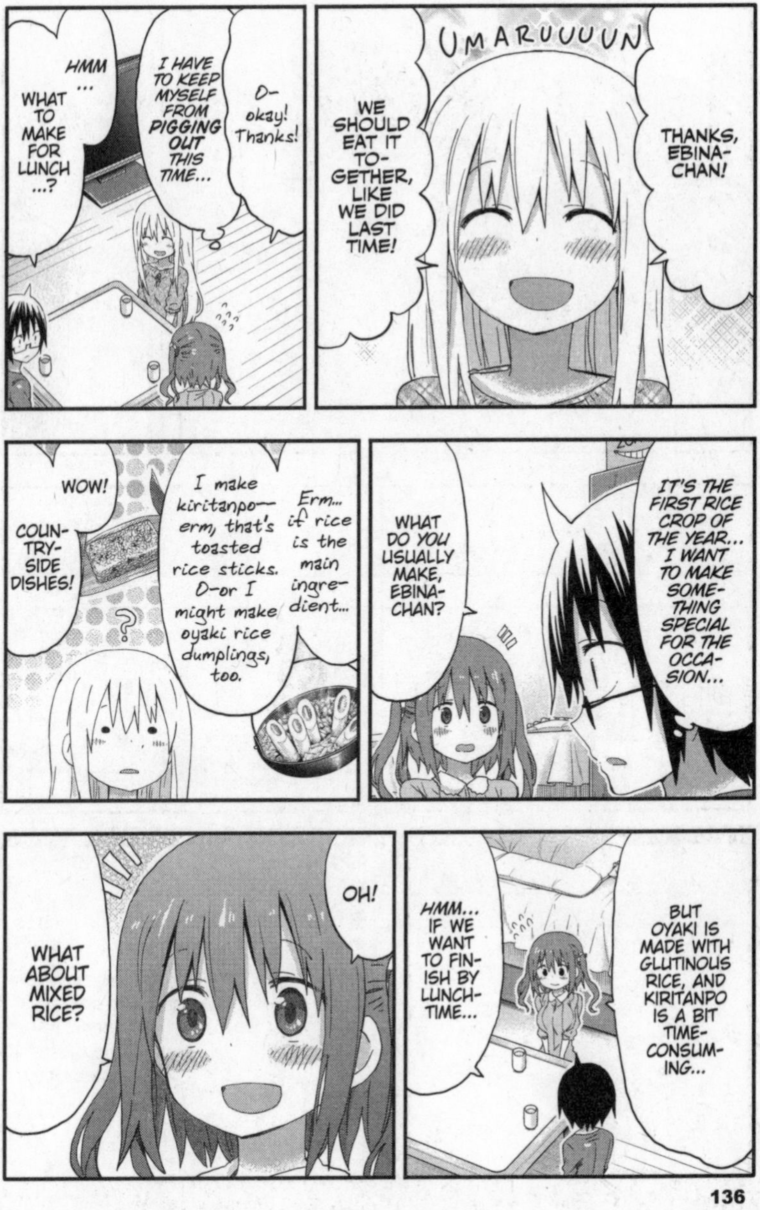
UMARUUUUN
THANKS, EBINA-CHAN!
WE SHOULD EAT IT TOGETHER, LIKE WE DID LAST TIME!
O-okay! Thanks!
I HAVE TO KEEP MYSELF FROM PIGGING OUT THIS TIME...
HMM... WHAT TO MAKE FOR LUNCH...?
IT'S THE FIRST RICE CROP OF THE YEAR... I WANT TO MAKE SOMETHING SPECIAL FOR THE OCCASION...
WHAT DO YOU USUALLY MAKE, EBINA-CHAN?
Erm... if rice is the main ingredient...
I make kiritanpo—erm, that's toasted rice sticks. O-or I might make oyaki rice dumplings, too.
WOW! COUNTRYSIDE DISHES!
BUT OYAKI IS MADE WITH GLUTINOUS RICE, AND KIRITANPO IS A BIT TIME-CONSUMING...
HMM... IF WE WANT TO FINISH BY LUNCHTIME...
OH!
WHAT ABOUT MIXED RICE?

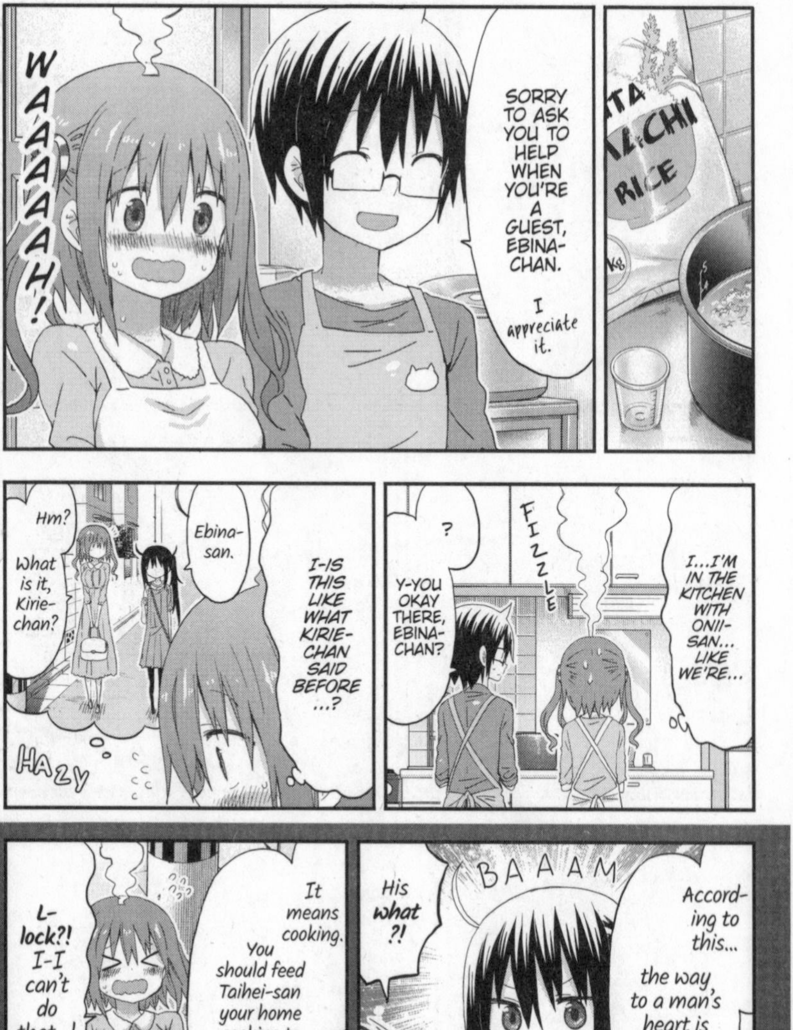
SORRY TO ASK YOU TO HELP WHEN YOU'RE A GUEST, EBINA-CHAN.
I appreciate it.
WAAAAAAAH!
I...I'M IN THE KITCHEN WITH ONII-SAN... LIKE WE'RE...
FIZZLE
?
Y-YOU OKAY THERE, EBINA-CHAN?
I-IS THIS LIKE WHAT KIRIE-CHAN SAID BEFORE...?
Ebina-san.
Hm? What is it, Kirie-chan?
HAZY
BAAAM
According to this... the way to a man's heart is through his **stomach**!!
His **what**?!
It means cooking. You should feed Taihei-san your home cooking to lock that man down.
L-**lock**?! I-I can't do that...!
Oh m'gosh!

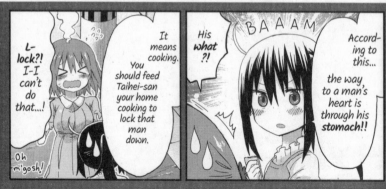

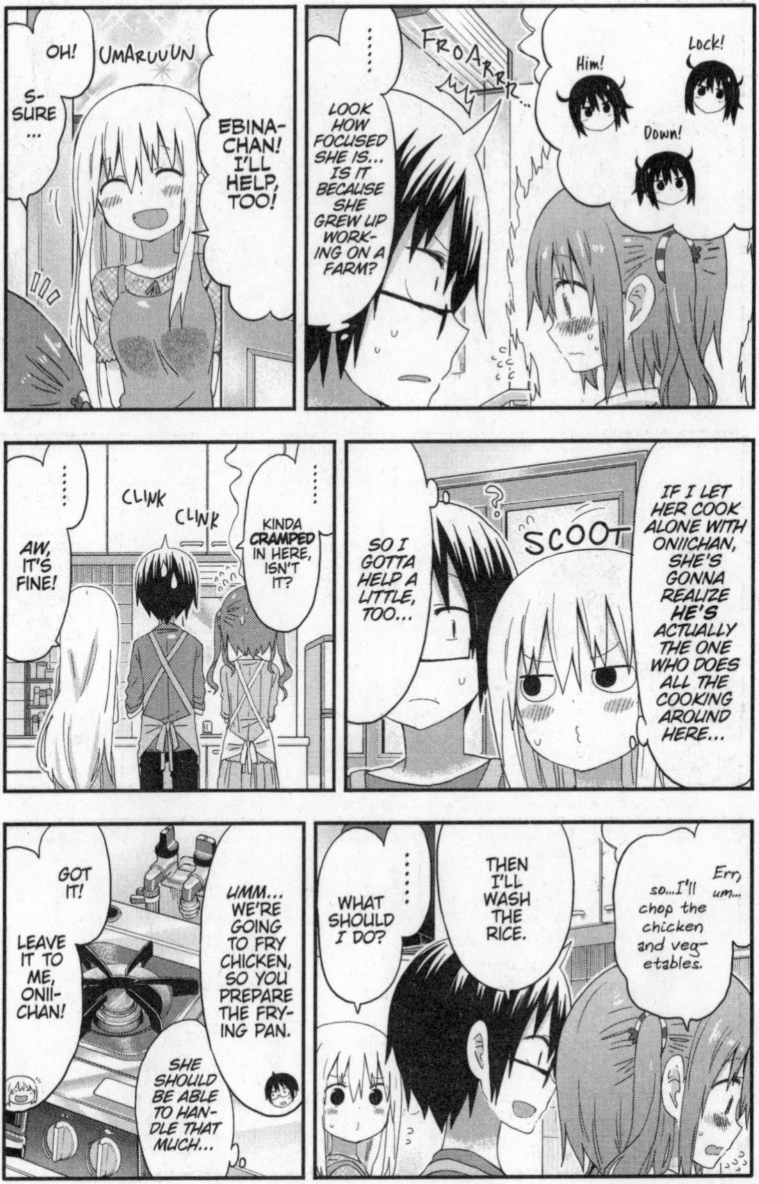
Him!
Lock!
Down!
FROARRR...
......
LOOK HOW FOCUSED SHE IS... IS IT BECAUSE SHE GREW UP WORKING ON A FARM?
EBINA-CHAN! I'LL HELP, TOO!
UMARUUUN
OH!
S-SURE...
IF I LET HER COOK ALONE WITH ONIICHAN, SHE'S GONNA REALIZE **HE'S** ACTUALLY THE ONE WHO DOES ALL THE COOKING AROUND HERE...
SCOOT
SO I GOTTA HELP A LITTLE, TOO...
......
KINDA **CRAMPED** IN HERE, ISN'T IT?
CLINK
CLINK
......
AW, IT'S FINE!
Err, um... so...I'll chop the chicken and vegetables.
THEN I'LL WASH THE RICE.
......
WHAT SHOULD I DO?
UMM... WE'RE GOING TO FRY CHICKEN, SO YOU PREPARE THE FRYING PAN.
GOT IT!
LEAVE IT TO ME, ONII-CHAN!
SHE SHOULD BE ABLE TO HANDLE THAT MUCH...

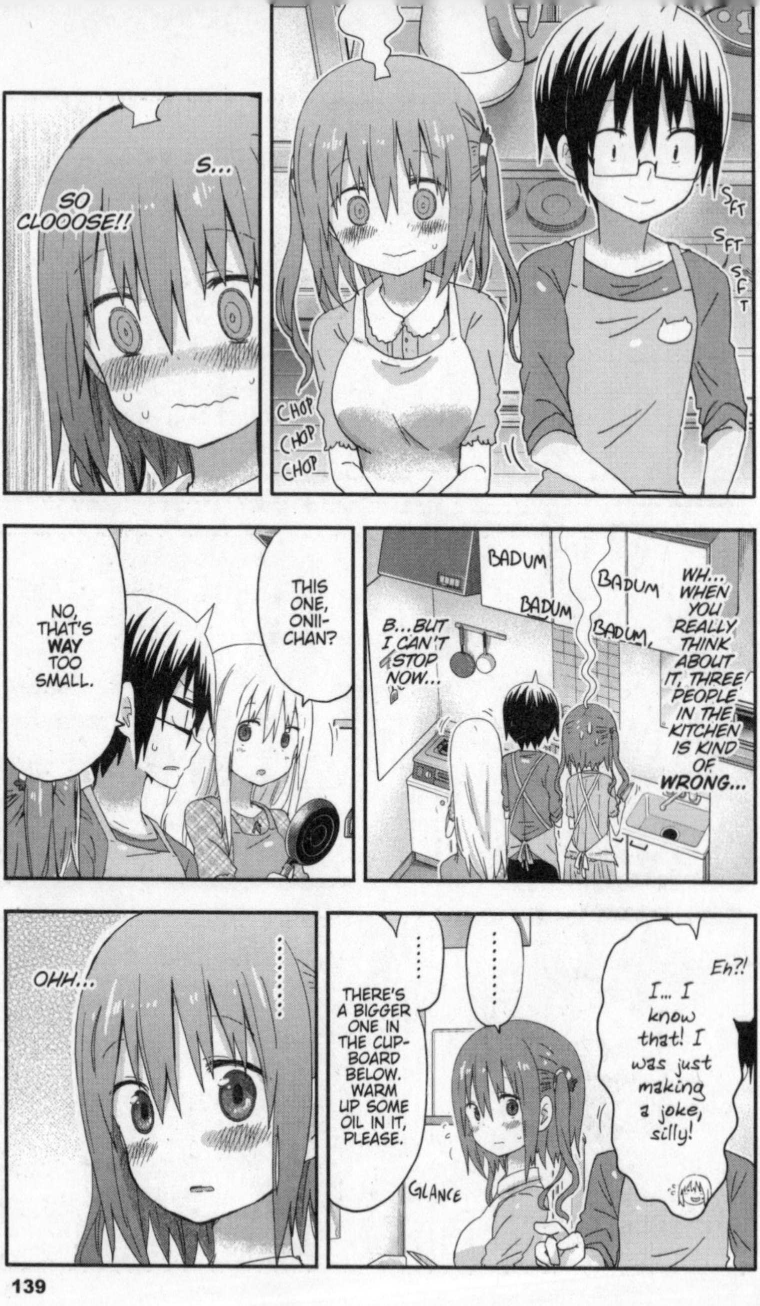
SFT
SFT
SFT
CHOP
CHOP
CHOP
S...
SO CLOOOSE!!
WH... WHEN YOU REALLY THINK ABOUT IT, THREE PEOPLE IN THE KITCHEN IS KIND OF WRONG...
BADUM
BADUM
BADUM
BADUM
B...BUT I CAN'T STOP NOW...
THIS ONE, ONII-CHAN?
NO, THAT'S WAY TOO SMALL.
Eh?!
I... I know that! I was just making a joke, silly!
......
......
THERE'S A BIGGER ONE IN THE CUP-BOARD BELOW. WARM UP SOME OIL IN IT, PLEASE.
GLANCE
....
OHH...

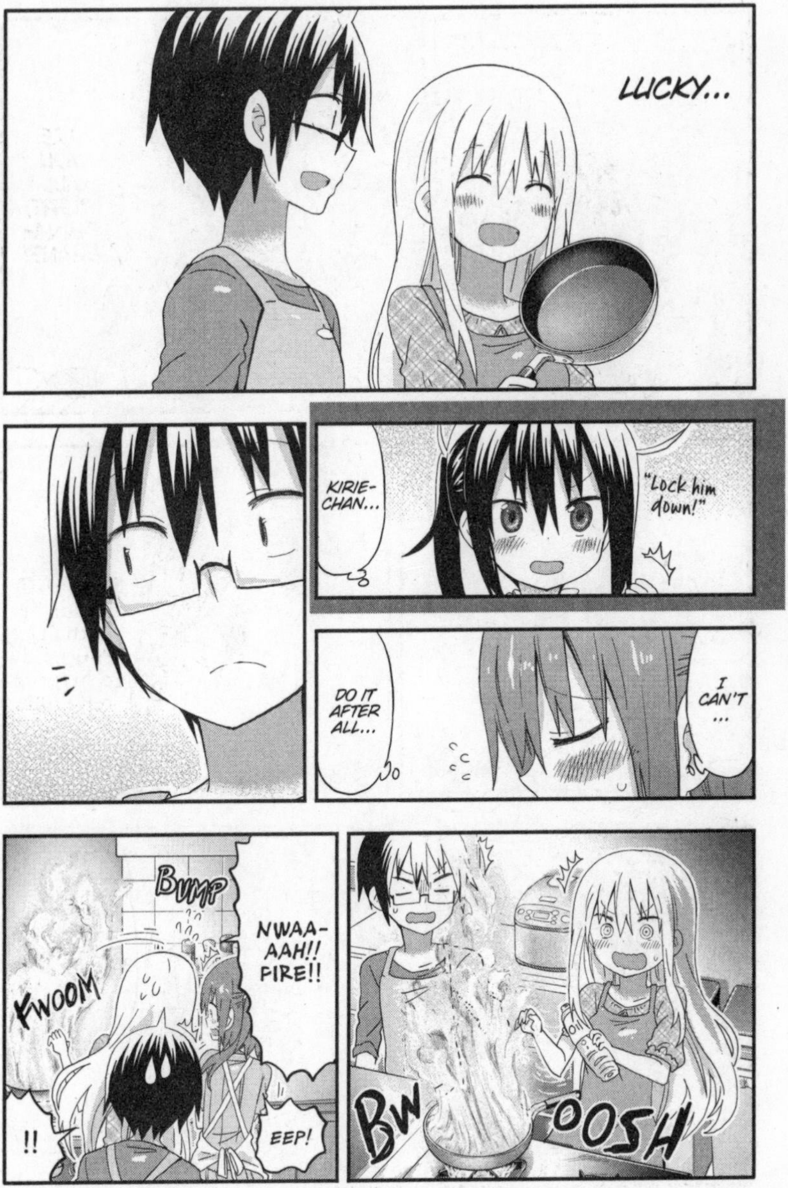
LUCKY...
"Lock him down!"
KIRIE-CHAN...
I CAN'T ...
DO IT AFTER ALL...
BWOOSH
BUMP
NWAA-AAH!! FIRE!!
FWOOM
EEP!
!!

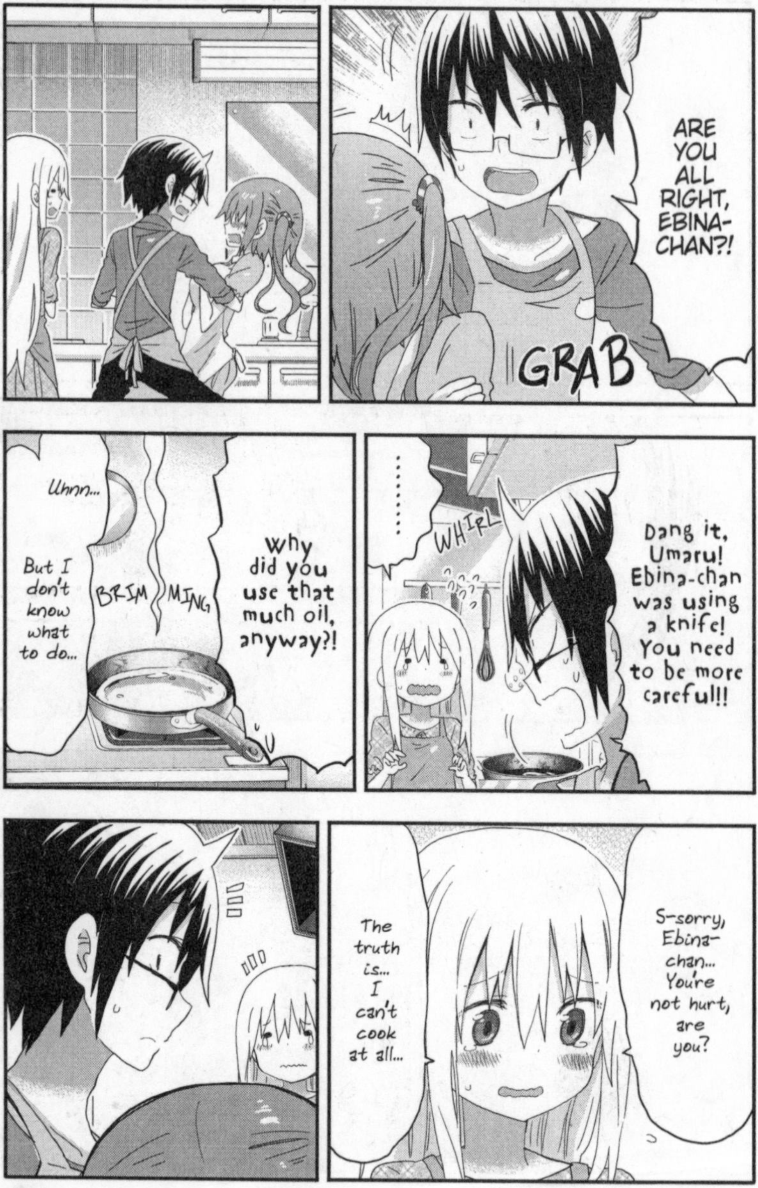
ARE YOU ALL RIGHT, EBINA-CHAN?!
GRAB
Dang it, Umaru! Ebina-chan was using a knife! You need to be more careful!!
WHIRL
......
Why did you use that much oil, anyway?!
BRIMMING
Uhnn...
But I don't know what to do...
S-sorry, Ebina-chan... You're not hurt, are you?
The truth is... I can't cook at all...

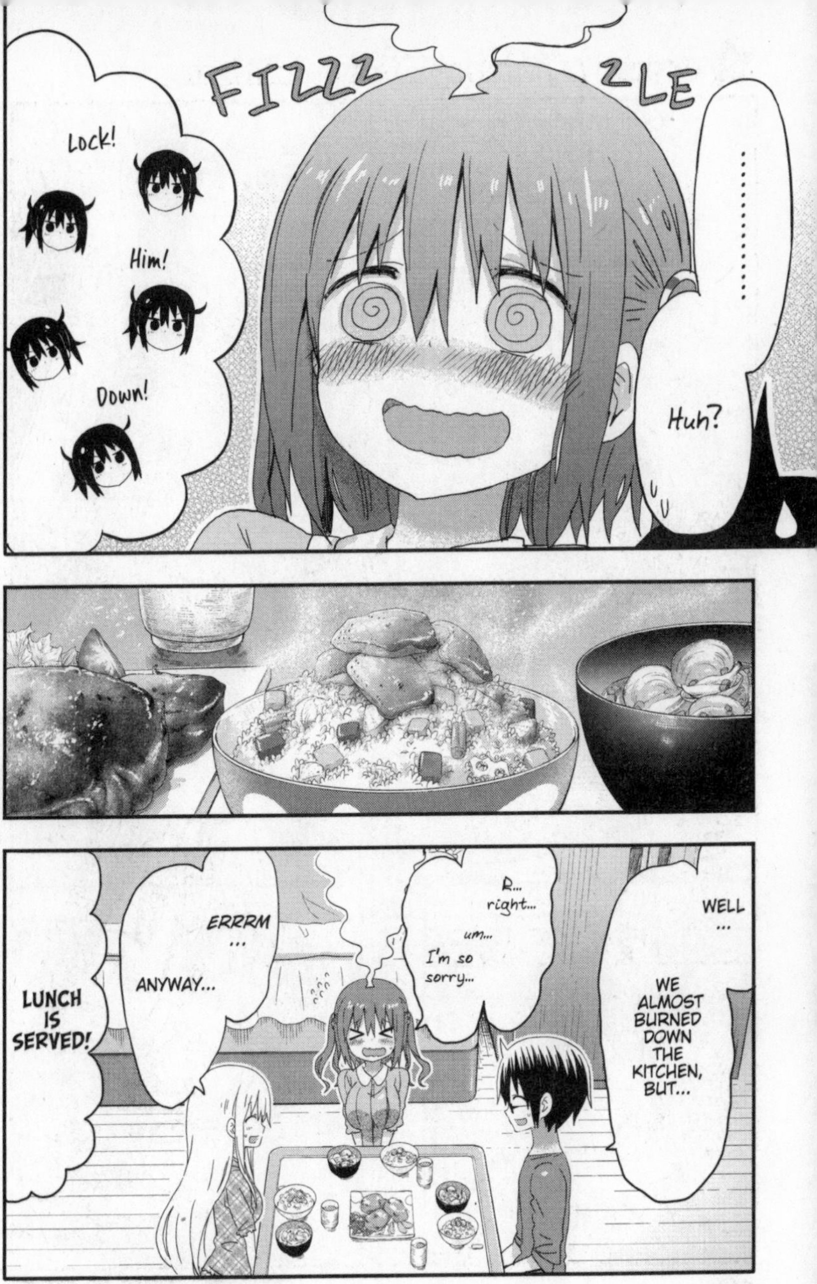
FIZZZZLE
......
Huh?
Lock!
Him!
Down!
WELL... WE ALMOST BURNED DOWN THE KITCHEN, BUT...
R... right... um... I'm so sorry...
ERRRM... ANYWAY...
LUNCH IS SERVED!

No. 123 Umaru & Hearing About Oniichan

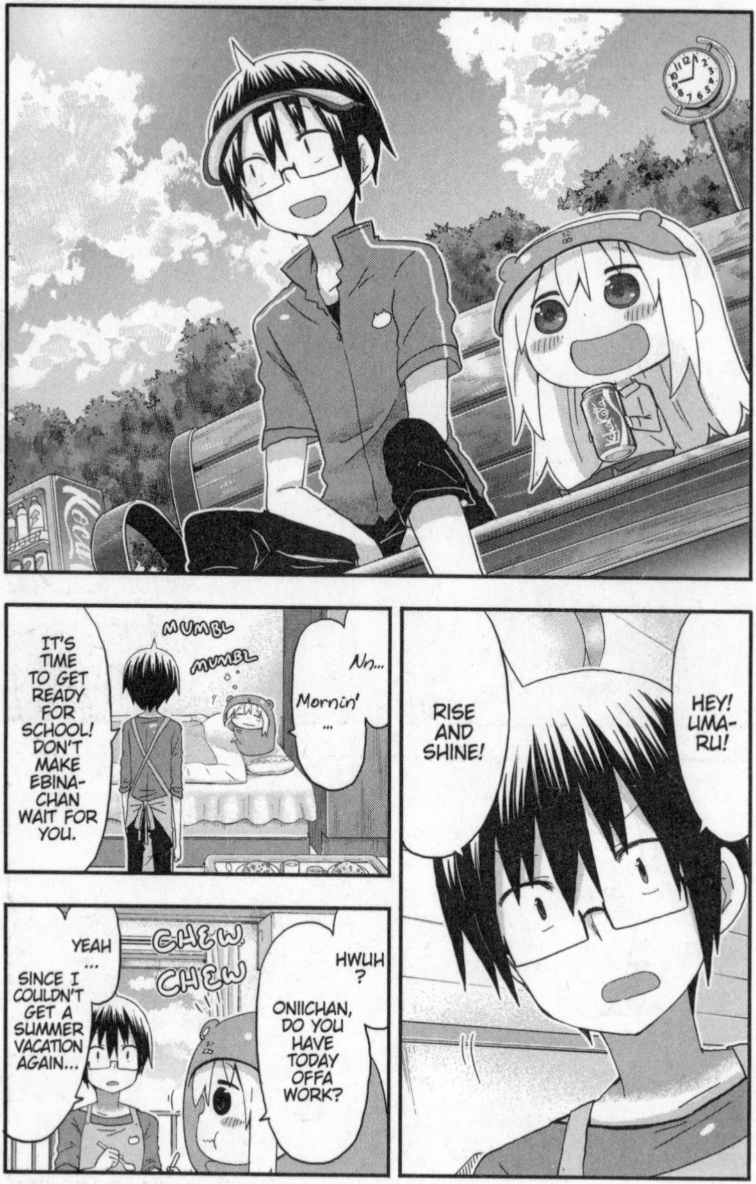
HEY! UMA-RU!
RISE AND SHINE!
Nn... Mornin' ...
MUMBL MUMBL
IT'S TIME TO GET READY FOR SCHOOL! DON'T MAKE EBINA-CHAN WAIT FOR YOU.
HWUH ?
ONIICHAN, DO YOU HAVE TODAY OFFA WORK?
CHEW CHEW
YEAH ... SINCE I COULDN'T GET A SUMMER VACATION AGAIN...

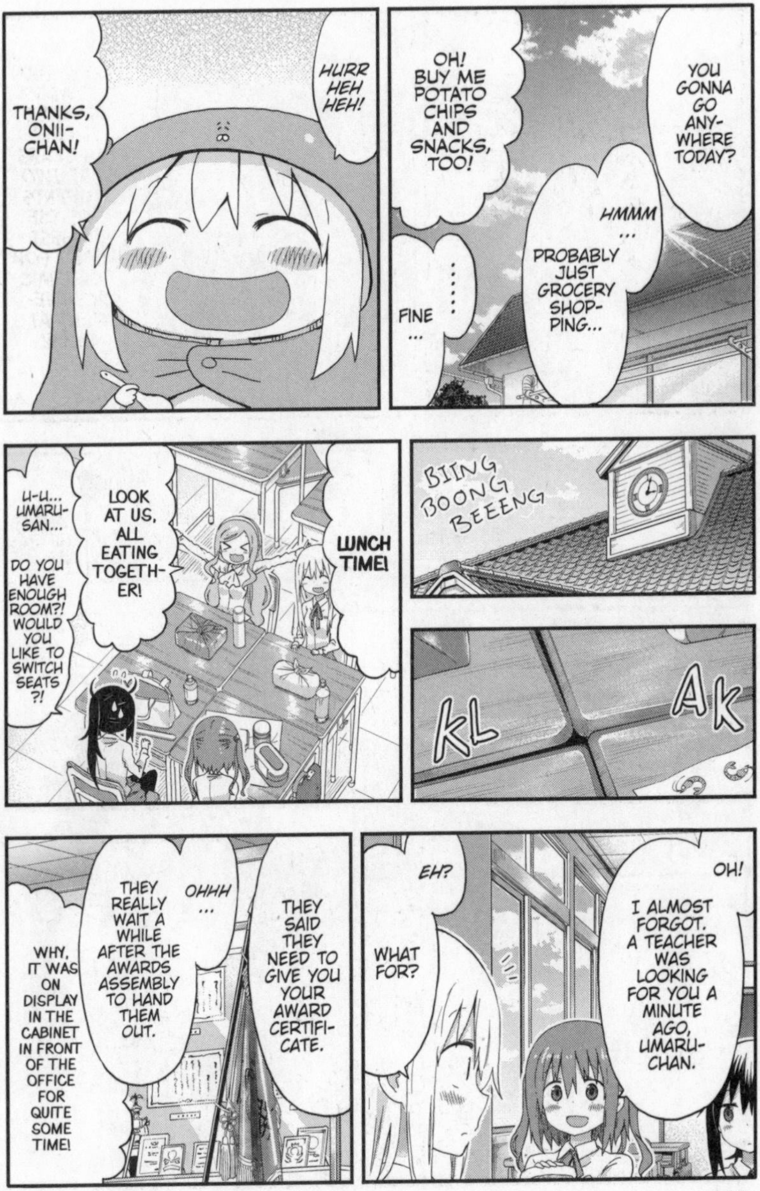
YOU GONNA GO ANYWHERE TODAY?
HMMM... PROBABLY JUST GROCERY SHOPPING...
...... FINE...
OH! BUY ME POTATO CHIPS AND SNACKS, TOO!
HURR HEH HEH!
THANKS, ONII-CHAN!
BIING BOONG BEEENG
KL Ak
LUNCH TIME!
LOOK AT US, ALL EATING TOGETHER!
U-U... UMARU-SAN... DO YOU HAVE ENOUGH ROOM?! WOULD YOU LIKE TO SWITCH SEATS?!
OH! I ALMOST FORGOT. A TEACHER WAS LOOKING FOR YOU A MINUTE AGO, UMARU-CHAN.
EH? WHAT FOR?
THEY SAID THEY NEED TO GIVE YOU YOUR AWARD CERTIFICATE.
OHHH... THEY REALLY WAIT A WHILE AFTER THE AWARDS ASSEMBLY TO HAND THEM OUT.
WHY, IT WAS ON DISPLAY IN THE CABINET IN FRONT OF THE OFFICE FOR QUITE SOME TIME!

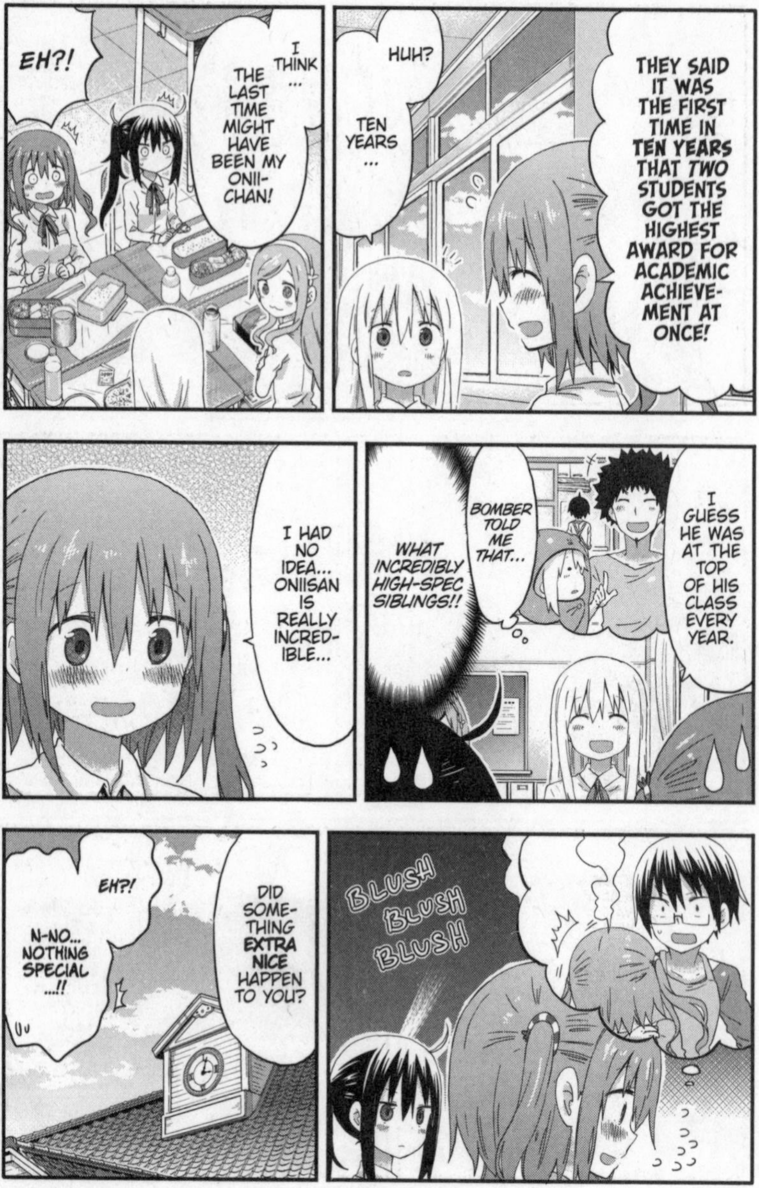
THEY SAID IT WAS THE FIRST TIME IN TEN YEARS THAT TWO STUDENTS GOT THE HIGHEST AWARD FOR ACADEMIC ACHIEVEMENT AT ONCE!
HUH?
TEN YEARS ...
I THINK ... THE LAST TIME MIGHT HAVE BEEN MY ONII-CHAN!
EH?!
I GUESS HE WAS AT THE TOP OF HIS CLASS EVERY YEAR.
BOMBER TOLD ME THAT...
WHAT INCREDIBLY HIGH-SPEC SIBLINGS!!
I HAD NO IDEA... ONIISAN IS REALLY INCREDIBLE...
BLUSH BLUSH BLUSH
DID SOMETHING EXTRA NICE HAPPEN TO YOU?
EH?!
N-NO... NOTHING SPECIAL ...!!

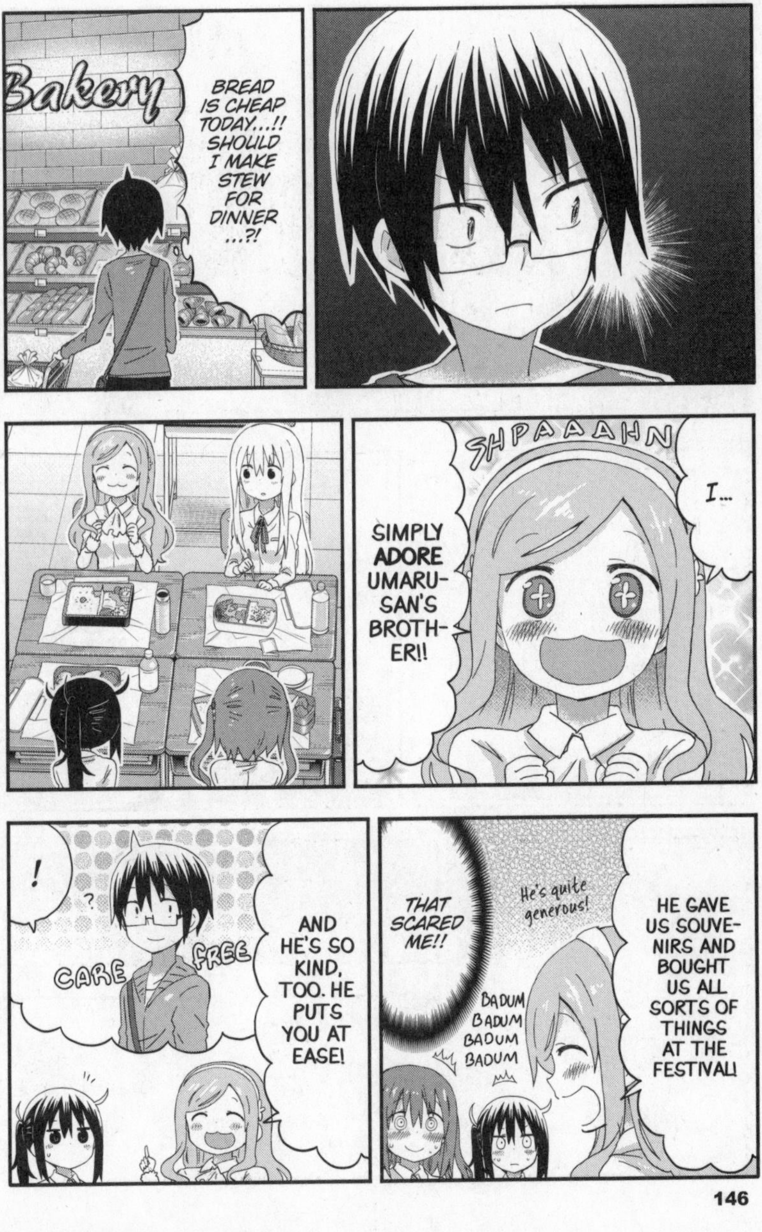
Bakery
BREAD IS CHEAP TODAY...!! SHOULD I MAKE STEW FOR DINNER ...?!
SHPAAAHN
I...
SIMPLY ADORE UMARU-SAN'S BROTHER!!
HE GAVE US SOUVENIRS AND BOUGHT US ALL SORTS OF THINGS AT THE FESTIVAL!
He's quite generous!
THAT SCARED ME!!
BADUM BADUM BADUM BADUM
!
?
AND HE'S SO KIND, TOO. HE PUTS YOU AT EASE!
CARE FREE

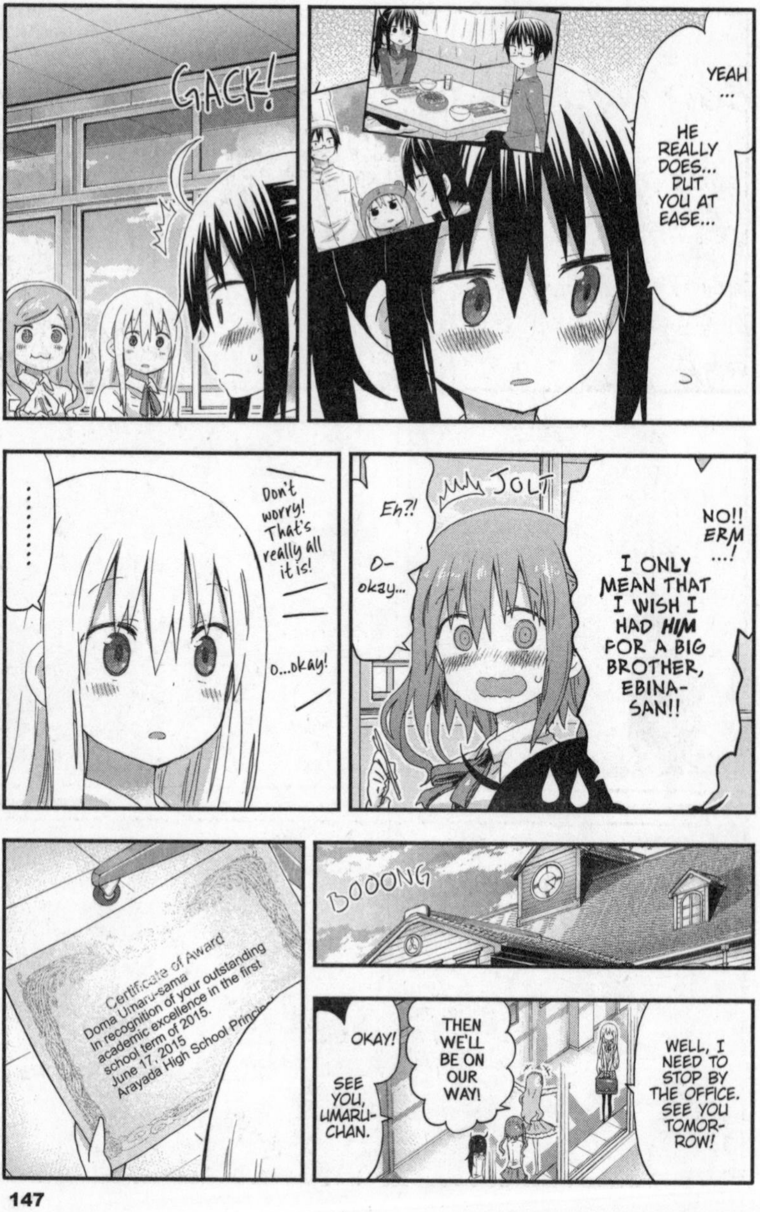
YEAH ...
HE REALLY DOES... PUT YOU AT EASE...
GACK!
NO!! ERM ...!
I ONLY MEAN THAT I WISH I HAD **HIM** FOR A BIG BROTHER, EBINA-SAN!!
JOLT
Eh?!
O-okay...
Don't worry! That's really all it is!
O...okay!
....
BOOONG
WELL, I NEED TO STOP BY THE OFFICE. SEE YOU TOMORROW!
THEN WE'LL BE ON OUR WAY!
OKAY!
SEE YOU, UMARU-CHAN.
Certificate of Award
Doma Umaru-sama
In recognition of your outstanding academic excellence in the first school term of 2015.
June 17, 2015
Arayada High School

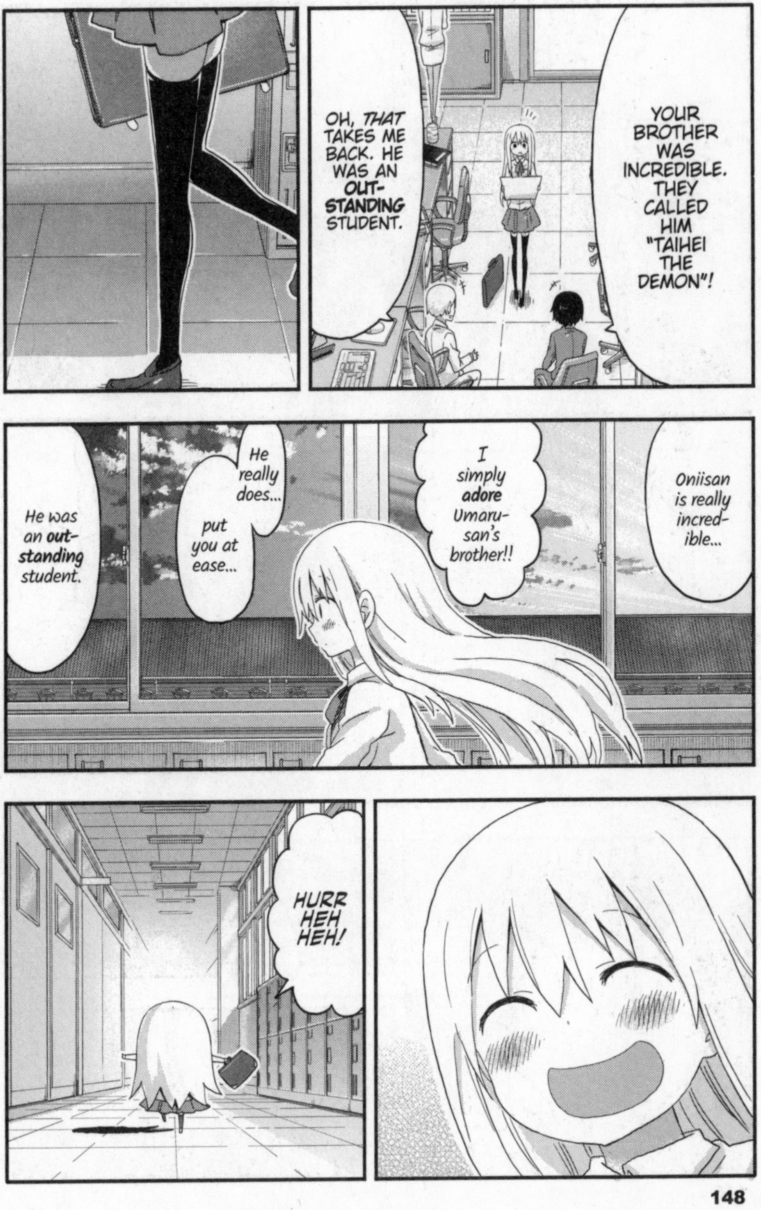
YOUR BROTHER WAS INCREDIBLE. THEY CALLED HIM "TAIHEI THE DEMON"!
OH, *THAT* TAKES ME BACK. HE WAS AN **OUT-STANDING** STUDENT.
Oniisan is really incred-ible...
I simply **adore** Umaru-san's brother!!
He really does... put you at ease...
He was an **out-standing** student.
HURR HEH HEH!

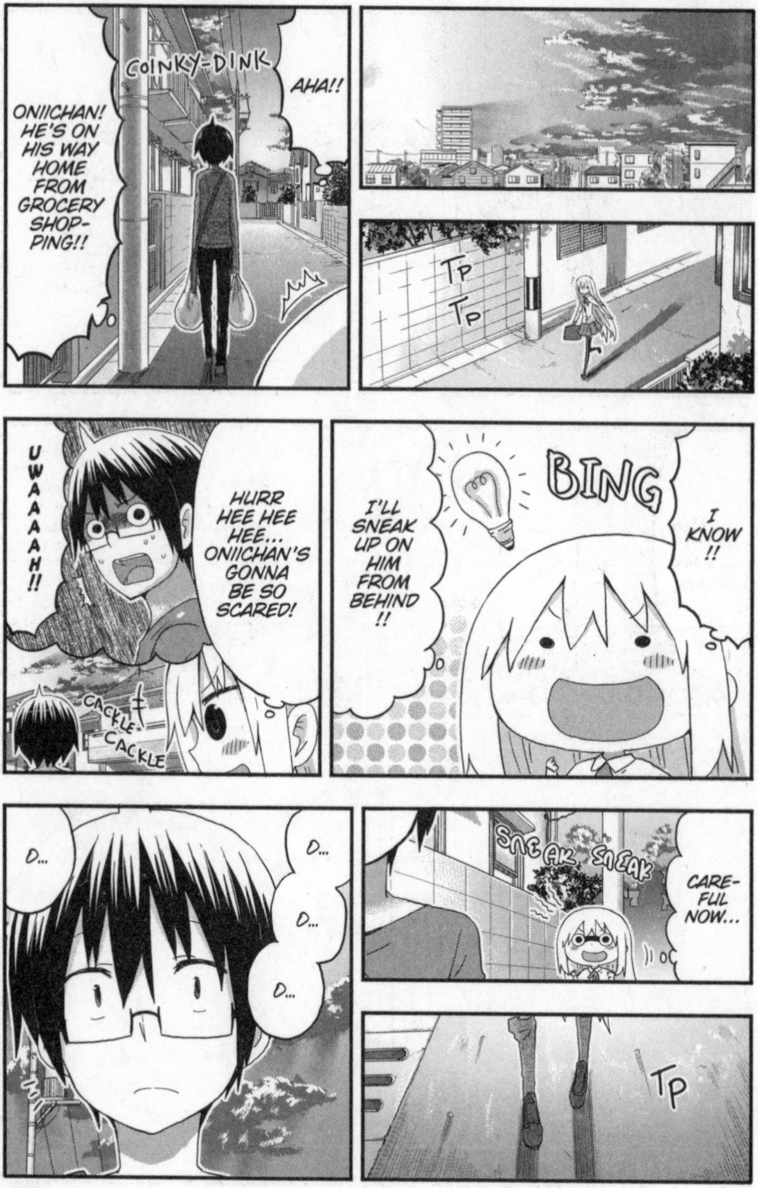
TP
TP
AHA!!
COINKY-DINK
ONIICHAN! HE'S ON HIS WAY HOME FROM GROCERY SHOP-PING!!
I KNOW!!
BING
I'LL SNEAK UP ON HIM FROM BEHIND!!
HURR HEE HEE HEE... ONIICHAN'S GONNA BE SO SCARED!
UWAAAAAAH!!
CACKLE CACKLE
CARE-FUL NOW...
SNEAK SNEAK
TP
O...
O...
O...
O...

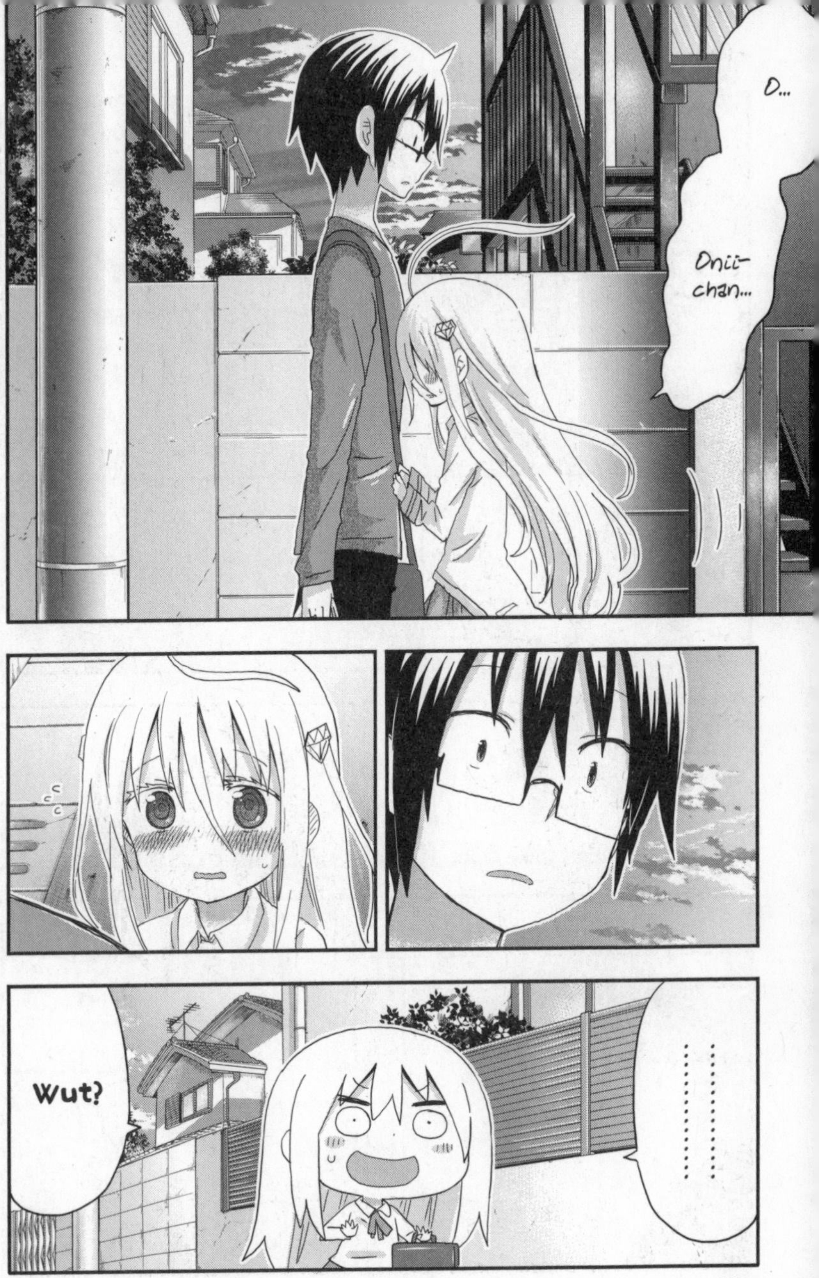
O...
Onii-chan...
......
Wut?

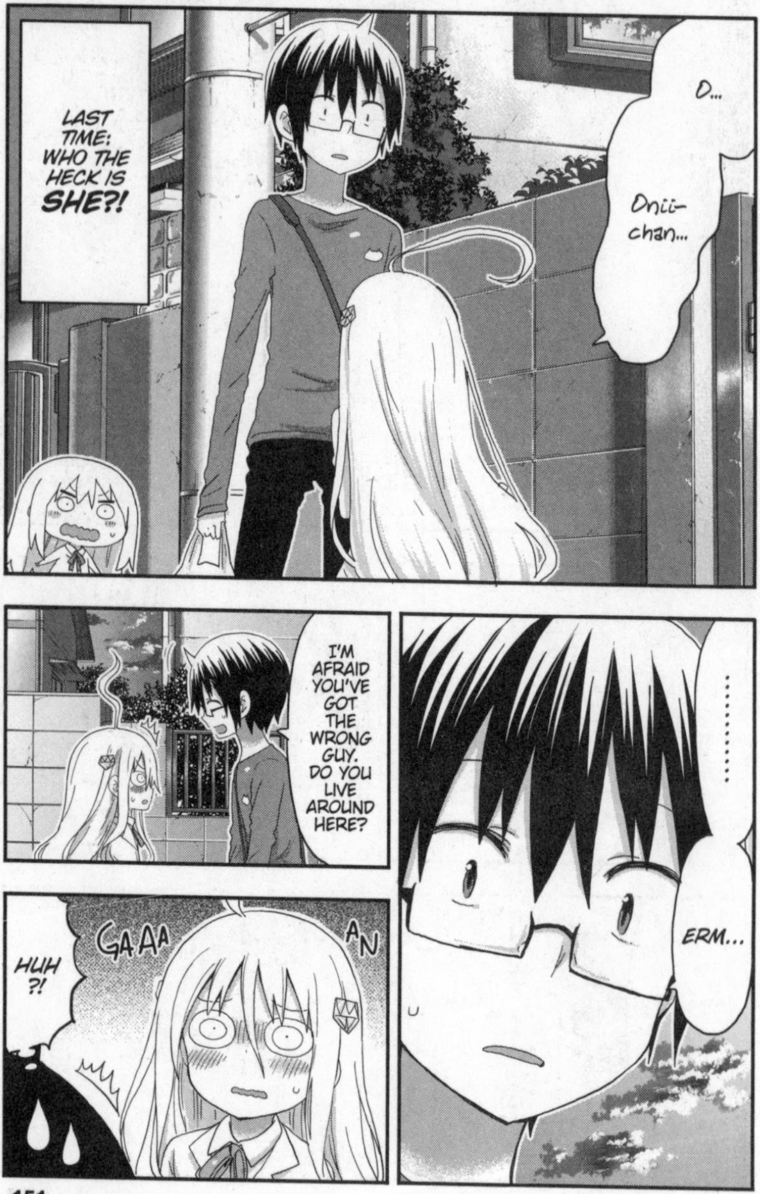
O...
Onii-chan...
LAST TIME: WHO THE HECK IS SHE?!
......
ERM...
I'M AFRAID YOU'VE GOT THE WRONG GUY. DO YOU LIVE AROUND HERE?
GAAAAN
HUH?!

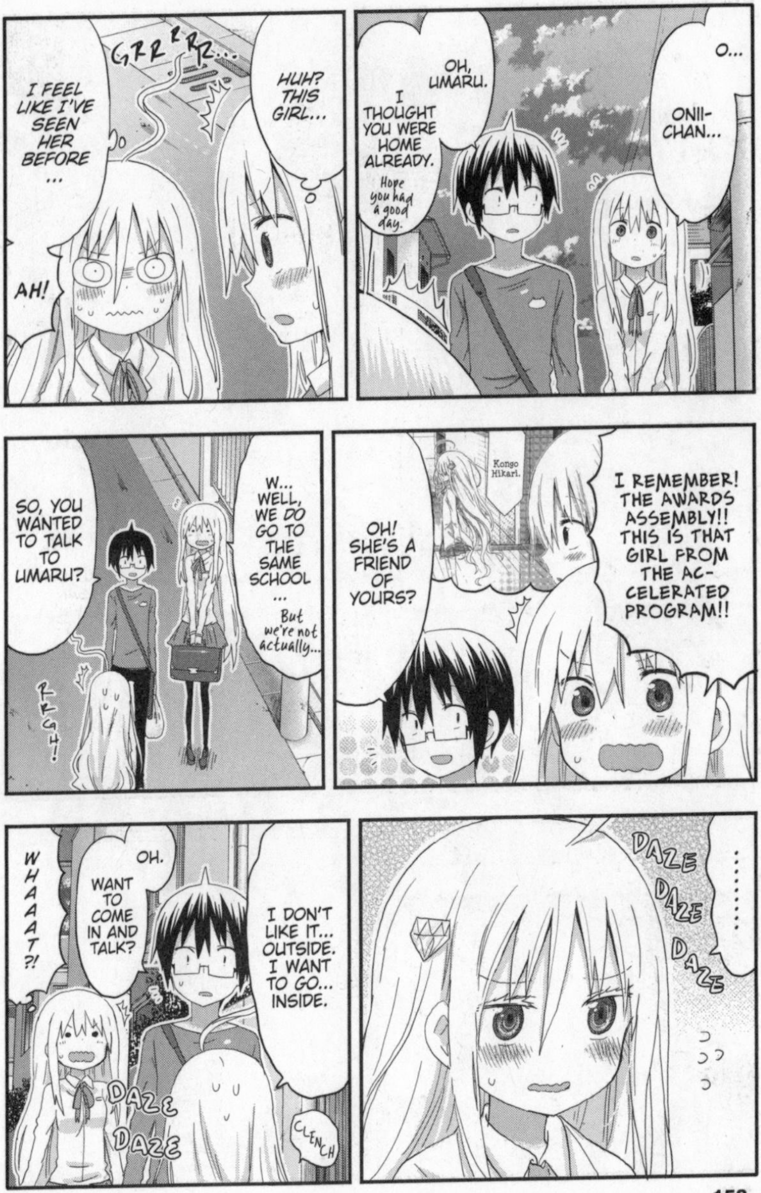
O... ONII-CHAN...
OH, UMARU. I THOUGHT YOU WERE HOME ALREADY.
Hope you had a good day.
HUH? THIS GIRL...
GRRRRR...
I FEEL LIKE I'VE SEEN HER BEFORE...
AH!
I REMEMBER! THE AWARDS ASSEMBLY!! THIS IS THAT GIRL FROM THE AC-CELERATED PROGRAM!!
Kongo Hikari.
OH! SHE'S A FRIEND OF YOURS?
W... WELL, WE DO GO TO THE SAME SCHOOL...
But we're not actually...
SO, YOU WANTED TO TALK TO UMARU?
RRGH!
......
DAZE DAZE DAZE
I DON'T LIKE IT... OUTSIDE. I WANT TO GO... INSIDE.
OH. WANT TO COME IN AND TALK?
WHAAAAT?!
DAZE DAZE
CLENCH

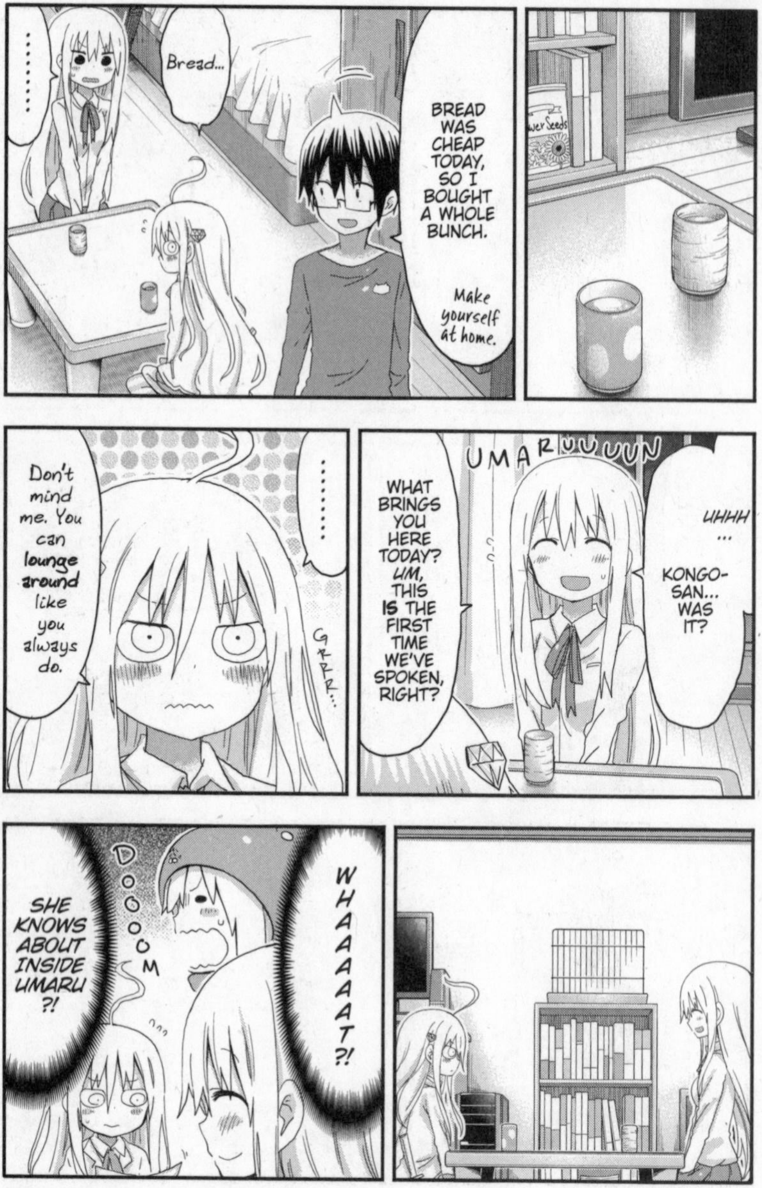
BREAD WAS CHEAP TODAY, SO I BOUGHT A WHOLE BUNCH.
Make yourself at home.
Bread...
......
UMARUUUUUN
UHHH... KONGO-SAN... WAS IT?
WHAT BRINGS YOU HERE TODAY? UM, THIS IS THE FIRST TIME WE'VE SPOKEN, RIGHT?
....
GRRR...
Don't mind me. You can **lounge around** like you always do.
WHAAAAAAT?!
DOOOOOM
SHE KNOWS ABOUT INSIDE UMARU?!

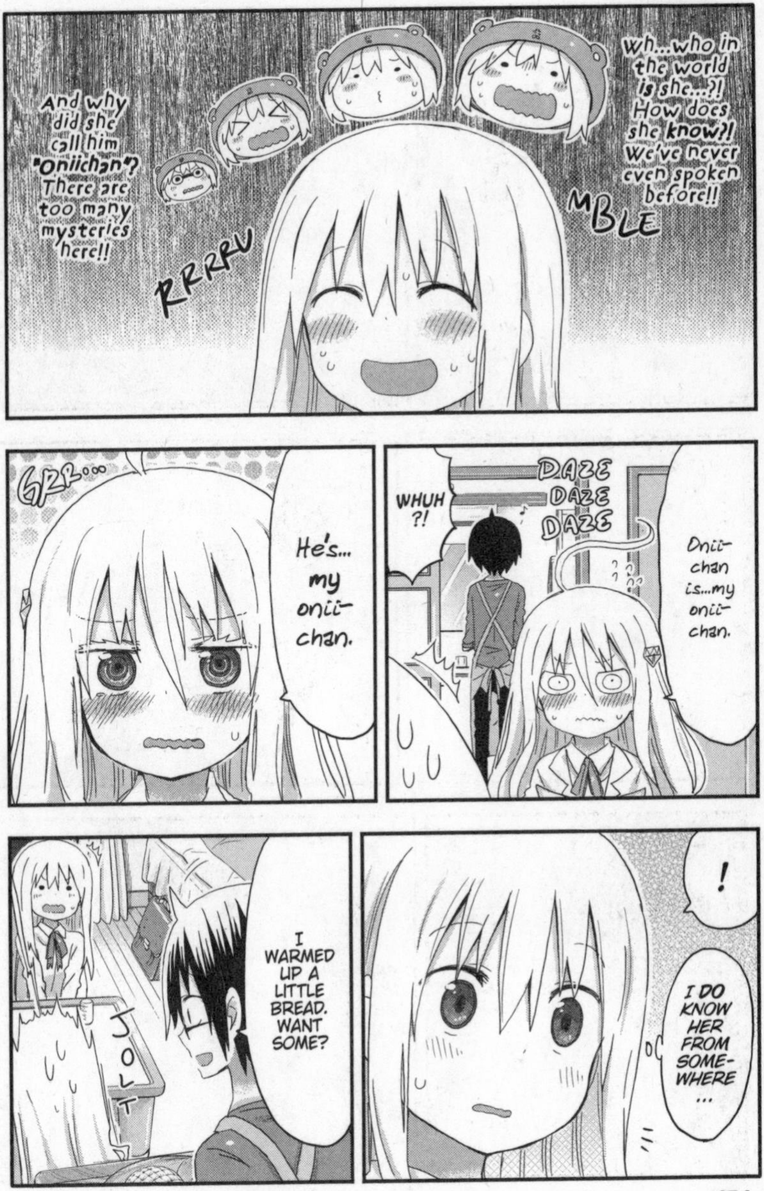
Wh...who in the world is she...?! How does she know?! We've never even spoken before!!
And why did she call him "Oniichan"? There are too many mysteries here!!
MBLE
RRRRU
Onii-chan is...my onii-chan.
DAZE DAZE DAZE
WHUH ?!
He's... my onii-chan.
GRR...
!
I DO KNOW HER FROM SOME-WHERE ...
I WARMED UP A LITTLE BREAD. WANT SOME?
JOLT

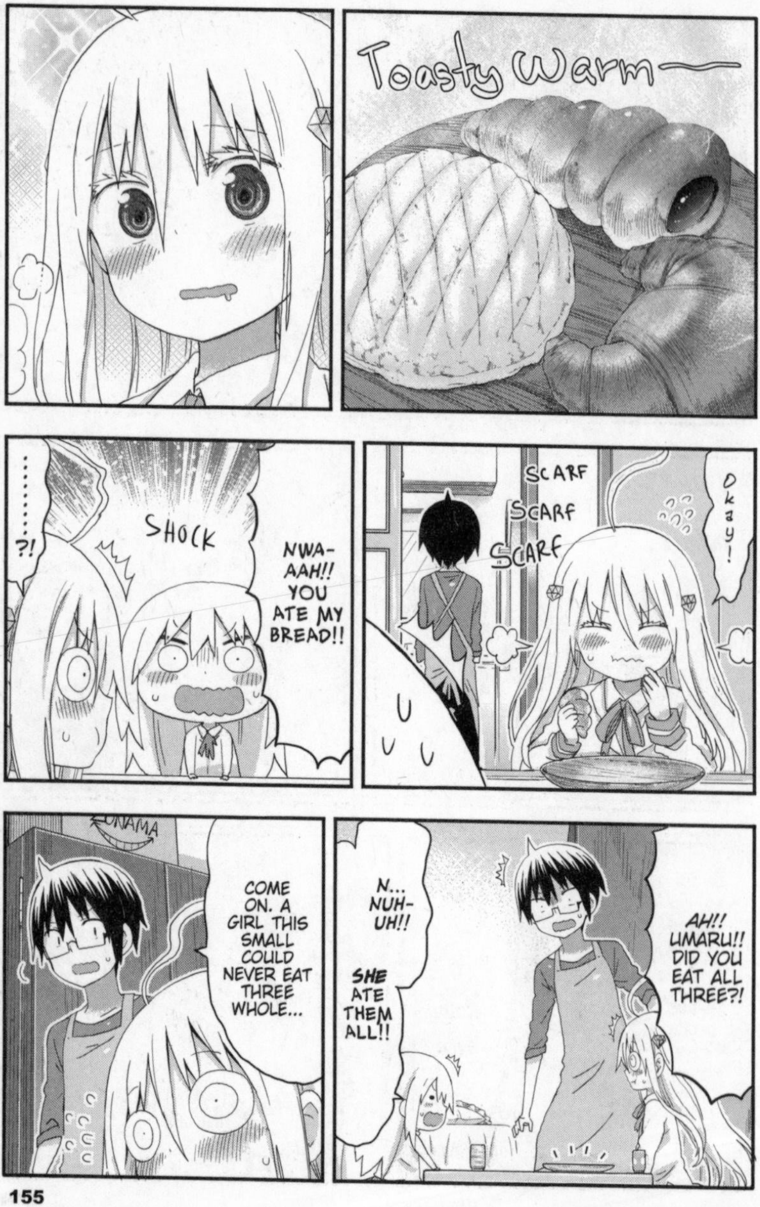
Toasty Warm——
SCARF
SCARF
SCARF
Okay!
......?!
SHOCK
NWA-AAH!! YOU ATE MY BREAD!!
AH!! UMARU!! DID YOU EAT ALL THREE?!
N... NUH-UH!!
SHE ATE THEM ALL!!
COME ON. A GIRL THIS SMALL COULD NEVER EAT THREE WHOLE...

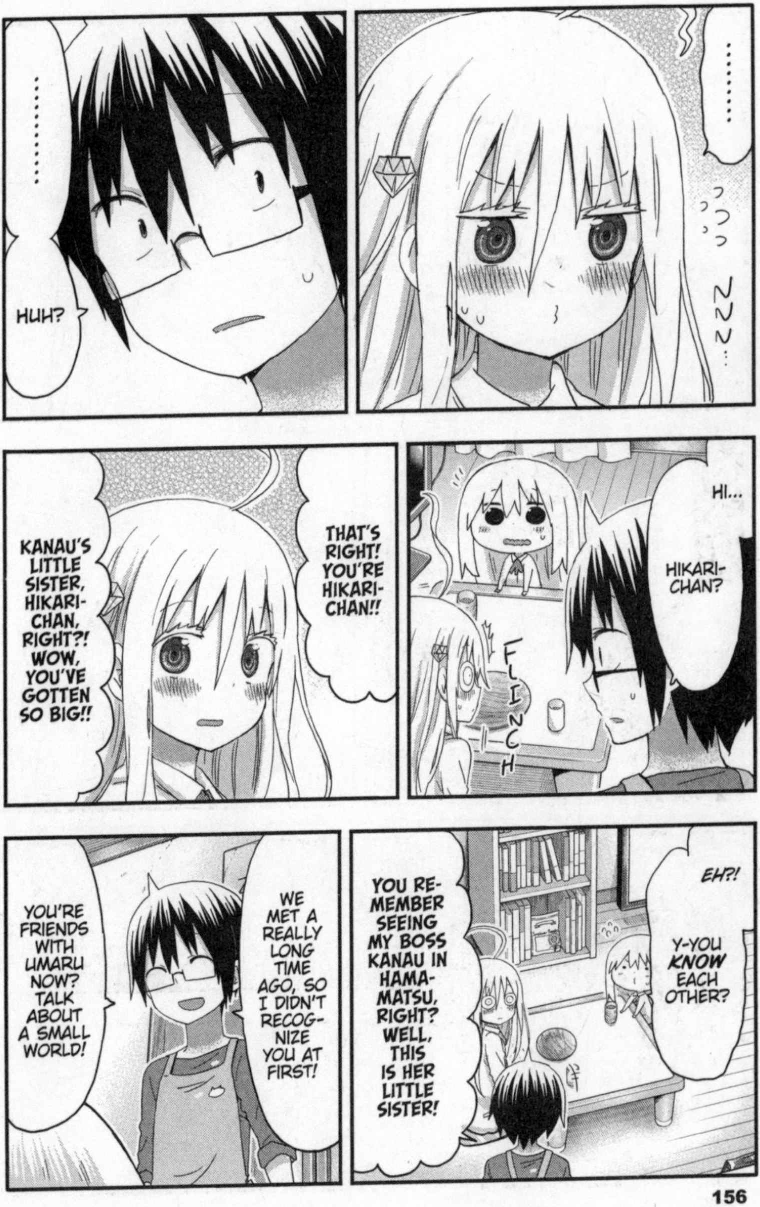
......
NNN...
...... HUH?
HI... HIKARI-CHAN?
FLINCH
THAT'S RIGHT! YOU'RE HIKARI-CHAN!!
KANAU'S LITTLE SISTER, HIKARI-CHAN, RIGHT?! WOW, YOU'VE GOTTEN SO BIG!!
EH?!
Y-YOU *KNOW* EACH OTHER?
YOU RE-MEMBER SEEING MY BOSS KANAU IN HAMA-MATSU, RIGHT? WELL, THIS IS HER LITTLE SISTER!
WE MET A REALLY LONG TIME AGO, SO I DIDN'T RECOG-NIZE YOU AT FIRST!
YOU'RE FRIENDS WITH UMARU NOW? TALK ABOUT A SMALL WORLD!

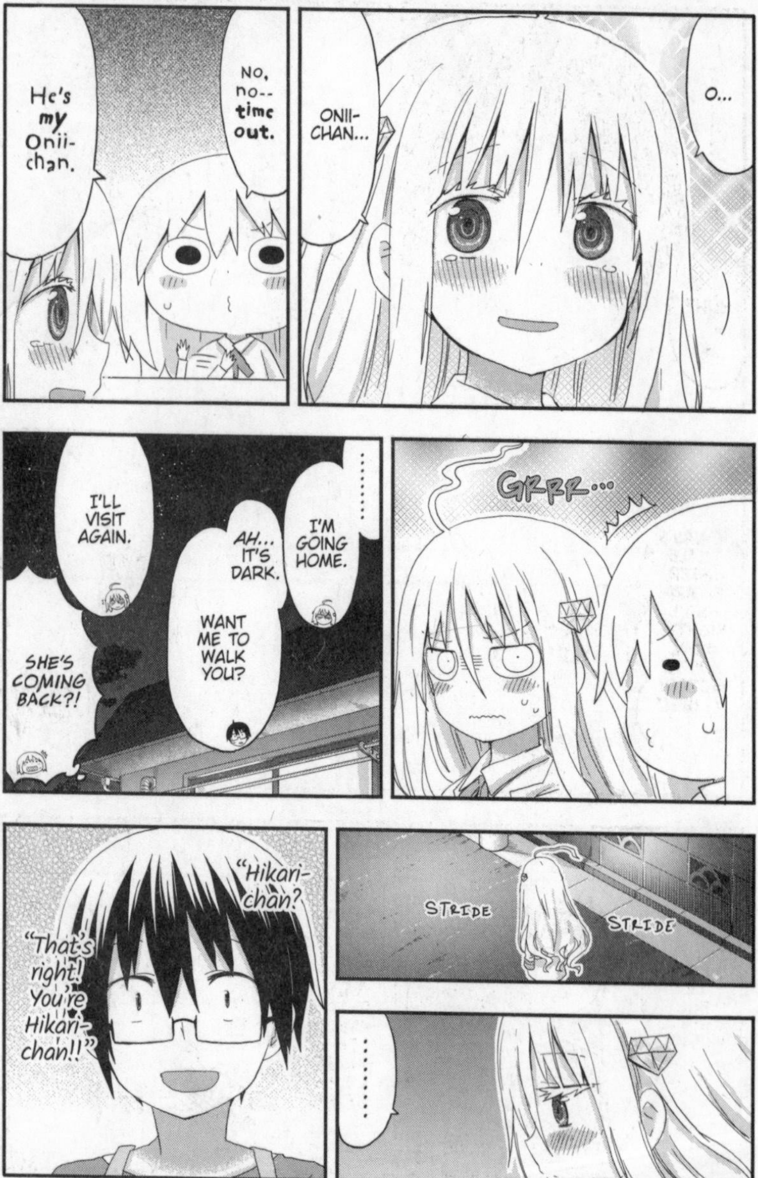
O...
ONII-CHAN...
No, no-- time out.
He's my Onii-chan.
GRRR...
......
I'M GOING HOME.
AH... IT'S DARK.
WANT ME TO WALK YOU?
I'LL VISIT AGAIN.
SHE'S COMING BACK?!
STRIDE
STRIDE
......
"Hikari-chan?"
"That's right! You're Hikari-chan!!"

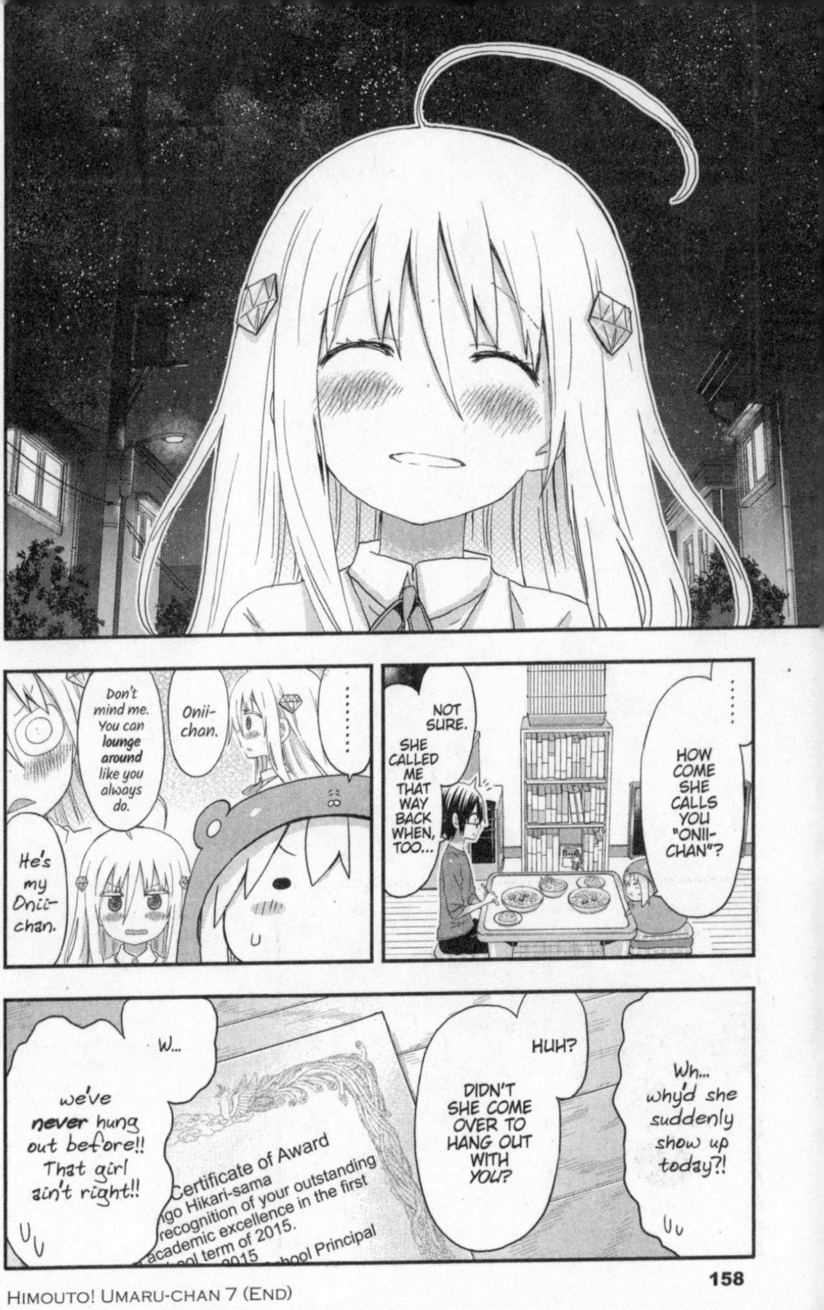
......
HOW COME SHE CALLS YOU "ONII-CHAN"?
NOT SURE.
SHE CALLED ME THAT WAY BACK WHEN, TOO...
......
Onii-chan.
Don't mind me. You can **lounge around** like you always do.
He's my Onii-chan.
Wh... why'd she suddenly show up today?!
HUH?
DIDN'T SHE COME OVER TO HANG OUT WITH *YOU*?
W...
we've **never** hung out before!! That girl ain't right!!
Certificate of Award
ngo Hikari-sama
recognition of your outstanding
academic excellence in the first
hool term of 2015.
2015
hool Principal

HIMOUTO! UMARU-CHAN 7 (END)

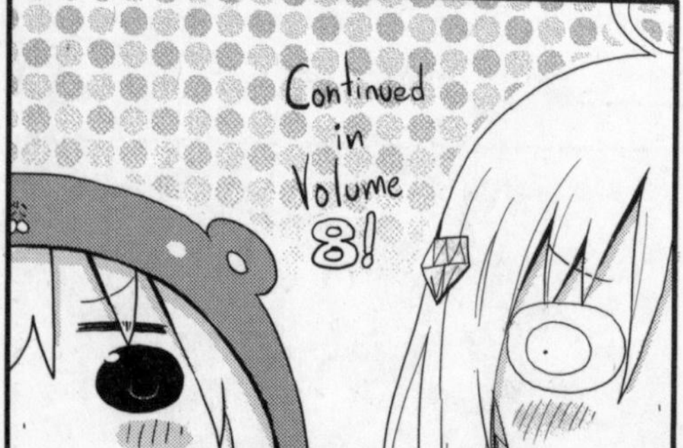
Continued in Volume 8!

HIMOUTO! UMARU-CHAN

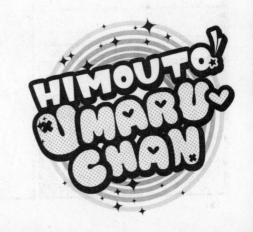

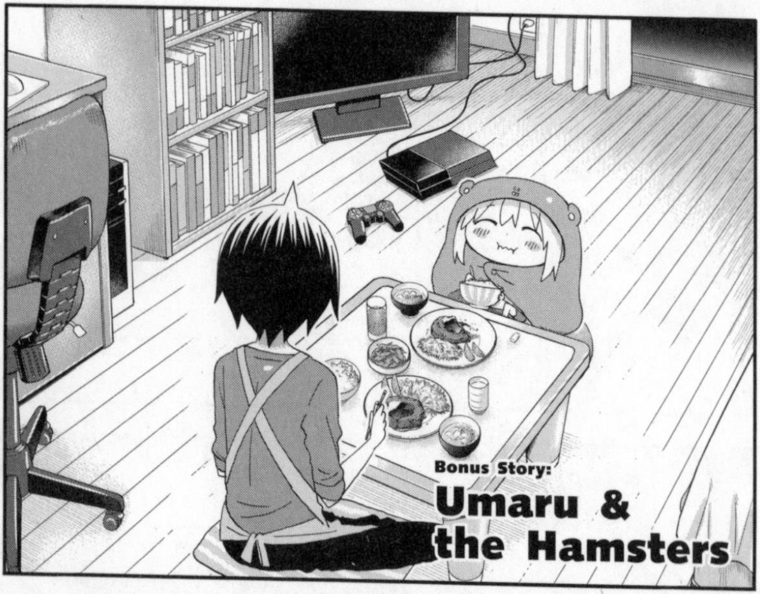

Bonus Story: Umaru & the Hamsters

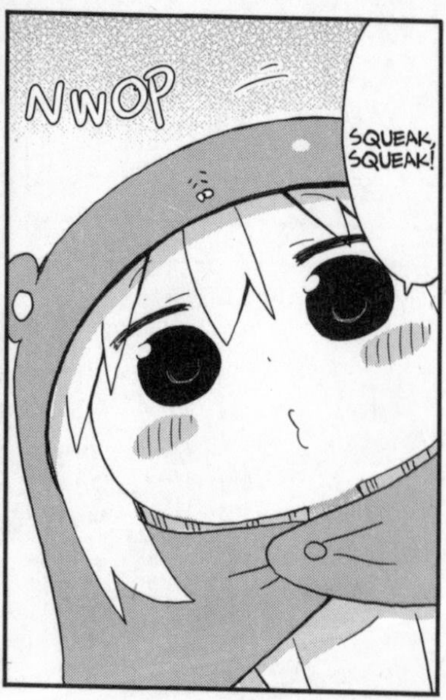
SQUEAK, SQUEAK!
NWOP

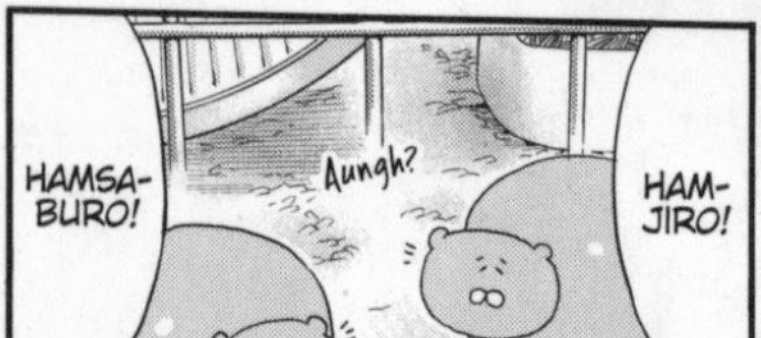
HAM-JIRO!
Aungh?
HAMSA-BURO!

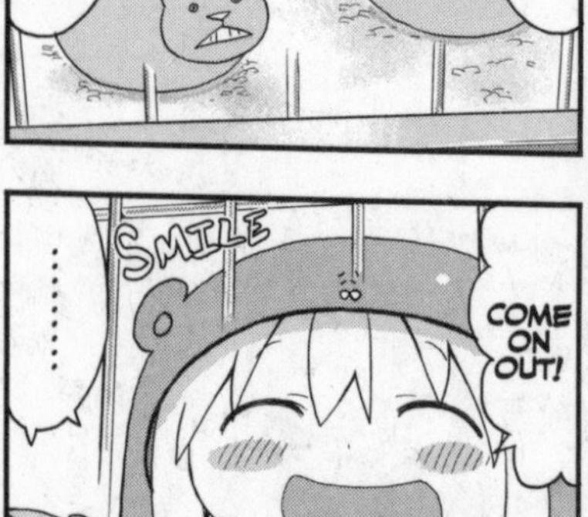
COME ON OUT!
SMILE
......

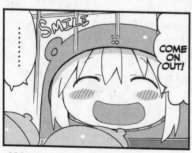

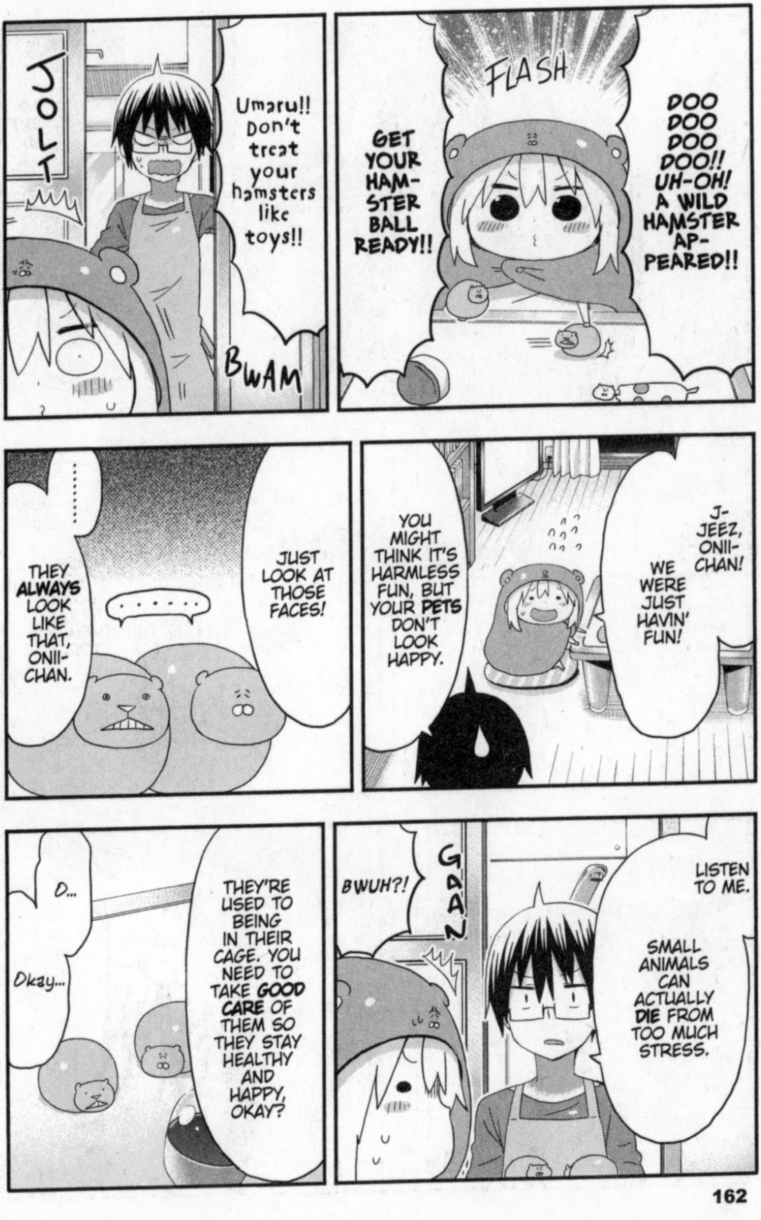
FLASH
DOO DOO DOO DOO!! UH-OH! A WILD HAMSTER AP-PEARED!!
GET YOUR HAM-STER BALL READY!!
JOLT
Umaru!! Don't treat your hamsters like toys!!
BWAM
J-JEEZ, ONII-CHAN!
WE WERE JUST HAVIN' FUN!
YOU MIGHT THINK IT'S HARMLESS FUN, BUT YOUR PETS DON'T LOOK HAPPY.
JUST LOOK AT THOSE FACES!
......
THEY ALWAYS LOOK LIKE THAT, ONII-CHAN.
.....
LISTEN TO ME.
SMALL ANIMALS CAN ACTUALLY DIE FROM TOO MUCH STRESS.
GAAN
BWUH?!
THEY'RE USED TO BEING IN THEIR CAGE. YOU NEED TO TAKE GOOD CARE OF THEM SO THEY STAY HEALTHY AND HAPPY, OKAY?
O...
Okay...

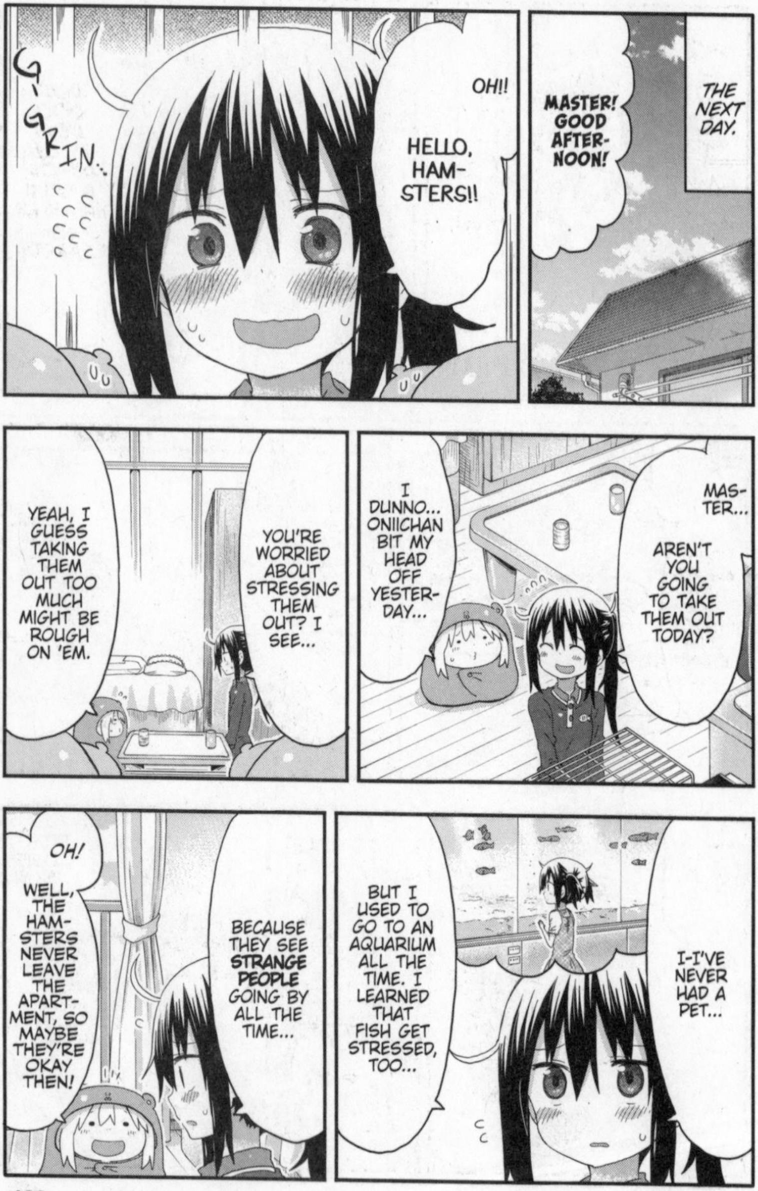
THE NEXT DAY.
MASTER! GOOD AFTER-NOON!
OH!!
HELLO, HAM-STERS!!
G-GRIN...
MAS-TER...
AREN'T YOU GOING TO TAKE THEM OUT TODAY?
I DUNNO... ONIICHAN BIT MY HEAD OFF YESTER-DAY...
YOU'RE WORRIED ABOUT STRESSING THEM OUT? I SEE...
YEAH, I GUESS TAKING THEM OUT TOO MUCH MIGHT BE ROUGH ON 'EM.
I-I'VE NEVER HAD A PET...
BUT I USED TO GO TO AN AQUARIUM ALL THE TIME. I LEARNED THAT FISH GET STRESSED, TOO...
BECAUSE THEY SEE **STRANGE PEOPLE** GOING BY ALL THE TIME...
OH!
WELL, THE HAM-STERS NEVER LEAVE THE APART-MENT, SO MAYBE THEY'RE OKAY THEN!

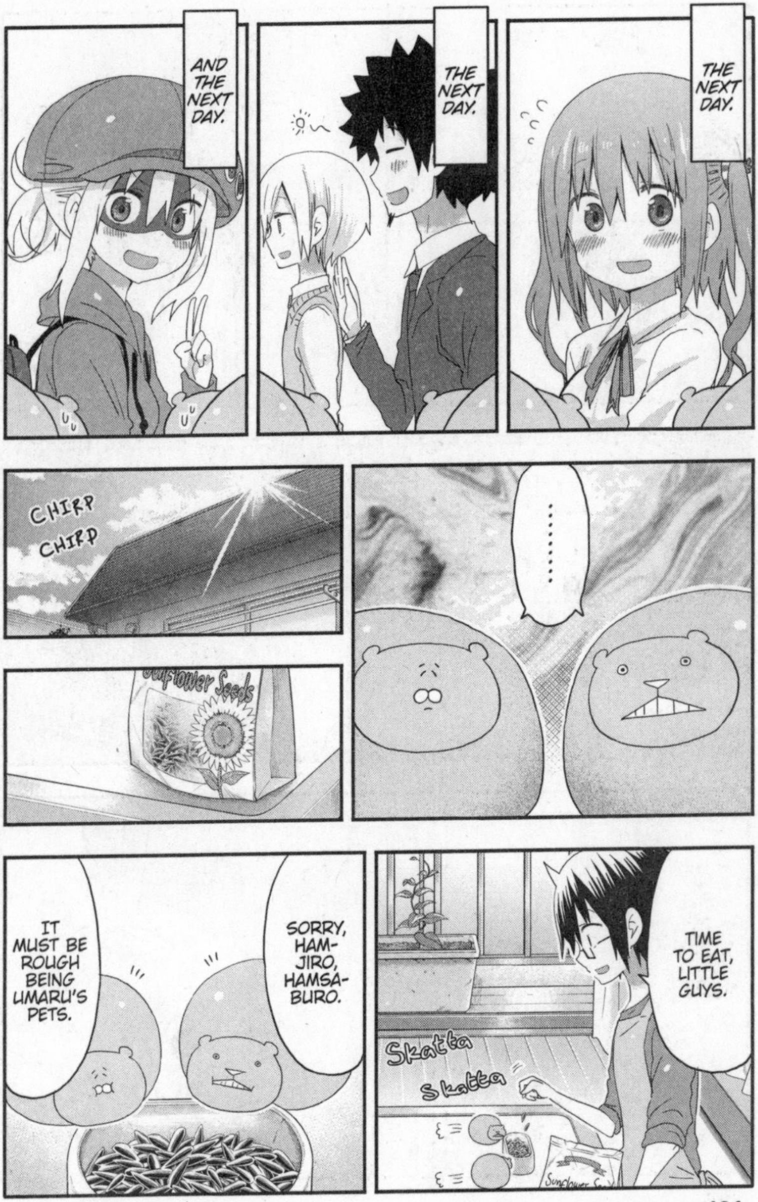
THE NEXT DAY.
THE NEXT DAY.
AND THE NEXT DAY.
......
CHIRP CHIRP
Sunflower Seeds
TIME TO EAT, LITTLE GUYS.
Skatta Skatta
SORRY, HAMJIRO, HAMSABURO.
IT MUST BE ROUGH BEING UMARU'S PETS.

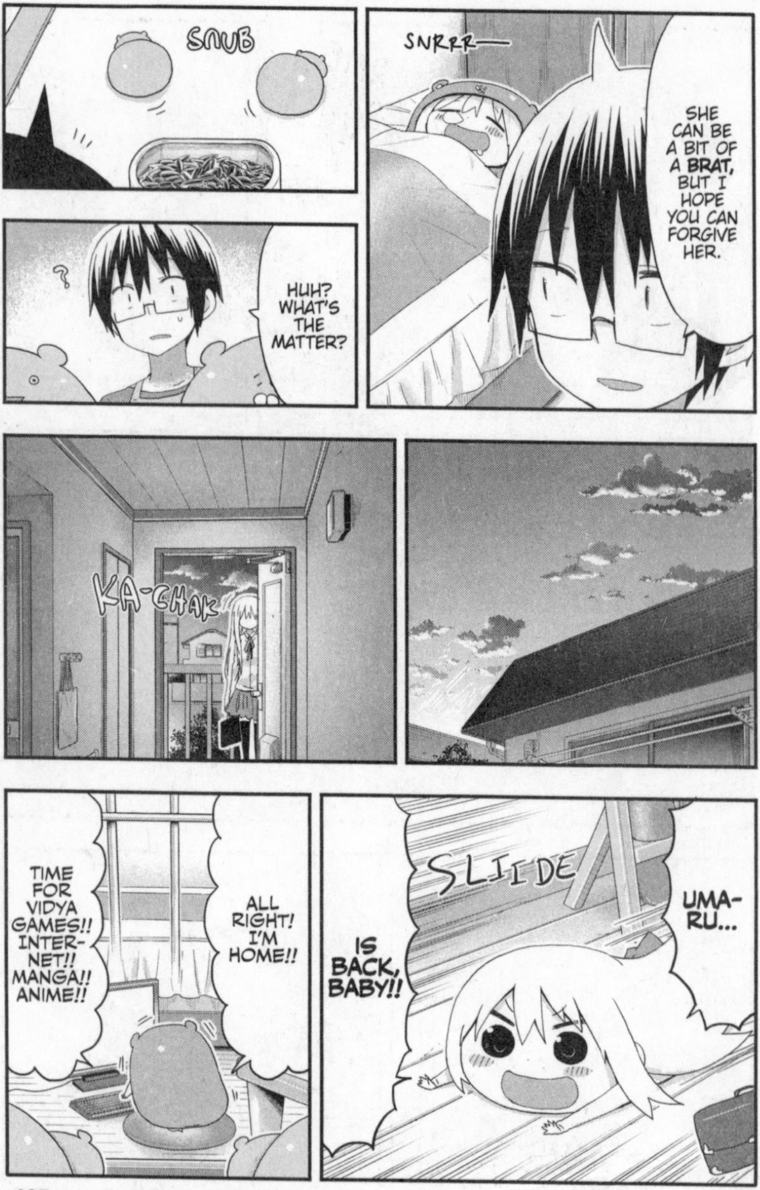
SNRRR—
SHE CAN BE A BIT OF A **BRAT**, BUT I HOPE YOU CAN FORGIVE HER.
SNUB
HUH? WHAT'S THE MATTER?
KA-CHAK
SLIIDE
UMA-RU...
IS BACK, BABY!!
ALL RIGHT! I'M HOME!!
TIME FOR VIDYA GAMES!! INTER-NET!! MANGA!! ANIME!!

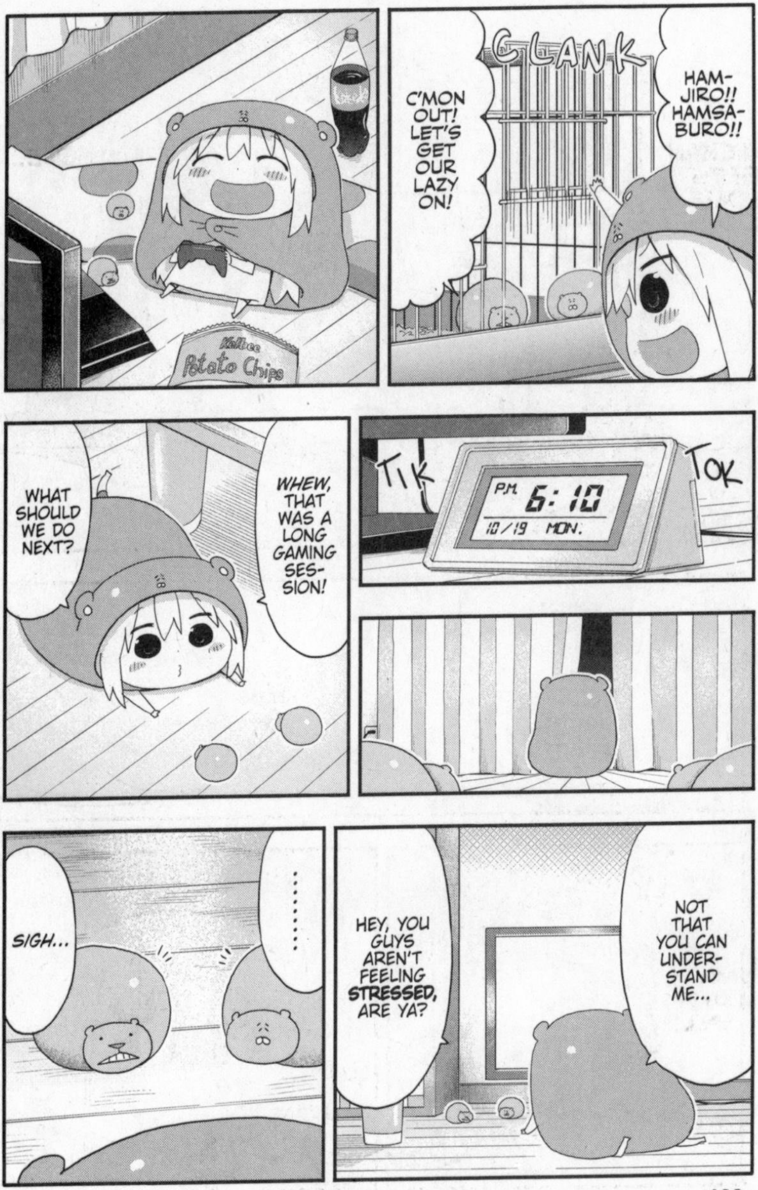
CLANK
HAM-JIRO!! HAMSA-BURO!!
C'MON OUT! LET'S GET OUR LAZY ON!
Kalbee Potato Chips
TIK
TOK
P.M. 6:10
10/19 MON.
WHEW, THAT WAS A LONG GAMING SES-SION!
WHAT SHOULD WE DO NEXT?
NOT THAT YOU CAN UNDER-STAND ME...
HEY, YOU GUYS AREN'T FEELING STRESSED, ARE YA?
......
SIGH...

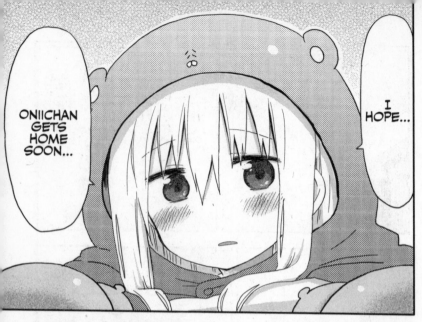

I HOPE...

ONIICHAN GETS HOME SOON...

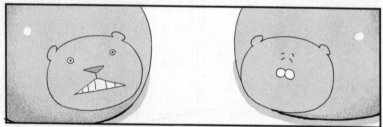

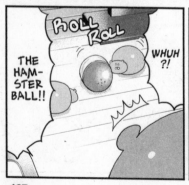

THE HAMSTER BALL!!

ROLL ROLL

WHUH ?!

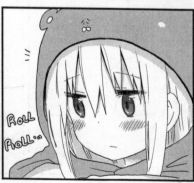

ROLL ROLL...

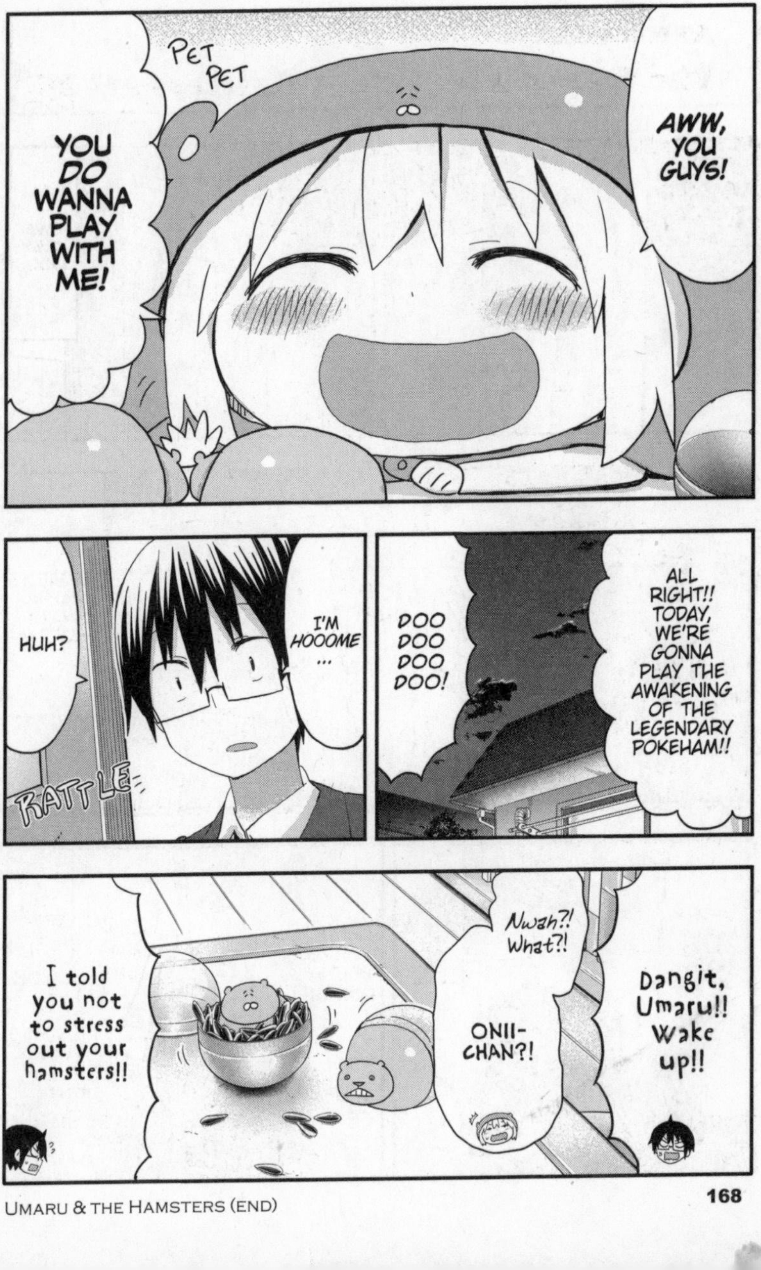
AWW, YOU GUYS!
PET PET
YOU DO WANNA PLAY WITH ME!
ALL RIGHT!! TODAY, WE'RE GONNA PLAY THE AWAKENING OF THE LEGENDARY POKEHAM!!
DOO DOO DOO DOO!
I'M HOOOME ...
HUH?
RATTLE
Dangit, Umaru!! Wake up!!
Nwah?! What?!
ONII-CHAN?!
I told you not to stress out your hamsters!!

UMARU & THE HAMSTERS (END)

AFTERWORD

The Creation of *Umaru* Anime: Part 2

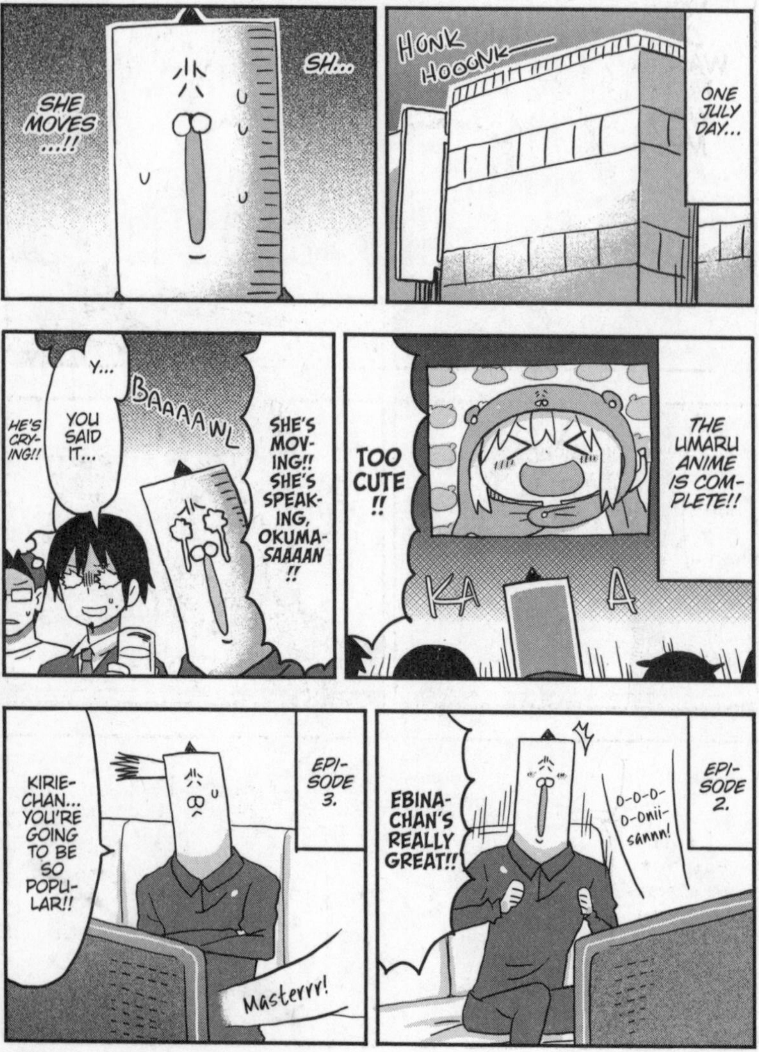

ONE JULY DAY...
HONK HOOONK
SH...
SHE MOVES ...!!
THE UMARU ANIME IS COMPLETE!!
TOO CUTE!!
KA A
SHE'S MOVING!! SHE'S SPEAKING, OKUMA-SAAAAAN!!
BAAAAAWL
Y... YOU SAID IT...
HE'S CRYING!!
EPISODE 2.
O-O-O-O-Onii-sannn!
EBINA-CHAN'S REALLY GREAT!!
EPISODE 3.
Masterrr!
KIRIE-CHAN... YOU'RE GOING TO BE SO POPULAR!!

Sensei is excited as the anime begins!! But a trap lies in wait...!!

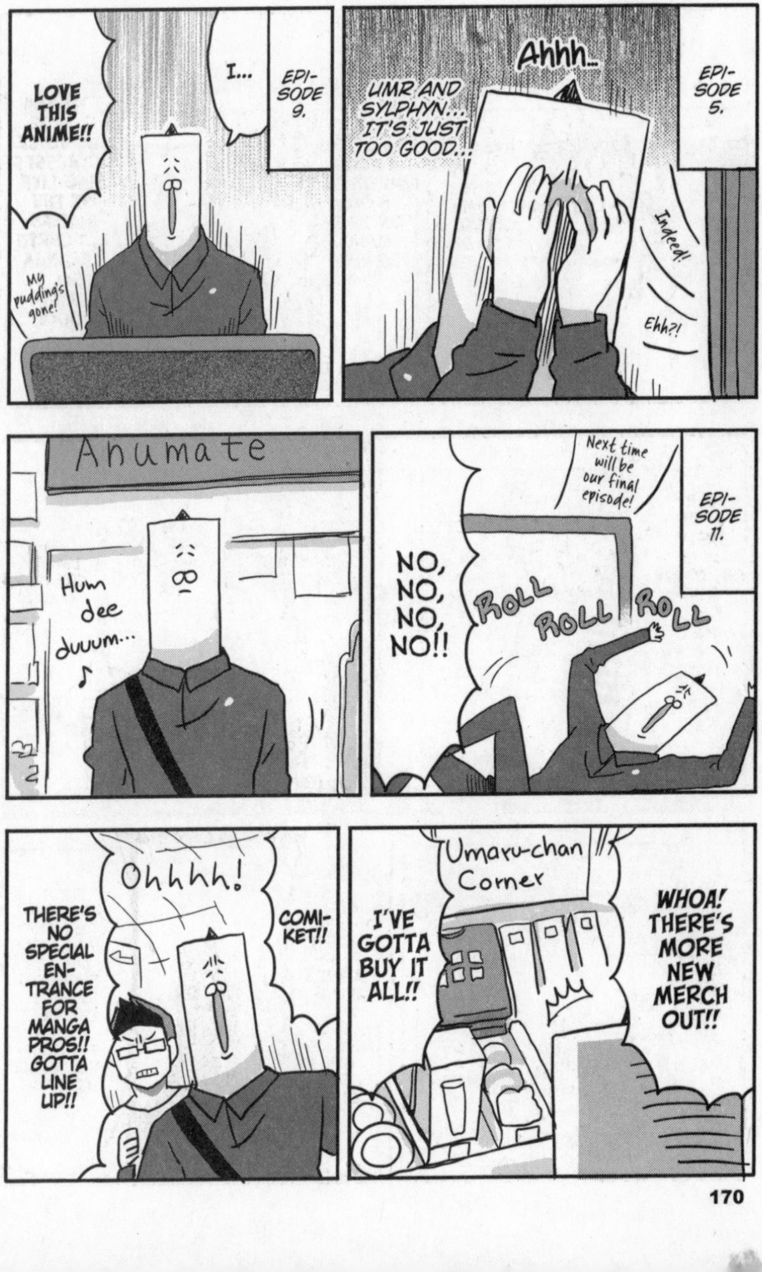
EPI-SODE 5.
Ahhh...
UMR AND SYLPHYN... IT'S JUST TOO GOOD...
Indeed!
Ehh?!
EPI-SODE 9.
I...
LOVE THIS ANIME!!
My pudding's gone!
EPI-SODE 11.
Next time will be our final episode!
NO, NO, NO, NO!!
ROLL ROLL ROLL
Anumate
Hum dee duuum... ♪
WHOA! THERE'S MORE NEW MERCH OUT!!
Umaru-chan Corner
I'VE GOTTA BUY IT ALL!!
COMI-KET!!
Ohhhh!
THERE'S NO SPECIAL ENTRANCE FOR MANGA PROS!! GOTTA LINE UP!!

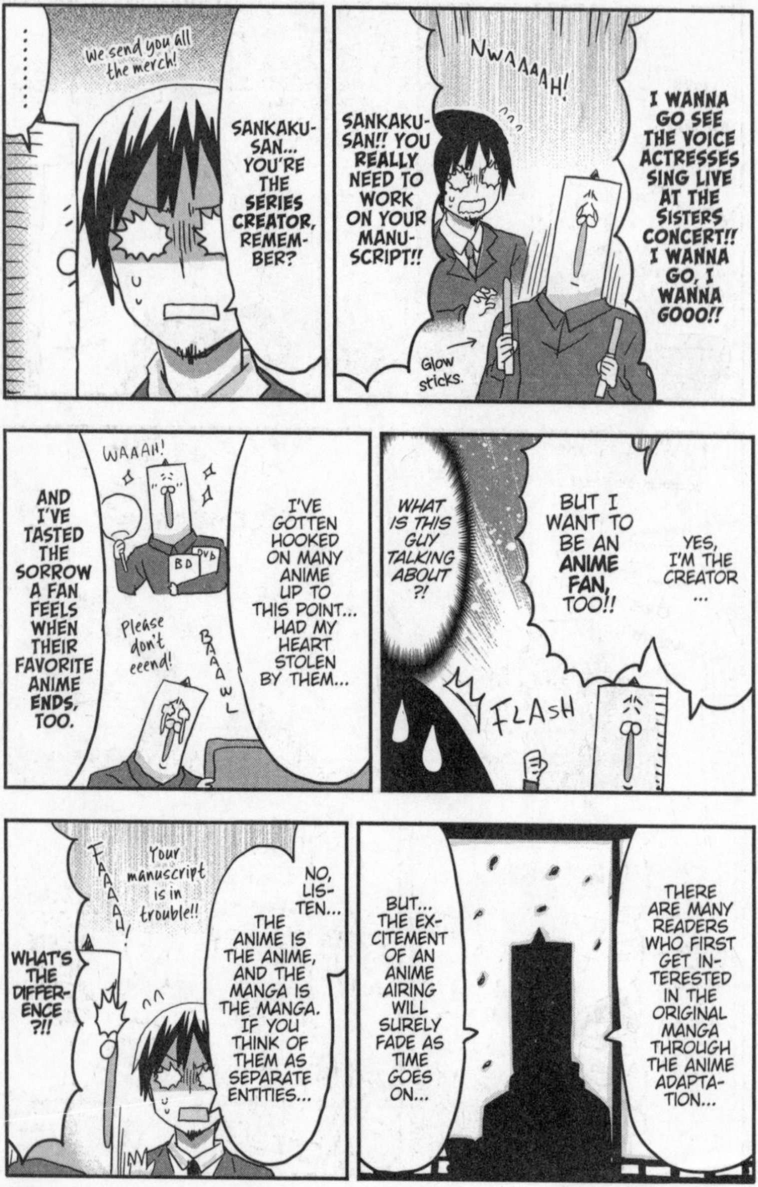
I WANNA GO SEE THE VOICE ACTRESSES SING LIVE AT THE SISTERS CONCERT!! I WANNA GO, I WANNA GOOO!!
NWAAAAH!
SANKAKU-SAN!! YOU REALLY NEED TO WORK ON YOUR MANU-SCRIPT!!
Glow sticks.
SANKAKU-SAN... YOU'RE THE SERIES CREATOR, REMEMBER?
We send you all the merch!
....
YES, I'M THE CREATOR ...
BUT I WANT TO BE AN ANIME FAN, TOO!!
WHAT IS THIS GUY TALKING ABOUT?!
FLASH
I'VE GOTTEN HOOKED ON MANY ANIME UP TO THIS POINT... HAD MY HEART STOLEN BY THEM...
WAAAH!
DVD
BD
BAAAWL
Please don't eeend!
AND I'VE TASTED THE SORROW A FAN FEELS WHEN THEIR FAVORITE ANIME ENDS, TOO.
THERE ARE MANY READERS WHO FIRST GET IN-TERESTED IN THE ORIGINAL MANGA THROUGH THE ANIME ADAPTA-TION...
BUT... THE EX-CITEMENT OF AN ANIME AIRING WILL SURELY FADE AS TIME GOES ON...
NO, LIS-TEN...
THE ANIME IS THE ANIME, AND THE MANGA IS THE MANGA. IF YOU THINK OF THEM AS SEPARATE ENTITIES...
Your manuscript is in trouble!!
FAAAAH!
WHAT'S THE DIFFER-ENCE?!!

Sensei...!! Are you totally hopeless?!

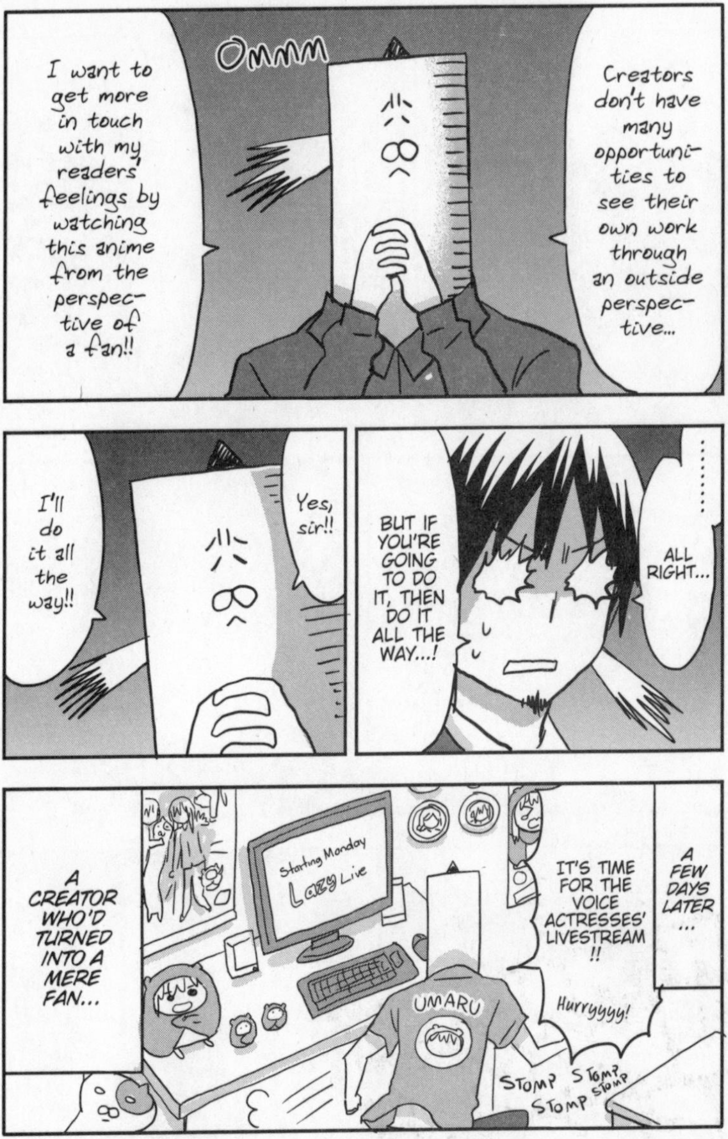
Creators don't have many opportuni-ties to see their own work through an outside perspec-tive...
OMMM
I want to get more in touch with my readers' feelings by watching this anime from the perspec-tive of a fan!!
......
ALL RIGHT...
BUT IF YOU'RE GOING TO DO IT, THEN DO IT ALL THE WAY...!
Yes, sir!!
I'll do it all the way!!
A FEW DAYS LATER...
IT'S TIME FOR THE VOICE ACTRESSES' LIVESTREAM!!
Starting Monday
Lazy Live
Hurryyyy!
UMARU
STOMP STOMP STOMP STOMP
A CREATOR WHO'D TURNED INTO A MERE FAN...

Special Thanks

My editor, Okuma-san; S-I-san; my assistants, Inagaki-san; Yamashita-san; Kitagawa-san; Nishizawa-san; my mom

HIMOUTO! UMARU-CHAN

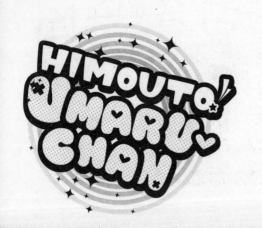

HIMOUTO! UMARU-CHAN

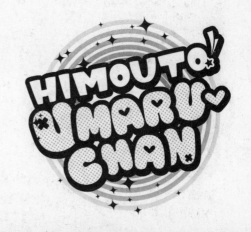

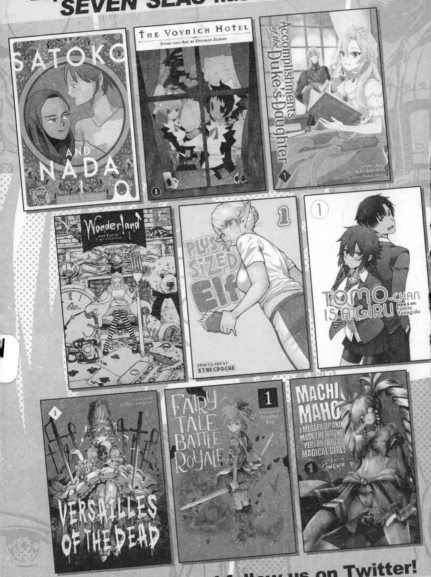

SEVEN SEAS ENTERTAINMENT PRESENTS

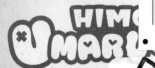

story a

TRANSLATION
Amanda Haley

ADAPTATION
Shanti Whitesides

LETTERING AND RETOUCH
Carolina Hernández Mendoza

COVER DESIGN
Nicky Lim

PROOFREADER
Janet Houck

EDITOR
Jenn Grunigen

PRODUCTION MANAGER
Lissa Pattillo

MANAGING EDITOR
Julie Davis

EDITOR-IN-CHIEF
Adam Arnold

PUBLISHER
Jason DeAngelis

Seven Seas press and purchase enquiries can be sent to Marketing Manager Lianne Sentar at press@gomanga.com. Information regarding the distribution and purchase of digital editions is available from Digital Manager CK Russell at digital@gomanga.com.

Seven Seas and the Seven Seas logo are trademarks of Seven Seas Entertainment. All rights reserved.

ISBN: 978-1-64275-718-7

Printed in Canada

First Printing: October 2019

10 9 8 7 6 5 4 3 2 1

W9-DEZ-791

FOLLOW US ONLINE: www.sevenseasentertainment.com

READING DIRECTIONS

This book reads from **right to left**, Japanese style. If this is your first time reading manga, you start reading from the top right panel on each page and take it from there. If you get lost, just follow the numbered diagram here. It may seem backwards at first, but you'll get the hang of it! Have fun!!

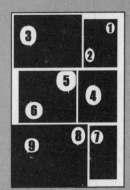

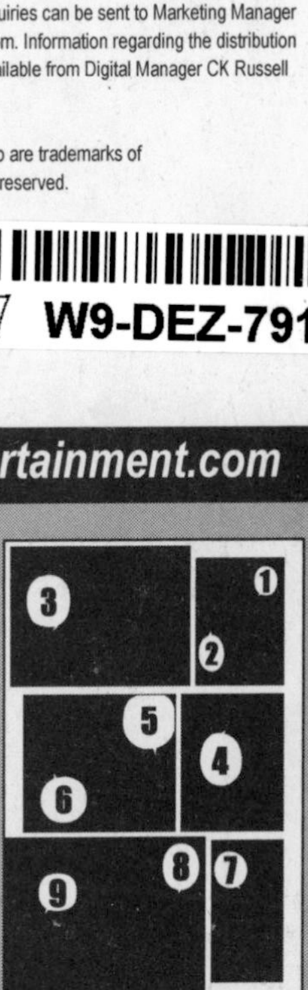